WOGAN

WOGAN

by

GUS SMITH

A STAR BOOK
published by
the Paperback Division of
W. H. Allen & Co. Plc

A Star Book
Published in 1988
by the Paperback Division of
W. H. Allen & Co. Plc
44 Hill Street, London W1X 8LB

First published in a limited paperback edition
for the Republic of Ireland by
Madison Publishers Ltd, 1986

First published in Great Britain by
W. H. Allen & Co. Plc in 1987

Copyright © Gus Smith, 1986, 1987

Printed in Great Britain by
Cox & Wyman Ltd, Reading

ISBN 0 352 32158 X

Contents

PART ONE: THE WOGAN PHENOMENON

1	*Wogan*	12
2	Shepherd's Bush	26
3	Wogan Towers	37
4	Celebrity Visitor	48
5	Wogan's Day	62

PART TWO: BANKER TO BROADCASTER

6	Nuns and Jesuits	78
7	Belvedere Boy	89
8	Radio Announcer	99
9	*Jackpot*	110
10	Terry in Love	119
11	Mark's Discovery	129
12	*Breakfast Show*	138
13	'Court Jester'	149
14	*Blankety Blank*	156

PART THREE: WOGAN AND GUESTS

15	'Over-Exposed'	170
16	Older Women	183
17	Out of Tune	191
18	Ideal Blend	197
19	Terry's View	204

20 Vadim's Women   212
21 'Emotional'   217
22 Royal *Wogan*   226

PART FOUR: WOGAN '87

23 Under Siege   236
24 Wogan's 'Crime'   250
25 New Challenges   260

Acknowledgements

Wogan was written with the co-operation of Terry and Helen Wogan, and their friends and associates, both in Britain and Ireland. I am indebted also to Terry's broadcasting colleagues for their generous assistance, to the library and P.R. departments of the BBC and Radio Telefis Eireann whose help and advice were invaluable in my research.

My further thanks must go to: Mrs Rose Wogan, Brian Wogan, Eamonn Andrews, Val Doonican, John Fisher, James Gilbert, Marcus Plantin, Alan Boyd, Carol Millward, Frances Whitaker, Mrs Jo Gurnett, Mark and Stella White, Gay Byrne, Andy O'Mahony, Fr Francis Shrenk, SJ Sisters Gillen and Lynch, Robert Morgan, William Ward, Maurice O'Doherty, Brendan Balfe, Patrick Weever, James Sexton, Roger Lewis, Ita Hynes, Bryan Kelly and Adrian Cronin.

I wish to acknowledge the following sources of information: *Radio Times, TV Times, RTE Guide, The Listener, The Observer, The Sunday Times, Sunday Telegraph, Sunday Express, Mail on Sunday, News of the World, Sunday Tribune, Sunday Independent, Sunday Press, Sunday World, Daily Mail, Daily Express, The Times, Daily Telegraph, Irish Press, The Irish Times, Irish Independent, The Sun, My Weekly, The Weekly News, The Northern Star, The Portsmouth News, Reader's Digest, Private Eye, Punch, High Life, Chat Magazine, Woman's Own, The Belvederian* and the following books: *Forty Years of Irish Broadcasting* by Maurice Gorham (Radio Telefis Eireann), *Jimmy Young* by Jimmy Young (New English Library), *Glued to the Box* by Clive James (Jonathan Cape), *The Last Laugh* by S. J. Perelman (Eyre Methuen Ltd), *Visions Before Midnight* by

Clive James (Pan Books), *The Best of Myles* by Myles na gCopaleen (Flann O'Brien) (Picador), *A Paler Shade of Green* by Des Hickey & Gus Smith (Leslie Frewin), *Portraits* (Belvedere College 1832–1982) edited by John Bowman and Ronan O'Donoghue (Gill and Macmillan).

Author's Note

I met Terry Wogan for the first time in Dublin in the early 'sixties at the start of his career in Irish broadcasting. I remember him as zestful and friendly, full of enthusiasm for the new challenge facing him. Clearly he recognised that banking – his previous occupation – and broadcasting were worlds apart; 'I'm prepared to learn,' was his motto.

Later, when I met him in London shortly after he joined the BBC, he was gaining in confidence, yet one detected in his attitude an air of caution as though he wondered if the gamble of leaving Ireland would pay off.

In 1986, when I talked to him in connection with this book, he was understanding about the project and appreciative of my interest in his career. The idea of a book tickled his fancy. 'A book on Wogan?' he gasped. 'You're joking! What'll you say about old Terence that the world wants to read?' He laughed as if at that moment Eamonn Andrews had suddenly dropped out of the sky with red book in hand to announce, 'Terry Wogan, This Is Your Life!'

The intervening years hadn't changed him; he could still laugh at himself. The Wogan smile was as much on his face as before, the Wogan wit flowed like Irish honey, and one could see the famous Wogan feet were planted firmly on the ground. But a book on Wogan . . . the prospect made him pace his dressing-room at Shepherd's Bush, halt in his tracks to gaze into the large mirror, and announce: 'I've got nothing to tell. I'm not a movie star. I'm not the President of America. I am *mere* Terry Wogan.'

I reminded him that Jimmy Young, David Frost and a host

of other broadcasters had jumped into print. But he still said: 'A book about Wogan . . . What 'll the world say?'

Wogan could not have been undertaken without the co-operation of Terry and his wife Helen, and indeed the Wogan clans in Ireland and England, so I am grateful for their personal reminiscences.

Gus Smith
March 1987

PART ONE

THE WOGAN PHENOMENON

Life is much too important a thing ever to talk
seriously about it.

—OSCAR WILDE

1   *Wogan*

'Wogan!' the voice on the telephone answered. It was the brisk voice of a woman, not the cheery voice of Terry Wogan. I had expected the voice to announce 'BBC' but it simply said 'Wogan'.

At that moment I had, I suspected, made contact with what I can best describe as the glamorous Wogan Industry, also the Wogan Phenomenon, located somewhere within the monolithic British Broadcasting Corporation. And the sweet-sounding young voice, at the end of the line, it transpired, was that of Carol Millward, public relations officer for the Wogan television show.

'Terry is giving no interviews at present,' she pointed out amiably, but firmly. 'He thinks he has nothing new to say at the moment. I suggest you get in touch with me again later.'

Although this was early April 1986, I remembered that Terry had been interviewed regularly for newspapers and magazines; in fact, scarcely a day went by without his name making the headlines. I asked Miss Millward to put my name on the waiting list. This was promptly agreed, though she could not promise anything. 'It could be weeks,' she added almost despairingly. 'Seems everybody wants to talk to Terry. He just hasn't the time to fit in everybody.' She agreed though that I could have a chat with the *Wogan* executive producer, Frances Whitaker.

There was nothing to be lost, I decided, in meeting the people closest to the Wogan Industry. It meant a journey to the BBC Television Centre in Wood Lane, which I found to be an imposing building within a stone's throw of White City underground. Inevitably, in these dangerous times, the security was tight, though not as tight as I had expected.

At the reception desk I explained briefly the purpose of my visit. Eventually Carol Millward arrived, a blonde with a cheerful manner. 'We go to the seventh floor,' she said, leading the way to the lifts. When we arrived, Carol said; 'This is where the *Wogan* show is planned.' As we stood in the corridor she pointed to at least four rooms where she said the *Wogan* team of producers, researchers and forward planners operated. 'There are twenty people here on the team,' she added.

I was told that by July of 1986 Terry Wogan had chatted to seven hundred guests and that many more were queueing up to appear on the show.

To celebrate the show's 100th birthday the year before, Terry released hundreds of colourful balloons into the night sky over Shepherd's Bush Green. He watched as many of the balloons failed to rise when released by his guests, *Eastenders* star Wendy Richard and singer/actress Nina. 'I do hope the excitement's not too much for you all,' he wryly told viewers. The prize for the balloon found farthest away was a ticket to *Wogan* and a *Wogan* mug. Typically low-key prizes.

'I will be more inclined to celebrate when we have done a thousand shows,' Terry wisecracked.

Inside the Wogan Industry there is an aura of power. Terry is in actual fact head of an industry that has an undeniable air of success about it. In Carol Millward's room off the corridor photographs of the great man adorned the walls, some featuring Terry with showbusiness celebrities. His face beamed down mockingly and reassuringly; a face dominated by a strong nose, perfectly-focused eyes and broad lips; a handsome face encircled by a profusion of dark hair; the face of a man confident of his own ability and conscious of his powerful position within the Beeb.

I heard Carol Millward say, 'I love my job. I have a wonderful product to sell'. I didn't argue. She talked about

the journalists who sought interviews with Terry. There
were two from Belgium where the show is now transmitted
by cable television. Women particularly want to interview
Terry's wife, Helen. Wasn't it natural, I asked, that people
should want to meet the woman behind the great man?

'I agree,' Carol said. 'But Terry nearly always says no to
them, otherwise he couldn't enjoy a private life.'

I began to see the logic of her statement. I said that I had
heard that Terry didn't suffer fools gladly and could be
difficult at times when things went wrong. 'We have never
found Terry to be temperamental or moody,' Carol assured
me. 'I find working for the *Wogan* team exciting. I meet a
lot of interesting people.'

Briefly she outlined how the Wogan show operated. There
was a Transmission Week and a Planning Week, which
meant that two different teams were at work all the time.
These included researchers, producers, their assistants, a
music researcher and a forward planner.

As I listened to her musical voice, the Wogan Industry
seemed to mushroom before my eyes. Clearly, the great
man had out-stripped his fellow Irishman Eamonn Andrews
in the number of people who depended on him for a living.
He now stood apart from the mortals in the business. Here,
at the pulse of the Wogan Industry, one felt among staffers
a deep sense of loyalty, an evident eagerness to make *Wogan*
the most exciting chat show on TV. Everyone was playing
for their captain; the secret was teamwork and Terry was an
inspiring captain.

But where was the great man himself?

Would I soon see him bounding gleefully along the
corridor whistling 'The Bold Fenian Men'? Could it be possible that the *Wogan* teamwork was by now so perfect that
the captain didn't need to be around? Great corporations
like the BBC do not revolve around one man, even the great
man himself; he, too, has to take his place among the BBC
hierarchy. There are other floors, other members of the hierarchy. Terry is not God. Nor does he want to be, he has
informed the world.

But that isn't the reason he doesn't often visit the seventh floor. Miss Millward explained: 'Terry hardly ever comes here. He lets us get on with what we're doing. He prefers to go straight to the BBC Television Theatre in Shepherd's Bush.'

I decided not to pursue the matter any further. I followed Miss Millward into an adjoining room where I was introduced to Frances Whitaker, who was then executive producer of *Wogan*.

I knew that Miss Whitaker was a key figure in the Wogan Industry. When it was decided to run *Wogan* three evenings a week she was invited to join the team and left the South Bank Studios in London Weekend Television in order to do so. By the end of the first year she had become Terry's close aide, adviser, friend and number one admirer.

She talked of her experience as producer with the Clive James and Michael Aspel chat shows and how different they were to *Wogan*. She was now, I could see, enjoying her stint with *Wogan*. It was part of her job to decide whom to invite, keeping the balance between showbiz people and newsworthy personalities. She was a strong influence on the show, although it is true that Terry is consulted about guests and he may make certain suggestions from time to time, but mostly he leaves the filling of the guests lists to his producer and team of researchers.

Terry has placed responsibility for a large portion of the success of *Wogan* on Miss Whitaker's expertise. 'We've never run out of guests and while the Boss is around, we never will. She's a brilliant "booker" and possibly the most experienced chat-show producer in British television.'

I decided to ask about Terry's wardrobe for the Wogan show. The wardrobe is of course all important to a superstar like Terry Wogan because it creates an image. I have always suspected that Terry treasures his wardrobe as a Hollywood star her glamour.

Miss Whitaker was prepared for my question. 'Yes,' she said calmly, 'Terry does have a large wardrobe for the show.

He has a slim wardrobe and a slightly fatty wardrobe, depending on how much weight he is carrying at the time.'

Were all his clothes provided by the BBC?

'No, not all.' Terry has about half a dozen favourite suits – greys and blues – which he likes to wear, particularly the blue shades. 'I think he likes blue but it is not his favourite.' She agreed that suitable clothes were important to Terry's image on the show. 'Terry is quite aware of this.'

I switched to the subject of pressure. The 'eighties were a time of pressure and stress. How immune was Terry? Or, if he was vulnerable, how did he disguise it?

'I don't think there is any personal pressure on him as such,' Frances replied. 'There is of course pressure to provide viewers with the best possible viewing and the best line-up of guests. Terry does not agonise before a show. He experiences as far as I know no tension or nervousness. He is as relaxed as he looks on the screen. If he is not enjoying himself, the viewers will not enjoy themselves. In fact, not only is Terry good at coping with crises that may arise on the show, he is expert at putting guests at their ease. He has this astonishing knack. That's why guests like to be interviewed by him. Even people who are new to television say he has made it all so easy.'

When I suggested that it might be difficult, if not impossible, to find suitable guests for a five-nights-a-week *Wogan*, Miss Whitaker assured me that she saw no difficulty. 'We have only scratched the surface. There are millions of potential guests in Britain alone. Problems do arise sometimes about guests. An American film star one has invited on the show in the morning may be unable to turn up because shooting on a film has overrun, so that leaves a gap to be filled, but we have a few people we can telephone and ask to come on the show. There are other people who want a day or two to ponder over an invitation and may in the end say no. A woman may want time to go to the hairdresser, or she may have a prior engagement. All the time people say no to going on the show. People have this mistaken idea that all one has to do is to make three telephone calls –

to the Pope, the Queen, and to Jackie Onassis and they will come on *Wogan*. Unfortunately it doesn't work that way.'

Proudly she disclosed that Terry Wogan was among the top five television personalities in the BBC. I remembered what a spokesman for the BBC had told me earlier: 'Terry's our biggest gun in the battle with ITV.' There had been reports that the Director-General wanted the show to become a little more up-market but the idea had met with a cool reception. The *Wogan* team saw *Wogan* in terms of entertainment and were suspicious of any move to make it educational.

Since Frances Whitaker was in charge of the show's editorial direction her opinion was sought. 'We could do a sort of chatty *Newsnight* at seven o'clock,' she said, 'but I don't think it would be as popular as the show we are now doing. In any case, the programme is changing all the time – you can never stand still.'

The show has not been without incident. Inevitably, traffic jams, delayed flight arrivals and the odd dose of back-stage drama (one actress managed to forget to take her insulin injection) have provided Terry with the occasional show-stopping moments. But through it all he has remained unflappable. He says that pre-show nerves don't figure in his routine. 'I just smoke my cigar and relax,' is his stock answer to questions aimed at finding the secret behind an almost unerringly cool and casual attitude.

The *Wogan* team will tell you that it is a 'happy ship'. They wouldn't want it any other way. Miss Whitaker said: 'It would be hard to work with somebody closely and as often as I do with Terry if you didn't actually think on similar lines. Terry has said quite often that he prefers to work in an atmosphere that is friendly rather than combative. He doesn't like working with argumentative and bad-tempered people and will not have them around him.'

Had not some critic claimed that he could be severe on those around him if errors were made?

'He has been known to go off in a rage,' Miss Whitaker said, 'but only after he's stamped his feet and slammed the dressing-room door on me! He compensates with the daily delivery of a box of chocolates, which reveals his rather soft centre.'

It is no secret that the *Wogan* team would like to see the show run five nights in the week. Not only would this boost the Wogan Industry considerably but a better balance could be achieved. One poor show, for instance, would be more readily forgotten and every effort made to provide an exciting one next night. But would five nights be altogether too much? Frances Whitaker did not think so. She agreed with me about the Englishman's fascination with chat shows and reasoned that it centred around the celebrities on the show and Terry's own image. 'I think also,' she added, 'the obsession has a lot to do with stardom. Viewers love to have stars brought into their sitting-rooms and chat shows do this superbly. They're glamorous shows and often can be informative about the stars themselves and their lifestyles. People just like the image presented by stars.'

Why did the show continue to be such a success and command such high ratings? Frances explained: 'First of all it's because Terry has this gift to communicate with people. They enjoy his sense of humour and obviously appreciate what he is doing. I am convinced there is no one who could do this show with the same ease as Terry. It's nice to know that whatever happens he is never going to embarrass his audience. He copes with most things and claims he learned that side of the trade in Ireland, working on shows that nobody was watching – things went wrong and it just didn't matter. *Wogan* is built round Terry and his personality, and even if the guests got stuck in one big traffic jam or, as was the case with Bob Geldof, were late arriving by air (the interview eventually came live from Hatfield Airport) he would sing, dance, talk to the audience and quite happily entertain them for the entire show. They would even be forgiven for forgetting there hadn't been a guest around within miles.'

Were the guests paid?

'Not a lot really. Nobody makes a lot of money in this

country out of appearing on chat shows. Anyway I don't think people go on chat shows for the money.'

It is reputed that guests are paid between £200 and £500. I am inclined to the view that some of the writers and film people would willingly exchange their fee for the valuable publicity. Terry says he has no 'real favourites' as regards guests. 'I just take 'em as I find them. If they go down well, it's all due to good production work.'

As I talked with Frances Whitaker I sometimes expected – hoped – that Terry might bounce into the office and surprise us all. But remembering what Carol Millward had said earlier, I realised that possibility was remote. I refrained from raising the likelihood with Miss Whitaker for fear of raising my own expectations too high. I recalled reading Terry's own explanation for staying away: 'It's essential that I don't get involved in the actual production of the show, otherwise it would become too stressful. I only get involved in that I like to know who is going to be on the show. I express my opinions as forcibly as I can, but that's as far as it goes!'

I hadn't finished with the Wogan Industry. There was Terry's fan mail; he attracts the BBC's biggest postbag, around 3,000 letters a week, and there is a staff to sort them out. And I was assured that only half the employees of the industry are to be found on the seventh floor of the British Broadcasting Corporation building; the other forty, mostly technicians, cameramen and lighting men, worked on the transmission of *Wogan* three evenings of the week from Shepherd's Bush.

Speculation about Terry's earnings has continued unabated. In Ireland he is now sometimes called 'millionaire Wogan' and this is not out of envy but admiration for his achievements. Once faced with the question: 'Are you a millionaire?' Terry replied: 'People say that I am a millionaire. I am not sure what they mean by that. I have always felt that the notion of a millionaire implies somebody who has enough money to keep him for the rest of his life, somebody who could stop work in the morning and never have to work again. If that's a millionaire then I am not one. I couldn't stop now and live on my money. The more you earn the more you spend and the greater the financial commitments you get into. To maintain my lifestyle and my family, I will have to work for many more years before I could think of stopping. Anyway, I have no desire to stop work. I enjoy broadcasting enormously and I intend going long after they are pushing me around in the old wheelchair.'

The fact is that of course he's a millionaire, a self-made one at that, so he doesn't have to wriggle in embarrassment. He has climbed from a humble banker to rank among the highest-paid television stars in Britain. Despite his claim that 'he will have to work many more years before he could think of stopping', there are those who believe he could take a year's sabbatical without the threat of starvation hanging over him.

Queried once about *Wogan*, he replied: 'I didn't need to do the show for the money or professionally. I did it for the challenge and all there is left now is to see the show run every night.'

There was a sensation not so long ago at the BBC when the computer leaked confidential information, including details of his pay. The figure mentioned was a staggering £350,000 a year from the Beeb. Instead of these details going to three senior people in the organisation, they were sent to dozens of others. For once the loquacious Terry said little. When asked about his pay, all he said was: 'No comment.'

He could argue of course that wealth is not discussed among the gentlemen of England, that it is actually caddish to indulge in such talk. When best-selling author Jeffrey Archer appeared as a guest on *Wogan* he was asked by Terry: 'How much are you worth now?' Quickly Archer replied: 'Not quite as much as you, Terry.'

As far back as 1982, when Terry was commanding more than £1,000 for a public appearance, British Broadcasting Press Guild Chairman Margaret Forewood commented: 'There's no way of really knowing how much the Wogan wonder earns in a year. But it's certainly enough for him to have turned down a contract with London Weekend Television on which £250,000 a show was going to be spent, with a lot of that going to Terry.'

It is accepted that by 1986 his earnings totalled at least £500,000 a year. Friends now say that he combines the broadcaster's flair with entrepreneurial vision, a claim that does not seem without foundation. Others prefer to call it the Midas touch. Although most of his earnings come from the Beeb, he and his family own 98 per cent of a showbiz agency called Jo Gurnett Personal Management, which guides his own career and those of Anna Ford and Gloria Hunniford among others, and is one of the founders of a company making video-tapes.

A realist, he recognises the ephemeral nature of show business. 'It changes so quickly, it's madness to rely on it.' In recent years he has been a big earner. In 1984 he was asking an Irish export firm for £100,000 to promote Irish beef in Britain. If the money is right, he will not think twice about hopping on a plane and doing a breakfast stint in a Dublin hotel.

In the advertising business he is known as One Take Terry. He has promoted margarine, fitted kitchens, rubber gloves and a variety of other products. The money for such work has been considerable. Each time he heard himself for thirty seconds on radio or television it was worth another £80 or so to the Wogan Industry. Even today, despite his busy commitments, he is heard in voice-overs on Irish radio.

Terry's recreations are listed in *Who's Who* as 'tennis, golf, swimming, reading and writing'. He is a member of the London-Irish Rugby Club, Lords Taverners and Stokes Poges Golf Club and Temple Golf Club. He entertains lavishly at home, something he has always been known to do since he first began to scale the broadcasting ladder in Britain. He can count on some loyal friends, although he rarely, it is said, puts showbusiness people on his dinner guest list. For relaxation between *Wogans* he and Helen may jet to their Spanish villa, or to New York. Like most modern rich and famous people, Terry tends to be guarded about his family for fear of the threat of kidnapping. There was a time when he welcomed journalists to what he jokingly calls Wogan Towers, his home in Berkshire, but this has changed. As Terry explains: 'The press jumps all over your bones every time you move. Your son gets mugged and they are living on your lawn, your wife goes into hospital and they're sitting in the car park.'

In 1984 his son Mark was viciously attacked by two muggers as he walked home one night after visiting neighbours. He suffered grazing and bruising, but beat off the two masked attackers, forcing them to flee empty handed. The incident changed Terry's attitude to publicity.

It is generally accepted that in America success is admired, whereas in Britain and Ireland it is more often envied. The Wogan Phenomenon is no exception. Terry, like others who have not inherited their wealth but worked for it, seems unaffected by it, just as he is unaffected by fame. His friends claim he is a workaholic despite his own plea that he is lazy. The truth is he cannot afford to be lazy, not with so many agencies requiring his services – these range from the opening of fêtes to making personal appearances. In this respect he has joined the Big League and is likely to ask for £5,000, which places him above Selina Scott (£4,000), Bob Monkhouse (£3,000 to £4,000) and Steve Davis.

From time to time he is approached by authors and journalists anxious to get a slice of the Wogan Industry. Terry is cautious at such moments, realising no doubt his own value in the literary market. He told me: 'I have been asked, it is true, many times in the past to have my life "ghosted" for me, but I'm in no hurry. When I've the time I'll reveal to the world the Wogan secrets!'

In Terry's case it is not all income, there is expenditure as well. His agent, Mrs Jo Gurnett gets between 15 and 25 per cent commission for looking after his show-business affairs, despite the fact that Terry is the biggest shareholder in the agency, of which Mrs Gurnett is also a director. She says she has derived great satisfaction during her eleven years' association with Terry, seeing him climb the ladder in radio and television. She considers his move into the thrice-weekly *Wogan* as a very important step in his development as a television performer. 'He's made it,' she adds with a smile. She can take some of the credit.

In June '86, the thriving Wogan agency moved into impressive new headquarters in Fulham. The company now caters for Anna Ford, Tony Blackburn, Gloria Hunniford, John Dunn, Diana Moran and the popular Kenny Everett. Furthermore, Terry is also one of the four founders and a significant shareholder in Film Training Aids, a video production company to make films such as *It's Your Business to Know* – a seventeen-part series that he presented and narrated. The marketing of it was handled by McGraw-Hill International Training Systems, part of the US-based world-wide publishing empire.

By September the Wogan Industry was spreading its wings from the BBC to ITV, when it was announced that he was one of the leading figures behind an animated children's series to be screened that autumn. Terry is the major share-holder of Queengate Productions, which has made the show called *The Trap Door*. The series, in twenty-three parts, would be screened every weekday from early October, each episode lasting five minutes.

Terry has made no apologies for combining a showbiz and business career. He explains: 'I have to diversify. The BBC could decide to dispose of my services at the end of the year. Popularity and success are such ephemeral things. When you've only got your voice and face between you and the workhouse, you have to make other arrangements.'

The workhouse? Some of the *Wogan* team were heard to gasp when they read the statement. It had curious Dicken-sian undertones. Worse, it underlined a gnawing and unnecessary insecurity on Terry's part. The more logical answer is that he is ploughing back into business the profits he is making from show business. Once, when I asked him in his dressing-room in Shepherd's Bush, what he actually did with all *that* money, he never quite answered my question adequately. Why should he? He did admit, though, that his annual tax bill was 'considerable'.

In the autumn of '86 there certainly seemed no reason for the remotest hint of self-doubt in Terry's mind. His star was floating high in the sky over Shepherd's Bush Green. On Monday, September 22, he celebrated his 250th *Wogan*, looking immaculate in his well-tailored suit. The close proximity of television survivor David Frost (his stand-in for a week) cannot have been reassuring; however, subsequent *Wogan*s proved that the slick Mr Frost lacked the charm of the down-to-earth Mr Wogan, which meant that he made an adequate stand-in, no more. Esther Rantzen, his stand-in for the second week, seemed badly miscast. Maybe Frances Whitaker was right after all – no one can adequately take Terry's place on *Wogan*.

Terry's earnings continued to attract the attention of the press. When he described his £350,000 a year salary as 'peanuts', it was bound to cause a critical stir in a country where unemployment is so high. As a qualification, Terry remarked: 'I don't think my salary is all that much.'

It was an accurate assessment compared with the earnings of others in showbusiness. Few people would have guessed that Max Bygraves and Michael Aspel each earns as much as Terry Wogan, or that Noel Edmonds and Bruce Forsyth command fees only £50,000 or so a year below Terry's. In the big television league, where ratings count for all, there seems no limit to the fees and salaries paid to the top audience-pullers. Jimmy Tarbuck is reputed to be a one-million-pound earner. He receives around £20,000 a show, hosting Yorkshire TV's game *Winner Takes All*.

Of course earnings fluctuate. It is reckoned that Bruce Forsyth's can vary between £250,000 and £500,000 a year. Although Max Bygraves has not had his own television series since *Family Fortunes*, he always fills theatres and halls in a dozen countries.

But Terry Wogan remains the BBC's top earner. It is argued that his annual earnings from the Beeb are now

pushing £400,000 a year, because his contract, signed two
years ago, stipulates an annual rise of 10 per cent or the
rate of inflation – whichever is the greater. The Jo Gurnett
Personal Management Agency continues to boom (even
Princess Margaret's former escort Roddy Lllewellyn has
signed up) and Terry himself is increasingly in demand for
TV commercials. Advertisers in both the UK and Ireland
pay him fat fees to publicise anything from Bovril cubes to
Flora Margarine.

Yet Terry never gives the impression that he is performing
only for the loot. He will tell you he immensely enjoys most
things, right down to voice-overs. And he doesn't demand
exorbitant fees for everything he is offered. There is the
story told of a small film producer in Dublin – a friend of
Terry's – who asked him to narrate for a film, carefully
adding; 'We can't pay you a lot, Terry.'

'How much?' asked Terry.

'Not a lot.'

'Don't worry, friend, I'll do it.'

Terry is loyal to his friends.

2　Shepherd's Bush

Wogan: the familiar name greets you as you approach the BBC Television Theatre in London's Sheppherd's Bush Green. The converted theatre is another integral link with the Wogan Industry and the Wogan Phenomenon. From here, on three evenings of the week, is transmitted to millions of viewers the popular Wogan show.

It is Terry's wonderful world for nearly three full days each week. And half-way up the front of the quaint building, visible to all from across the green, is the name 'Wogan'.

Somewhere inside, the great man was preparing for his next show. To get a glimpse of him, to be part of the show and its celebrities, his admirers had come to Shepherd's Bush on foot, by car, tube and coach, from near and far, each the proud holder of an admission ticket with the name 'Wogan' colourfully printed on it.

The set for *Wogan* covered the width of the stage. The two familiar chairs were there, one facing the other, and the backdrop reminiscent of a disco with its twinkling lights and glittering colours. By now the warm-up comic was doing his stint. The audience was in good spirits and sympathetic. Cheerfully he enquired: 'Is Emma's group from Essex here?' Immediately a roar went up from a part of the audience. The audience were prepared to laugh at the drop of a hat.

'It's Terry you've really come to see, though,' 'aven't you?' asked the comic wistfully.

'Yeah!' the audience roared, their impatience obvious. They could barely wait for Terry to appear.

The comic asked the audience to clap to give the

soundman a level. Afterwards he asked us to try again. We obliged but the applause wasn't loud enough. After some more minutes of constantly interrupted gags and much clapping a genuine roar from the audience on one side shook the theatre as the star was spotted. The comic introduced the star of the show at the top of his voice, 'Good old Terry!' Everyone in the theatre responded at once with cheers and applause. Terry called for applause for the departing comic and everyone clapped again.

Terry, in a friendly voice, said: 'We'll start the show now. It's not that serious you know. It's not the Eurovision Song Contest.'

People around me were straining their eyes to catch a glimpse at last of Terry in the flesh. Looking immaculate in his well-tailored bright blue suit, red tie and light-blue shirt, he appeared not at all different from the image we had come to expect from his countless television shows. He was no bigger, no smaller, no skinnier, no more red-faced. His personality exuded friendliness. He chatted to the audience, made them feel totally at ease, and acknowledged their applause with a slight wave of his hand.

The familiar began. The overhead monitors displayed the opening sequences, the music played, and then suddenly we saw the whimsical smile of Terry in close-up. He made some amusing introductory remarks, an essential and enjoyable part of any *Wogan*, and by the time he had finished a guest had been eased into one of the empty chairs facing the star. It was noticeable from the start that Terry was intent on taking his audience with him and a number of his witty asides were intentionally aimed at making us all part of the show. It was like real theatre, except for the flashing lights, the cameras and the technicians.

The successful Wogan technique was immediately apparent. Terry was talking to his guests just as he might chat up a friend in his local; he cultivated a nice informal air which seemed to put guests at their ease. They had no reason to be nervous about possible 'loaded' questions. It was a simple approach and it seemed to work admirably. It was persuasion without aggression, blarney without bluntness, wit without wickedness. The Wogan recipe was working like a charm. As a critic put it: 'It was his self-deprecating charm and gift for creating a unique intimacy with his viewers that won his show an audience of up to 13 million – enough to put *Wogan* regularly in BBC TV's top ten'.

The show proceeded without a hitch. People around me were clearly enjoying themselves. Those who had made the long coach journeys to see the great man were not disappointed. But there was one more hurdle left to jump before the show was over. I wondered if it would present Terry with any problem. It centred round his next guest, Anna Ford, a single-minded woman with considerable experience of working on television. She had been invited on the show that evening because of her best-selling book *Men*. It was regarded as controversial, very outspoken, and not at all nice to the much maligned male species. She was guilty of *the* unpardonable sin – she had investigated the sexual behaviour of the male, and even for a smart lady like Miss Ford that was a daring experiment to undertake. Some of the answers she got in her research on the subject would not be considered suitable material for airing on an early-evening show in case grand-dad was watching the box. So I wondered if Terry would skip over the salacious bits and concentrate instead on the more amusing parts.

Perhaps it is well to put Terry's chat-show approach into some perspective. Unlike Harold Williamson ('I always think that the best second question is not to speak'), he does not aim to draw out the darker side of the human soul for public inspection. Terry's skill lies elsewhere. With three or four guests to get through in forty minutes he hasn't got time for any soul-searching. But he is never shy to take on people in a lighter vein. As a former rugby player, the great man knows that the bigger they come the harder they fall.

On Anna Ford's book jacket there is a splendid photograph of Anna, which shows off her well-chiselled profile. Now, as she faced Terry, she looked confident, as one might expect from a woman well versed in current affairs on television. A smiling Terry said: 'Welcome back to the old haunted fishtank.'

FORD: (*With a show of slight bewilderment*) The haunted . . . fishtank . . . ?

WOGAN: You did miss it, didn't you?

FORD: I did.

WOGAN: The excitement of it all (*After a pause*) You got mixed critical reaction for your book?

FORD: Mixed critical reaction? The critics got at it because they didn't like it. It's reasonable for them to say they don't like the book, but when they say they don't like the author it's a bit personal. I've heard of men who visited bookshops at lunchtime and leaving with the book beneath their mackintoshes.

WOGAN: They were probably looking for dirty pictures.

FORD: But the women have been nice about it.

WOGAN: You didn't paint the men in a very favourable light, did you?

FORD: I didn't paint men. I simply interviewed them. Condemned out of their own mouths, I am afraid, by what *they* said, not what I said.

WOGAN: Maybe you'll tackle an agony column soon now?

FORD: I'd find that difficult. I've trained myself to listen. I think it would be hard finding answers. It's hard enough to find answers to one's own problems.

At this point Terry deftly switched the conversation round to Miss Ford's home life, which he described as 'conventional for her'.

FORD: I don't think I lived a wildly unconventional life before.

WOGAN: I remember they used to call you the darling of the smart set?

FORD: (*slightly annoyed*) Did they?

WOGAN: I mean . . . you taking your clothes off at the Embassy Club?

FORD: I don't remember that.

WOGAN: You have conveniently forgotten about it.

FORD: Yes, I have. (Pause) I remember having my photograph taken from time to time but I don't remember living a wild unconventional life.

WOGAN: In your book you wrote that men are simple, clever and dependent. You implied that women were stronger. If men are simple, clever and lonely, do women have any problems?

FORD: I think women who have become very independent are very strong. I think that women are more mature than men. (*Audience breaks into laughter*).

WOGAN: Why not more women in politics then?

FORD: I have a feeling when it comes to the crunch women are too sensible to go into Parliament. My own view is that politicians live a miserable sort of life.

WOGAN: Do you think women are afraid then?

FORD: They may be afraid. I think they look at the life they are going to have if they go into politics.

WOGAN: If I was writing a book and came to you and asked you: "Do you think sexual chemistry works?" – what would you say?

FORD: (*Unsmilingly*) I think that is a loaded question. I didn't invent that phrase. It was David Frost who invented it. There was no sex chemistry between me and him.

WOGAN: The trouble about Frost is that he thinks he invented sex as well. (*After a slight pause*) Do any men live up to your expectations, or do you find that generally you are disappointed?

FORD: No, they get better as they get older.

WOGAN: Better at what?

FORD: They're very interesting and more handsome and more charming, more mature and sophisticated.

WOGAN: Do women improve with age?

FORD: I think they do.

WOGAN: Do you feel totally self-assured?

FORD: I feel more confident. I am forty-two years old. As you get older you feel more confident. I worry less about things I used to worry about. My life is going extremely well.

Terry thanked Anna for coming on the show and went straight away into the list of guests for his next *Wogan*. The forty minutes seemed to have slipped away more quickly than I or anyone expected and left some of the audience rather puzzled. Slowly they lifted themselves from their seats and wandered towards the exits. To those unacquainted with Miss Ford's *Men* the Wogan interview probably meant very little, save perhaps affording a chance to see Anna as she really is off screen and in conversation with Terry; otherwise book talk didn't interest most of them.

However, the interview did achieve, to my mind, something very significant – it underlined clearly the world of difference between Terry's approach and that of Joan Rivers. Joan, in similar circumstances, would probably have come armed with a copy of *Men* and shocked all and sundry with her direct, unbridled approach based on the book's intimate details of men's sexual behaviour.

Terry avoided such shock tactics and instead concentrated more on Anna Ford's views than on the sexual behaviour of the men in her book. It was an intriguing approach and achieved a positive result. The interview between Terry and Anna also illustrated Terry's exquisite light touch as opposed, for instance, to Joan River's often vulgar self-indulgence.

Wogan audiences have come to expect good taste from the host and are rarely disappointed. What they enjoy are his witty asides, ironic comments and his own intelligent brand of conversation with guests. Terry says: 'A chat should be a little untidy, rough at the edges, live and spontaneous. Its entertainment-level will vary with its guests. The chat show is the lucky dip of television. You switch it on and then, just as quickly, switch it off. But it should always be worth a peek.'

He dismisses the notion that it should be 'serious and profound'. By his own admission 'the chat show is bread-and-butter television, easily digestible, regular and filling the empty schedules. Its function is usually to shore up the empty weaker parts of the television day, early afternoon, early evening and late evening. It's designed to keep the audience mildly entertained, interested and still viewing until the big prime-time block-buster comes up, until it's time to put the cat out. As with a daily radio show, the television chat show's great strengths are its regularity, its familiarity and, certainly, the very predictability of its host to the show's constant viewers.'

To Terry, the *Johnny Carson Show* in America is a good example of what he was trying to convey. 'People in Britain,' he argues 'are constantly telling me how awful Carson's show is, on the basis of a couple of nights' viewing while on holiday or on business in the States. But a whole generation of Americans have grown up with Carson. They understand him and he understands them. They can anticipate his every word and every nod and wink. His every move and gesture denote a man confident of his public, secure in their affection. He's been there twenty years, day in, day out, week in, week out. Criticism has long since become redundant. It's only lately that British television has seen the chat show for the mundane and ordinary thing that it is. Hitherto it's been confused with a "major" entertainment.'

For Terry the evening was not over. It is a ritual with him to join his guests after the show in the Green Room. There he can relax over an informal chat and have a glass of wine or two. It is said that half the fun of being a guest on *Wogan* is speculating which fellow guest you're likely to meet in the Hospitality Room – or as it has now ironically become known, the 'Hostility Room'. The atmosphere is warm as film stars mix easily with soap-opera stars, rock singers with authors, politicians with captains of industry.

Terry had already met the guests briefly before the show when they gathered in the Green Room. But he avoided giving any hint of what his chat with them would be. Now it was different. There was no need for inhibition. Stories abound about happenings to *Wogan* guests. There was the reported case of singer/actress Cher. Her car was caught in traffic and it was touch and go whether she would make the show at all, never mind the pre-show party. The *Wogan* team had to hastily rearrange the timings, in the hope that she would turn up before the show was due to end. It was such a close thing that Cher had to hotfoot it into the studio as the final minutes ticked away. Terry remained calm as usual. Eventually a breathless Cher made it and chatted amiably for eight minutes with Terry.

Sir Les Patterson, Australian 'Cultural Attaché', alias actor Barry Humphries, caused a sensation before he appeared on the show. To give himself that 'disgusting image', Sir Les slapped his hand in the cheese dip in the Green Room, and smeared it all over the front of his suit before going out to meet Terry.

Victoria Principal and Terry together now make compulsive viewing. Their first meeting was tempestuous. In fact, five minutes after the show, Victoria roared off into the night in her black limo, refusing to set foot in the hospitality room. But now they get on famously.

Things can also go wrong off-screen. Sharon Glass, star of *Cagney and Lacey* can testify to that. When she left the Shepherd's Bush Theatre in the evening, having enjoyed the after-show party, she was mobbed by fans. In her frantic efforts to escape she ended up in another part of the building and shouted, 'Let me in! I'm Sharon Glass – you know, from *Cagney and Lacey*.'

'Oh, yes,' came the reply behind the BBC door, 'and I'm Margaret Thatcher!' and the door stayed shut.

Eventually a much relieved Sharon was escorted to safety by two passing women police officers.

Technicians can vividly recall when Terry started off the Sophia Loren interview with a couple of sizzling questions: 'Are you still drinking?' and 'Let's have the truth about your affair with Dudley Moore?' Immediately the technicians were seen to burst into laughter. In fact, Ms Loren wasn't even there and knew nothing about the bizarre enquiries. For sitting in the chair reserved for the Italian film star was one of the *Wogan* floor assistants playing the role of Sophia in the afternoon rehearsal of the evening show.

When it came to the actual show that night, Terry dropped the 'loaded' questions, but the real ones were still pointed enough to make his audience sit up. Like: 'You are the epitome of beauty – but you are fifty . . .' A surprised Loren snapped: 'What's wrong with that? I feel only twelve inside. And that's what counts. How old are you yourself?'

Terry beamed: 'I'm forty-six. A mere slip of a lad.'

Loren: 'Then you need to read my book on beauty. Especially about the legs.'

Ever since that interview in October 1984 Terry's legs have held a curious fascination for the guests. Although Miss Loren turned down the opportunity to touch his legs, since then half of Hollywood's female stars haven't been so coy.

Sometimes Terry genuinely regrets that he hasn't sufficient time to talk with guests. As he explained: 'We had only five minutes with Howard Keel, which was a great shame. Of course we can invite the same guests on the next night, like Paul Hogan and June Havoc, but it's not always possible for them. Howard Keel was so good you just wished you had another five minutes. But there's little you can do. You can record the extended interview and keep it for the next day, but you lose the live feel of the show.'

Although his chat with Princess Anne on *Wogan* was recorded and as a result 'missed that electricity of the live show', Terry enjoyed it. It was the first time he had set out to meet his guest before a show.

'I saw her at Buckingham Palace. It was quite a feeling going through those gates, I can tell you. But she didn't lay down the law at all about what I could and couldn't ask. We got on very well and she was so pleased with how the show went that she even had drinks with us afterwards. I don't think our chat did her image any harm. She came across very well.'

In the course of the chat she was asked what she would do if the monarchy was abolished. The Princess replied she'd have to work harder on the farm, or get a job as a long-distance lorry driver.

Terry says his most disappointed guest was Omar Sharif. 'He told viewers he was interested in finding a wife. He got this tremendous postbag, full of naughty suggestions. The trouble was we mislaid the mail. But Omar still lives in hope.' Terry has become known for his flirting (on *Wogan*) with the world's most alluring women. Only Raquel Welch took exception to his style. She seemed to want the discussion to be a ten-minute promotion of her book on beauty. Terry wasn't having any of that. In retrospect, she was one of the few lovely women to be rude to him – and that's not a bad record.

It's doubtful whether Terry will get the opportunity to welcome onto his show the most wanted woman in Britain for chat shows – the Prime Minister, Margaret Thatcher. When they met after an invitation to Downing Street, Mrs Thatcher said to him: 'What would you like to drink? It's on the taxpayer.'

Terry chuckled: 'I'm a taxpayer. I'll have some water, if you please.'

Needless to say, he hasn't been invited back!

Leaving the BBC Television Theatre, one encounters another side of the Wogan Industry. In the foyer there are Wogan souvenirs for sale, including T-shirts. I watched as girls snapped them up. Others waited hopefully for a glimpse of the great man. In the street outside a few people had heard a rumour that 'Terry would be coming by soon', but it was groundless. It is well known that he doesn't greatly care for such public adulation.

When he slips into Dublin for an international rugby match he has left his hotel next morning before the Dublin reporters realise it. But he does have special affection for *Wogan* audiences. They are after all part of the Wogan Phenomenon and help to maintain it.

Talking about the show, he has been quoted as saying: 'The theatre is not the ideal place to do *Wogan*. It's not big enough and I would like to have the audience closer. I would like more freedom to take the cameras outside and I would like more freedom to comment on other TV programmes. At the moment this isn't really in the brief. But if I have my way we will gradually become more flexible.'

In a rare moment of whimsy, he remarked: 'The wheel of God moves slowly' – and, he hoped, 'surely'.

3   *Wogan Towers*

Terry admits that the Wogan Phenomenon and the Wogan Industry probably wouldn't exist without his stable marriage and happy home. Away from the glitzy world of television, he is essentially a family man and obviously intensely proud of the private world he has created. Here such trite Fleet Street lines as 'TV Megastar Terry Wogan, the Guinness-smooth talker from Limerick who put the corn into leprechaun' seem curiously unreal.

His wife, Helen, is a shrewd and intelligent woman who, after nineteen years of living in England, still speaks with a soft Irish brogue, has what she good-humouredly calls 'Irish freckles' on her pale-skinned face, and is a very supportive wife and mum. One suspects, though, that she is seriously underrated as an influence behind the Wogan Phenomenon, and perhaps too the Wogan Industry. She can certainly dispense useful advice; she has watched enough television to know when a performer is wearing the wrong shade of suit or when a show is not quite right. Yet she is adamant she is not a critic. 'Criticising performers demeans them and serves no purpose,' she says.

To meet this unusual woman, I made the journey to Wogan Towers, as Terry jokingly calls their house in the heart of leafy Buckinghamshire. From the narrow, winding road the house is partly hidden behind high pebble-dashed walls, with lockable gates that surround the forecourt. Built at the turn of the century in that mock Tudor-style that is at once quaint and typically English, it has been the Wogan home for about twelve years now.

They used to live not far away and became friends of the occupants. One evening after a dinner-party Terry said: 'I really love this house, Helen. One day we are going to buy a house like it.'

After the birth of their youngest child, Katherine, they decided to buy a bigger house and approached an estate agent. By a lucky coincidence the house in Buckinghamshire was on the market.

'We pulled out all the stops to buy it,' Helen recalls. 'I was attracted to it because it seemed a nice family house, not too big. It had nice-sized bedrooms and a large hall that I adored from the moment I saw it. It's always nice to get your hands on a place and do it up the way you want it. Structurally, we had little to do, but set about improving the décor, recarpeting and buying the kind of furniture and curtains to suit the new décor.'

Wogan Towers is the perfect retreat for the private Wogan, an idyllic house that affords a panoramic view from the terrace across the broad fields of Buckinghamshire with Windsor Castle in the distance. Terry jokes that on a clear day he and the Queen wave at one another. At the age of forty-eight, he is rich and famous and has the status symbols to show for it. Parked in the drive alongside the Rolls Royce is a Jaguar and near by Helen's Mercedes sports car.

Terry's study is situated off the drawing-room; it's a compact room, yet spacious and well lit. Its walls are festooned with photographs of Terry with other celebrities and friends; in between are some of the best cartoons of the great man. His antique desk is small but large enough to accommodate his famous legs. 'Terry doesn't spend a lot of time in his study,' Helen remarks.

The drawing-room is particularly refreshing, at once ornate and brightly lit, with its apricot décor and french windows that afford a view over the countryside. More poster-sized family photographs adorn the room; even the top of the small grand piano is littered with them, one of Terry and Helen together immediately catching the eye. The colour scheme of the room, from the pale sofas to the shining silverware and sober mahogany, is easy on the eye and shows excellent taste. One of the large prints on the wall facing the French windows depicts a Dublin scene, a reminder of the Wogans' Irish links. There is a brilliance of cut glass, and a fireplace alcove with a carved beam overhead, and fake coal-fire beneath.

Helen takes pride in pointing out various pieces which she says she picked up in antique shops and at auctions. Obviously transforming Wogan Towers into its present stylish interior has taken the best part of a decade. The most striking feature about the dining-room is the mahogany table with its matching chairs for twelve diners.

'Usually we have eight or ten people,' Helen explains. 'I can't stand large parties, nor do I care for buffet parties. I like people to sit at table and eat in comfort. There is nothing worse than standing with a plate in one hand and glass in the other.

'We never feel it necessary to entertain on a business level. We invite old friends as well as new friends. I always try to make a bit of an effort when I'm cooking. It is so easy to plunk a roast in the oven and say that's it; but I like to do something different. Terry may give out to me occasionally and say, "You go to too much trouble." I never think it's too much trouble if people enjoy themselves. I may serve up a nice chicken dish. I like doing different sauces.'

During the run of *Wogan* she will cook a dinner for seven o'clock for the children, Alan, Mark and Katherine; then at nine o'clock, when Terry returns from the Television Theatre in Shepherd's Bush, she will have a drink ready for him and afterwards they'll sit down to dinner together. Usually she will have seen that evening's *Wogan*, but over the meal she will only briefly refer to it. She might remark that such an interview was good or so-and-so was responsive.

'I never criticise,' remarks Helen. 'I know that Terry wants to relax. He does not ask for a video-tape of the show. He never looks at himself on television. When one *Wogan* is over, he is looking forward to the next one. He doesn't believe in post-mortems.'

Over coffee in the drawing-room she does admit to me that at the outset of *Wogan* she was unhappy about the format. She knew that Terry was anxious to get the show exactly right, but she felt the balance wasn't correct in the first few weeks. They weren't getting quite what they wanted; it was a bit of everything. Eventually they got the balance right. Helen agreed that a lot depended on the calibre of the guests. 'I think it is difficult to get the right mix thrice a week. Sometimes it happens, but not always. Five nights of *Wogan* might be too much and too risky.'

She makes no secret of the satisfaction it has given her to find Terry so relaxed before his television appearances. It wasn't always that way.

'At one time,' Helen recalls, 'Terry tended to become up-tight before a show. I put this down to lack of confidence, his experience with *Jackpot** in Ireland. Confidence came back to him gradually. To a television performer like Terry, confidence is essential. I suppose it comes with success. Now he sails through *Wogan*.'

On the sun-drenched terrace, Helen pauses for a moment to drink in the fragrance of the plants and flowers. She turns round as I ask: 'How does it feel to be a millionairess?'

She laughs that infectious laugh of hers as she replies: 'I wouldn't say I'm a millionairess. Not when you have three children to educate.'

By now I have been introduced to Katherine, a confident and pretty girl, who in two years would be sitting for her O Levels, and also Alan, a sturdy and likeable young chap, who would shortly be starting his university career at Warwick. They show no surprise that their mother is devoting most of her morning to talking about the Wogan Phenomenon. They have become accustomed to journalists, mostly women, calling to Wogan Towers and talking either to their Dad or Mum.

At that moment a big grey dog with blue eyes, a Weima-

* See Chapter 9.

raner, pads in and out again. In the house the atmosphere
is leisurely.

Helen expresses some surprise at the growth of the Wogan
Phenomenon, but she feels that it shouldn't detract from
the special talent Terry possesses.

'I think that many people who have started out life like
Terry haven't been nearly as successful as him. I am sure
that a lot of his success is due to his not pushing himself.
Terry has remained himself. He retains that certain charisma. Not everybody in this business possesses the same
kind of charisma. I suppose we have both remained the
same. I know that people look at Terry and exclaim: "Gosh,
you haven't changed!" It doesn't change people fundamen-
tally if they are financially well off or if they are famous;
underneath they are the same people. The way we do
change is by becoming more mature as persons, more able
to cope with success or fame. Unfortunately you do come
across people in this business who, the minute they are
successful, become big-time. Terry has never been that. He
has remained level-headed about fame and money; he hasn't
allowed adulation to turn his head as it easily might have.
I think this factor has contributed enormously to his success
as a performer and his acceptability as a person.'

We stroll round to the other side of the house where
the heated swimming pool is located. On warm summer
evenings Terry is known to relax here, swimming the length
of the pool with Helen or the children. Or he may play
tennis in the court near by. It is the Wogan recipe for relaxation, away from the pressures of Shepherd's Bush or his
modern business offices in Fulham. He has learned to live
with the pressures of the Wogan Industry without being
overwhelmed by them.

Helen employs a gardener to keep the place trim. But
some of the time she takes care of the new plants and flowers
herself. The rich profusion of flowers is very attractive to
the eye.

'I enjoy watching the shrubs and the plants grow,' she
muses.

Back in the drawing-room she pours more coffee. In a soft voice she says she has grown accustomed to living with the Wogan Phenomenon.

'You find that people are quite pleasant, although occasionally you'll find the odd one who is rude and he or she may say bluntly: "Put your autograph on that" instead of saying: "Please, will you . . ." Sometimes I suppose I get tired of smiling but it's all part of the business – show business, if you like to call it that.'

She talks of the children's attitude to their Dad's fame: 'They, like myself, have come to accept what it means and they know they've got to live with it. A few years ago at school they experienced some trouble when other kids taunted them. A boy might say: "I think your dad is great" or "He's a twit". It's up to them how they will react to what the children say. Usually they will walk away, but Mark might stay and throw a punch at the offender. Once or twice Katherine got annoyed when people pointed at her and said: "She's Terry Wogan's daughter." But she can cope; indeed, there are times when we have all to try to cope.'

The sedate way of English life appeals to her. She has good friends and enjoys going out to dinner-parties.

'I am the sort of person who likes to make friends,' she says. But she has firm convictions about a woman's place in marriage: 'I think it's most important that one has women friends so that one can make a life outside of marriage. I feel it's important to do separate things, not to be always dependent on your partner. It's nice to have one's own special interests. I play golf. My free time is between 9.30 and 3.00 during the day and I use this time myself and I don't feel I'm neglecting Terry or the family.'

She agrees wholeheartedly with Terry that the stability of their marriage has meant a great deal to his career and to her own life, and her definition of a happy and successful marriage is simple: 'I suppose we both have a healthy sense of humour; that's important in any relationship. What is more important perhaps is to go through married life without finding too much fault with one another. To me, a lot of couples as the years go on get irritated with one another. I agree that everybody has faults but why look for them? And yet I also agree there are a lot of unhappy people back in Ireland who live together because they can't get a divorce. One is lucky if it works out. I do feel in the context of divorce that it should be harder to get married. Maybe there wouldn't be half the number of divorces if they made it more difficult to get married. The truth is you really don't know anybody until you live with them.'

Somewhere in Wogan Towers the great man is preparing to go to the Television Theatre in Shepherd's Bush for another show. He has had a bath, the cleansing ritual is over, he is almost prepared to face his millions of adoring viewers. Monday . . . Wednesday . . . Friday . . . the week has become routine, yet *Wogan* dominates Wogan Towers. The show is never far from Helen's mind. Without wanting to take the place of Frances Whitaker, or the team around Terry, Helen does sometimes discuss different aspects of the show and how it is developing.

'If Terry asks for my opinion or for a suggestion I will be happy to say what I think,' she reflects, 'but he would never discuss the day-to-day details of his work with me. I don't try to influence him. But he will listen. The great thing is that he can switch off at home. For a performer that is important. Rarely would he think of going out socially without me being with him. We usually go to dinner-parties together.'

That infectious laugh again when I ask: 'Do you have any fear that some day Terry will dash off with a pretty television presenter or producer?'

Helen is frank in her answer: 'I'm not saying it couldn't happen, but I think the chances are remote, or I would like to think so. We are mature enough to discuss matters honestly and know where we stand. I would be very hurt, but I know too that he would be equally hurt if I, as you put it, dashed off with a Don Juan. People come to me and ask, "Is he as nice at home as he is on the box?" I honestly tell them that he is. He is very even-tempered. I may make him sound like a saint, but there is no point telling lies. I know there are characters on television who can be quite different at home.'

Since I had discussed Terry's wardrobe for *Wogan* with Frances Whitaker, I thought it appropriate to ask Helen the same question.

'Terry is definitely a suit man,' was her quick response. 'He's not got the figure for casuals. I know what suits him and what doesn't. I think he looks well in blue. I don't like brown on him.'

How does she see his career evolving? She could not visualise Terry going into administration at the BBC. 'I think that as long as he is on television or in radio he will always be a performer.'

It is time to go. Since I am bound for Dublin the conversation inevitably comes round to Ireland. Helen goes back there once in a while to see her father, who retired to County Carlow; her mother died a few years ago. Although she has settled into the elegance of country life in Buckinghamshire and apparently thrives on it, and cannot see herself coming back to Ireland in the foreseeable future, she said with conviction: 'I love Ireland. I love going back to see my father.'

I rise and look again through the French windows onto the terrace and the pastoral view beyond. It is peaceful – the kind of peace you might expect in a monastery garden. Someday someone might describe Terry as the Monk of Wogan Towers; anything is possible where the great man is concerned. He would see the fun in it. That's where he scores over so many of his English colleagues: his unerring sense of humour never fails him. I have almost forgotten that I am about to say goodbye to Helen. Quickly I ask, as though as an afterthought, for the three highlights in her life.

Almost casually she replies: 'I suppose the first must be Terry's great success as a broadcaster; secondly, being successful as a couple; and lastly being able to enjoy the rewards of that success.'

Playing the role of modern housewife does not detract from Helen Wogan's enjoyment of life. Nor is she envious of women like Esther Rantzen who can combine a career with looking after the home. It is Helen's own choice. Friends say that with her keen business acumen – she was trained in Ireland as a professional model – she could run a successful business, but she is not interested at the moment. Maybe when the children have graduated from college.

Spacious Wogan Towers requires her presence; keeping the lawns and gardens attractive also requires her guidance. 'I find so much to do,' she will tell you. This may also embrace collecting her children at the railway station or driving her eldest son to university. Helen carries out these chores cheerfully and denies that such routines can become boring.

Life of course has its compensations for a well-off modern housewife. She has time to meet friends for coffee, as Helen Wogan likes to do, and to take a holiday in the sun when she feels the need. As far as Terry is concerned, he is delighted to have Helen waiting for him at home after the rigours of his television show. He would have it no other way.

The taxi is waiting for me. We shake hands at the white-coloured gate. I look back for a quick glance at Wogan Towers. It is a fitting home for Terry and Helen. You expect the great man to come dashing headlong out of the front door and straight into the swimming pool beyond, but I am spared that magnificent spectacle for he is, I know, already on his way to Shepherd's Bush.

It seems that Helen is correct in her assessment of her husband, that he cannot stop performing. Being on screen fires his imagination, boosts his adrenalin, and keeps him bubbling over.

Helen has sacrificed her own career to keep Terry happy. It is not such a common occurrence today when ambitions have to be satisfied.

As I set off along the winding roads in the taxi towards

Heathrow Airport, I wondered if the private view I had formed in my mind about Helen Wogan was correct. The answer at that moment seemed important to me, for not only does she invest Wogan Towers with character but clearly brings to her husband's hectic lifestyle an essential balance. And it had been thoughtful of Terry to let us talk alone. Columnists had often fallen into the trap of trying to interview the celebrated pair together at Wogan Towers and this inevitably resulted in the limelight being almost entirely focused on Terry, understandable, perhaps, though that is in the circumstances.

Not that he ever wants to talk for Helen; that is something he has always tried to avoid. Left to herself, one felt she talked with more ease, particularly about their early romantic days. The magic of their love is still palpable. She doesn't wear a mask, although for an Irish woman she is less effusive in conversation than one would expect. As one visitor remarked, 'Mrs Wogan's voice is very calm, with long, peaceful stretches of silence.'

Yet, in retrospect, she had not that day deliberately tried to avoid my questions, except to say on occasions, 'I think you'll agree that is a question for Terry to answer' or, 'Where did you hear that about Terry? But at no time was she trying to create an impression.

One came away from Wogan Towers remembering this unusual woman of composure and determination. True, for Fleet Street tabloids in search of the sensational she will never remotely rank alongside Joan Collins, yet editors of glossy magazines constantly contact her for interviews. Occasionally she will say yes, but most times it will be a gracious no.

One got the impression that she is highly organised and, as far as the family is concerned, a good planner. She is energetic and strives in an unobstrusive way to make visitors to Wogan Towers thoroughly welcome – 'an Irish trait', she says.

Helen Wogan's maturity as a woman shows in her attitude to life. One remembered her saying, 'Ageing doesn't worry me. I take each day as it comes. I enjoy what I am doing. I try never to lose my sense of humour, even when things go wrong, as they sometimes will.' She avoids the Irish failing of sentimentality, yet she can be 'soft' occasionally with the children.

She has never failed to be amused by some of the things written about Wogan Towers, such as colourful descriptions of the furniture, the wallpaper, the size of the swimming pool, the ages of the surrounding trees. Some of the more personal pieces about herself have almost embarrassed her.

Frank Delaney had remarked, 'She's the most beautiful woman imaginable.' To the world, it sounded like Irish blarney, but Frank swears he meant every word of it. Someone else commented, 'You can see at a glance from her lake-blue eyes why she was coining good money as a fashion model, while himself was toiling in a bank for a few quid.' And in a lovely flight of fancy in the early eighties, Jean Rook told her readers, 'Helen Wogan still has a waist like a Kerry fiddle. Her cheekbones sweep down like the Mountains of Mourne.'

Helen takes it all in her stride. By the time she has a round of golf played she will probably have forgotten the 'delightful flattery'. If nothing else, she is a practical person and allows her famous husband to luxuriate in his high profile; in her own more leisurely world she sees little wrong with a low profile. Visitors, like myself, come away from Wogan Towers remembering her cooking, easy manner, and the serenity she has managed to convey. Small wonder that Terry wants to lock the high gates behind him, park his car, and bask in the idyll.

Helen admits that life has been good. She is the first to acknowledge this truth. But as a realist, and a mother, she also admits that it can never be without anxiety. At that moment one remembered her infectious laugh; not a loud laugh, but a kind of good-humoured laugh that was appealing to visitors. Wogan Towers is unthinkable without it.

4 Celebrity Visitor

Rose Wogan, Terry's vivacious mother, is a frequent visitor to Wogan Towers and may stay for up to four months at a time, looked after by Helen Wogan and cheered by the Wogan children. Once, after a particularly lengthy stay, when she expressed a wish to return to her home in Dublin, Terry joked: 'You can't do that, mum. You can't leave now.' She relented.

Rose is a small, frail woman in her mid-seventies with a refreshing sense of humour and a good memory. She likes to talk about the elegance of Wogan Towers, where Terry's friends regard her as a celebrity in her own right. In the course of an evening she may be introduced to David Frost or Val Doonican, or at the weekend join Terry and Helen for dinner with a television producer or popular chat-show host. Rose dresses neatly for these occasions, always ensuring that her auburn hair is styled. 'I must look my best before Terry's friends,' she will laugh. A perceptive woman, she feels being Terry's mother places a responsibility on her to project a pleasing image, but she remains the chatty warm Mrs Wogan.

A victim of chronic arthritis, she gets around Wogan Towers with some difficulty. Once she confided to Helen Wogan that she would love to see the 'lovely shops' in central London but wondered if she would be up to making the journey. Next morning Helen packed her mother-in-law's wheelchair into her car and together they set off shopping. For hours Helen wheeled Rose around Harrods.

'I was in my wheelchair,' recalls Rose, 'and all these

people were around me, some looking at me. When you are in a wheelchair, people tend to think you are a little daft. I was enjoying myself no end.'

On another occasion Helen drove her to Harley Street, where Terry had arranged an appointment with a specialist. Mrs Wogan frets about the hours Helen and Terry devote to her as their guest at Wogan Towers. 'They are wonderful to me,' she reflects, 'and the children are wonderful too.'

Occasionally she feels hurt by Fleet Street reports about her son and her perception tells her that Terry is vulnerable in his role as chat-show host and cannot of course be universally popular. She says that in company she senses when people do not like Terry or his show. As long as they are not rude it doesn't upset her. 'These people are entitled to their views.'

Obviously she has learned to live with Terry's success. Curiously it has not surprised her.

'I've never been surprised where Terry is concerned. He was always surprising me I suppose. What pleases me most is the way he has kept his head. He could have gone the other way. I think that's important.'

Sometime ago Des O'Connor wanted her to be a guest on his chat show along with five other famous mothers, but despite his persistence she was unable to accept his invitation. A few days earlier she had come out of hospital after two operations to relieve her arthritic pains.

'I told Des I wouldn't look well on his show. I think I would have enjoyed it.' Being regarded as a celebrity at Wogan Towers amuses her no end. She likes to say she gets on well with the English.

Terry's annual invitation to his mother to visit Wogan Towers underlines his genuine concern for her. Because of her painful condition, he has involved himself in Arthritis Care. He has also contributed much to Children in Need, for which he heads a team of presenters each year linked to every BBC local radio and television station so that viewers can phone in pledges of support. By the middle of 1986 more than four million pounds had been received for distribution to some 4,000 projects all over the UK ranging from play groups to mini-buses for the handicapped.

Friends claim that Terry has never lost his consideration for others. It remains one of his most salient characteristics. Mrs Wogan says her son never lets a fortnight go by without telephoning her in Dublin. 'Usually it's about ten o'clock on a Sunday night. He will ask how I feel, if the pain has got worse. He tells me to try to be cheerful. We share a joke together. We have much the same sense of fun.'

She recalls a time when Terry and Helen invited herself and her late husband, Michael, on a holiday to Portugal. 'I thought that was very good of them because most married couples would much prefer to holiday on their own, but Terry wanted us to see Portugal for the first time.'

Rose jokes that she's Terry's biggest television fan. Instinctively she feels that Terry, who is approaching fifty years of age, may be at the turning-point in his career. She is confident though that when the time comes he will make the correct decision.

'Terry knows that his show cannot go on for ever. Sometimes I think it would be nice if he tried a travel show like *Whicker's World*. He is observant and I think he would make a success of it. But Terry knows best. He has always been lucky.'

When friends suggest that Terry has inherited her expressive and warm smile, she does not disagree; in fact, she is rather proud of it.

When the time comes for her departure from Wogan Towers she is driven by Terry to Heathrow Airport. The English country air has brightened her pale cheeks and she vows she will be back. In Dublin she will stay as usual with her son Brian, his wife and children in a semi-detached house a few miles from the airport. Here Brian has built an annexe for his mother; in this room she will sit by the windows and try to forget the pain. Occasionally her world is interrupted by a reporter seeking an interview or a photographer asking for a special picture.

Strangely, she wonders about Terry's popularity in

Ireland, now that he has been out of the country for nineteen years. She asks herself how many people watch *Wogan* in Ireland and if his popularity has waned among the Irish. She is not certain. However, she is aware of the interest in his show. As Terry's mother she is regarded as a celebrity in Ireland, although she says the English have more time for their celebrities.

Brian Wogan and his family are also visitors to Wogan Towers. Brian is not unlike his famous older brother – he is dark-haired, softly-spoken and easy-going. Soon you discover he is by no means overwhelmed by the Wogan Phenomenon. It's no secret that for years he has been evading the Dublin and overseas press.

'I tell them that I'll spill the beans on Terry for £50,000,' he quips. He has a laugh not unlike Terry's. For twenty years, ever since Terry became a star of Irish radio and television in the 'sixties, Brian has been content to live in the shadow of his brother. He is reluctant to discuss Terry with the press.

'Why should I? Terry is his own man.'

When he does talk about him, he invariably uses the words 'my brother' in a natural and earnest manner. Being an admirer of Flann O'Brien (Myles na gCopaleen) Terry would probably be tempted to call Brian 'the brother' after one of O'Brien's amusing literary characters.

Mention of the Wogan Phenomenon brings a slight look of puzzlement to Brian's deep-set eyes, as though uncertain of how to explain it. He admits that he was just as surprised as anyone else when it materialised. I can't explain it any more than anybody else can. My brother is successful I suppose because of his talking ease, his ability to get points across without a script; but honestly I can't put a finger on the whole truth any more than anyone else can.'

He was of the opinion that the real transformation took place in Terry's broadcasting career in the late 'sixties when he joined the BBC. Everything clicked for him.

'I suppose there was an element of luck involved allied

to Terry's own inbuilt talents. Not everyone makes it in broadcasting despite my brother's repeated claim that it is an easy job, which we all know it isn't. I mean, any of us who ever sat in a radio or television studio knows it can be a daunting experience.'

On reflection, Brian felt that Terry's imaginative approach and racy style were just right for British audiences, who were looking for something new, as were the BBC top brass. Furthermore, the BBC was changing and the corporation's new image fitted Terry like a glove.

'I cannot explain,' mused Brian, 'why my brother possessed star quality and others did not. It may have something to do with certain people's appeal to listeners or viewers. Terry has this special appeal, in particular in the case of mums and dads and younger married couples. As far back as I remember, he had a way with people and such a characteristic cannot be hidden. I attribute it to his own family and educational background.'

As brothers they have kept in contact despite the distance. With six years between them Brian found they had nothing in common until he reached his teens.

'Certainly I wasn't aware of my brother as a pal,' he recalls. 'I think we are close because we are good foils for each other. In some respects though, we have the same temperament – and I do enjoy his company. I like to think that like Terry I have a calm disposition and a sense of humour. Our lives to a certain extent followed the same pattern. At college we played rugby, acted in plays, sang in musicals, and generally found college life stimulating. Afterwards I studied dentistry before joining Aer Lingus.'

Acting on stage, they discovered they possessed one thing in common – both were nervous at the start, but once they settled into their parts they thoroughly enjoyed the experience. Later, Brian aspired to be a broadcaster and scripted some shows for RTE.

'I would have enjoyed life as a broadcaster,' he says today, 'despite the inevitable comparisons that would be made between Terry and myself. I saw broadcasting as a challenging career.'

Once, when asked if he saw anything exceptional in his brother, Brian replied: 'I remember Terry had what I like to call a great pen, a gifted facility with words and phrases. He started writing when he was about ten years of age. When I went to Germany for a while to school he used to write to me regularly. These letters were extremely funny and very descriptive. I began to think that one day he would be a novelist or a Fleet Street journalist.'

For some years Brian was a prominent amateur actor on the drama scene in Ireland. From time to time he was exposed to savage criticism from eccentric adjudicators at drama festivals, so he quickly became aware of the risk of 'going public'. So it comes as no surprise to him to find Terry incurring the wrath of critics; in his view entertainers cannot afford to be over-sensitive to criticism.

'If you are exposed for three nights every week on television as Terry is, you are actually pushing your luck,' Brian Wogan argues. 'In the case of *Wogan* one has got to appreciate that it was something new to British viewers and when Terry reached a pinnacle of popularity he quickly found he was not going to be popular with everyone. I think he knows by now the criticism he can expect. It was inevitable sooner or later that his family would be targeted. As a family man he is more vulnerable; if he wasn't a family man the sniping wouldn't hurt as much.'

There has been a general consensus among the Wogan clans in London and Dublin that *Wogan* on five nights a week would be excessive, possibly also a grave mistake. Brian Wogan feels that Terry would not have any difficulty presenting the show itself because by now he has developed the technique successfully; the problem in his view would arise from lack of suitable guests to maintain the show at a consistently high level of entertainment. To Brian, three nights is quite sufficient.

Friends of Terry's in Ireland and the UK claim he hasn't changed. To them, he still retains a lively sense of humour and is unmistakably Irish. But to Brian Wogan his famous brother has changed in certain ways, not all of them apparent.

'As a brother I can notice some changes. To deny success would be silly. I think being, as he has, a number of years away from Ireland has changed his thinking and some of his attitudes. If one's everyday contacts are with English people it is bound to influence one's attitude. We do get his television shows in Ireland, but they are essentially aimed at the British viewer. Yet because Terry is cynical about himself I think there is no danger of him becoming a boor. It would be easy for him to be a boor – I mean, if you are being lauded most of the time, isn't there a possibility it may affect you?'

Brian feels that because Terry chooses to live in Britain and hasn't sought refuge in a tax-free haven while still earning large sums of money on the British mainland, the people of Britain have come to respect him.

'You see my brother cannot be accused like some other star entertainers of being an interloper who is there to rake off the goodies, an accusation they are inclined to throw at others.'

One aspect of the Wogan Phenomenon that intrigues Brian Wogan is that it has never caused friction or jealousy among the Wogan clans. He is aware that this isn't always the case. If the Wogan family had been six children instead of two it might have led, Brian believes, to jealousies, even rivalry, between brothers and sisters. Once when a newspaper wrote that Brian was envious of Terry's success the allegation angered Mrs Rose Wogan. She felt the claim was untrue. She said that Brian never felt himself inferior to his famous brother. Brian was more inclined to laugh at the allegation.

As brothers, they remain close and friendly. Brian visualises no change in their relationship.

'I like Terry's company. I enjoy talking to him. I look forward to visiting Wogan Towers and having a game of tennis with Terry – and beating him!' But he is still greatly puzzled about the Wogan Phenomenon. As hard as he tries, he cannot explain it. He wonders if anyone can.

More than three hours earlier Terry had left Wogan Towers for the Television Theatre at Shepherd's Bush Green. Now, at exactly 5.45, Carol Millward told me he was ready to see me in his dressing-room, which is to be found off a corridor on the ground floor inside the stage door. Terry looked surprisingly at ease considering how soon he would be hosting another Wogan show and after the tiring press-interviews he had given that afternoon. On the floor, under the television set, were strewn a number of newspapers, mostly tabloids, and on a small side-table across the room were two bottles of soft drinks and two drinking glasses. A long grey-coloured couch, spanning almost the entire wall facing the door, dominated the ornate room.

'Is that machine working?' Terry quipped in mischievous mood, throwing a quizzical glance at my small Sony tape-recorder. It was a typical Wogan approach, the old puckish humour asserting itself. As an afterthought, he wise-cracked: 'That suit you're wearing – it's bloody awful!'

I had by now learned when to take him seriously; not everyone has been so lucky and some have consequently paid the price. Terry's whimsical humour and sharp wit are not universally popular: only southern Irishmen and Cockneys can really appreciate it.

Out of the blue he said: 'Did you know that friends sometimes denigrate one another?'

I told him that I found it hard to get away from the ubiquitous Wogan. 'Why's that?' he asked, as he poured himself a Perrier water and afterwards filled my glass with orange. I explained that on my flight with British Airways I was handed a copy of *Highlife*, the airline's magazine, and found an article in it in which he was discussing his favourite drinks. I remembered one remark he had made in it: 'Summer drinks are all very well, so long as you have a summer to drink them in.' He admitted that from time to time he dabbled in writing – and enjoyed the exercise.

As he sat opposite me on the couch he looked comfortable and listened to what I had to say. Contrary to what some critics claim, he can listen. In fact I found him a good listener. We talked about other journalists who had visited him in his dressing-room.

'A while back,' he said, 'a woman reporter from a glossy Sunday magazine came here to talk to me and later suggested in her piece that I tried to dominate her and tell her what to write. I don't dominate anybody – do I? I just answer the questions.'

I told him that I had read the interview and considered it curious, as though the young woman was implying he was a bully.

'I'm nothing of the sort!' Terry bellowed, holding back a smile. 'As you see, I'm not an aggressive person, am I?'

I told him it was too early for me to say and this amused him. He was by now joyously perched on the couch, as cool as a cucumber, and delighted to be holding court. I sensed his moment had arrived. When I commented on this remarkable state of affairs, he quickly corrected me: 'I am cool. I have to be cool. You simply couldn't sustain this show thrice weekly if you weren't relaxed and tried to take it as casually as you can.'

At that moment I was puzzled why, on the afternoon of *Wogan* he had agreed in the first place to be interviewed. Why wasn't he sparing his voice for the show? Why wasn't he relaxing alone, reading a book, instead of trying to find answers to questions? I could only assume there was a psychological reason. Perhaps the great man was disguising his nervous tension by working right up to the hour of the show. Indeed, was my own presence in that dressing-room really another way of making him forget the obvious tensions involved in presenting a live show? For years I had known actors who wouldn't dare entertain friends in their dressing-rooms before they went on stage.

I sipped my orange. I let him talk. Terence Wogan is a truly compulsive talker. Someone once hinted that the real reason why he likes to give interviews was to listen his own golden tones; it is only partly true. The truth is he simply loves talking. In Dublin he cultivated a love of chat and it has stayed with him. Watching him across the room, I discerned no uneasiness, no nervous tension. Not once did he get up and pace the room. He smoked a large cigar and seemed content with the world. It was an amazing performance.

It struck me forcibly that he was still sensitive to press criticism. I pointed out the folly of this, but he couldn't quite agree.

'Critics I can take – and criticism,' he said earnestly, 'but personal criticism is entirely another matter. As far as I am concerned, the critics said it, not the viewers.'

Evidently what has hurt is the popular media's intrusion into his private life. He finds this unforgivable.

After a pause to sip his drink, he referred directly to *Wogan:* 'I can't see the show having the same longevity, say, as Johnny Carson's show in America. However, it has become bigger than I imagined. It takes two or three years for a show like this to establish itself. The strong point now is the viewers' familiarity with the show. That's important. Of course the show fluctuates, as do the ratings. Better guests ensure good nights, but you can't let the bad nights worry you. The great thing is there's always another Friday night or Monday night or Wednesday night.'

One suspected that he wasn't entirely satisfied with the show. He said he had his own ideas about how it should develop in the future. Relating the show more to the day's particular happenings was important, and development along these lines would make *Wogan* less predictable. It bothered him that the show was criticised for being nothing more than a platform for the free advertising of the latest book or film. He didn't believe in being used as a sounding-board for someone to launch their ego at him.

'I'm not a sponge, or a blancmange, or a piece of blank paper for people to write on. I'm there for an interchange of conversation. Of course I'm interested in the guests on the show, but I have to say I forget who they are almost

immediately I've done the interview. I don't tend to dwell.
It is said that I am bigger than the people I interview. That
of course is the essence of the show. In terms of popularity,
notoriety or fame – whatever you call it – I'm as big if not
bigger than the people I'm interviewing. That's why people
watch.'

Contrary to what some people have claimed, he said he
was not good at sycophancy and all that.

Someone remarked not long ago that Terry Wogan is a
man slightly confused by success. As he stretched his arms
that moment in the room, he looked anything but confused.
He looked in control of himself and his emotions, eagerly
awaiting the moment to get on with another *Wogan*. He
beamed like someone enjoying success and, largely unper-
turbed by the critics. He is a man wound up like a clock,
refusing to accept the ordinary pace of lesser mortals. He
makes no secret of the fact that he likes fame and money
and life itself, but he is at pains to stress that he works hard
for any success that comes his way.

At that moment Frances Whitaker popped her head into
the room and reminded Terry that he had three minutes to
go. He seemed almost unconcerned as he shrugged: 'Television is a question of confidence. You have to have confidence. It has taken me sixteen years to reach this point
where I am confident.'

Did he find the thrice-weekly show fulfilling?

'It's not a question of fulfilment. I'm not doing the show
to be fulfilled. I like doing it. It is a job. It's a hard show on
my production team, but they do a great job. Can't you
imagine what it would be like if we ever decided to go five
nights a week?'

There was a sharp rap on the door. A woman's voice
called out that he must go. 'I must be off,' Terry said at the
door, and vanished into the corridor outside.

By 6.45 the warm-up comic Felix Bowness, a stocky figure
in a smart beige jacket, was addressing the audience. The
show, he told them, was live and they were expected to be

part of it and respond. He was a useful link between stage and balcony, for in a converted theatre where television cameramen and technicians were conspicuous all round, there was a strange air of unreality. The audience could easily seem an anachronism. Now this witty little man made things look more real, as though the show was really for the audience and not for the millions of television viewers. Bowness said in a cheeky voice: 'We are going to put a camera on you tonight. We like to do queer things!'

Felix Bowness is a cheerful fellow and doesn't look his sixty-one years. At that moment while continuing to balance himself precariously on a shaky wooden chair, he warmly welcomed the various parties to the show. There was a spontaneous cheer when he called out to welcome the nurses from Guy's Hospital, another more robust cheer for the farming group from Surrey, and even louder applause for the cameraman perched on a mobile machine whose wife had given birth that day to a baby girl. Bowness had managed to put most of the audience in cheery mood.

Suddenly Terry appeared on the balcony steps, within touching distance of those people seated on the outside seats. Heads were instantly turned in his direction, as though some people were assuring themselves that at last the great man had come miraculously amongst them. For a few more fervent Wogan admirers it might well have been the second coming of Jesus Christ; a hand or two went out to touch his coat. Others simply stared at the chat-show host, obviously not knowing what to think. Terry's presence generated quiet excitement, but it never threatened to overwhelm the star.

With a glass of red wine in one hand and a large cigar in the other, and dressed immaculately in a blue jacket and grey trousers, Terry beamed all over. He spoke quietly: 'Relax, will you. You have nothing to worry about. Enjoy the show. Have fun.' He sounded like a magician preparing his audience for his next trick. Then he looked down towards the stalls and uttered what seemed some more words of encouragement. He lifted his gaze towards the

stage – and Felix Bowness. It was the little man's cue to
chuckle; he looked proud to be addressed by the great man
himself.

Terry thanked him for his co-operation, and Bowness
quickly disappeared, not at all disappointed that he was
deprived of the fruits of his labours. After his years as a
popular warm-up comic Felix Bowness knows his place. He
has brought his art to an enviable level, hence his long
survival.

'I never tell gags,' he says. 'Seen youngsters come on in
this job, start tellin' gags, get a big "woof" from the audience, go on an' try and slay 'em, think the producer'll spot
'em and give 'em a show of their own. Out the next week
and dunno why.'

At seven o'clock the familiar *Wogan* signature tune,
composed by trendy pop star B. A. Robertson was played
and immediately afterwards Terry's introductory remarks
came across in a voice that struck me as tired, but then that
was an impression gleaned from my seat high up on the
balcony; television viewers would hardly notice. I wondered
if, after all, it had been wise on his part to talk so much all
that afternoon. However, there was a sparkling opening to
the show. Seated on a high chair in front of a large screen,
Terry chatted by satellite to Cockney actor Robert Lindsay,
star of the musical *Me and My Girl*, which was due to open
that week on Broadway.

Lindsay is a bubbly character, quick-witted and funny and
reminiscent of Tommy Steele. For ten minutes Terry kept
the chat at a lively level of entertainment and the audience
enjoyed it; it underlined once more how successful satellite
link-ups can be on *Wogan*.

A deeply suntanned Christopher Plummer next took his
seat opposite the chat-show host and in a rather routine
conversation talked about his film roles, in particular in
The Sound of Music, which had taken everybody in the film
business by surprise with its astonishing success. Plummer,
urbane and chatty, then reminded his audience: 'Unfortunately some of my best stage parts are seen by comparatively

few people – I mean in comparison with my film roles. This is something all of us actors regret.'

It was an entertaining show but by no means a memorable *Wogan*. Plummer required more time to elaborate on theatre and film topics, but extra time wasn't available. It is one of the problems with the show – an interesting actor or writer may be cut off abruptly, yet there is little Terry Wogan can do about this. The show is meant to be fast-moving and entertaining, not long and profound. Afterwards, though, in the Hospitality Room, where Terry mixed easily with his guests, he said he thought the show had 'gone very well' that night. He urged his guests to taste the BBC's wine and most of them responded. Terry was patient and courteous, even when a photographer asked if he could have a picture of Terry with a guest.

Meanwhile, outside the theatre, his chauffeur waited at the wheel of his car, which was by now surrounded by a score of people waiting for the great man to emerge from the theatre. It was pushing 8.20. Terry had already been six hours in the theatre. Yet when he eventually stepped towards the car he obliged autograph-hunters. Then he dived into the front seat beside the driver, signed some more autographs, and said to his chauffeur: 'Let's get out of here.'

As I stood watching the car vanish into the distance, I remembered the question I had put to Terry earlier that evening in his dressing-room: 'Are you pleased with the way your career has progressed?'

Terry's answer had been made in a quiet voice: 'The opportunities came along, I was ready to take them. And when the popularity happened I was able to cope.'

5   Wogan's Day

Drawing a distinction between the Private Terry and the Public Terry is none too easy. Maybe the answer is to be found somewhere in his own words and those of his wife Helen.

TERRY: (*Commenting on his joky television image*) It's surprising how many people don't realise that it is really an act.

HELEN: If he went on like that at home, I'd go mad.

It is amazing the curiosity that exists about Terry's home life and his show-business career. *A Day in the Life of Wogan* still excites the curiosity of magazine and newspaper writers. Terry is prepared to go half-way in his description; he draws the line at the more intimate details. He admits that since he gave up his early-morning radio programme his lifestyle has altered. For one thing, he doesn't have to rise at the crack of dawn and motor off to the radio studio. His 'new day' is more civilised.

As he says: 'I lie there full of good intentions, like making three-course breakfasts, before falling back exhausted at the thought of all that activity and sleeping until nine o'clock. The strain of it!

'I then leap athletically from my bed, choose what I'm going to wear for the show, dive into the bath and emerge spruced and refreshed for a bracing cup of Bovril. My next task is to have a glance through the research for the evening's show. Then I decide what my opening remarks will be and how I'm going to introduce the guests, all of which I write out in laborious long-hand. This is for the autocue. In a show like *Wogan* you need a few crutches and these act as signposts for me so I know where I'm going in an interview.

'I don't have lunch. I've lost nearly a stone and a half over the past year, mainly because I don't eat much on Mondays, Wednesdays and Fridays when the show goes out. I prefer to wait until I get home in the evening before having a meal.

'At 2.00p.m. the car arrives to pick me up and thirty-five minutes later I'm walking through the stage door to the Television Theatre, Shepherd's Bush. Ensconced in my dressing-room, I chat about the night's show. We also look at what the papers have been saying about us, as well as doing forward planning. When it comes to selecting the guests somebody will ask: "What do you think of so-and-so?" I'll say what I think. Seriously, though, you've got to be flexible and I'm prepared to take a chance with anybody. All I'm looking for is somebody who will respond.

'I rarely go to the Television Centre, where the production office is based. Having your own desk at HQ may be all right for some people, but for me it would only add to the pressure of doing a live television show three times a week. Basically, I'm very lazy. I prefer to work intensely over short periods. Anything that requires a great deal of preparation and thought doesn't suit me, I'm afraid. I'd love to write short articles for magazines, but I'd never write a novel.

'At 4.00p.m. the researchers come in and brief me on each of the guests. We talk about what sort of people they are, how we want the interview to go and so on. Then it's out on the stage for a walk through the various positions, a look at the autocue, and a chat with the cameramen and stage crew. I put my feet up for a while before putting my suit on and going into make-up. Before the show I always make a point of calling into "Hostility" – Wogan-speak for Hospitality Room – to make contact with guests. I don't talk to them about the interview, though. It's just a matter of touching base before we go on the air.

'By then it's nearly seven o'clock and it's time to walk out and do the show. It's always the quickest forty minutes I've ever experienced. Afterwards I go up and have a drink with the guests and the production team. I think it's very important to do that – it would be very bad manners not to. My experience of American chat shows is that you never see the host at all, either before or after the show.

'If I go out, it's usually on the night of a show because it means I have the following day off. Obviously, I'm not going to go out too late on a Tuesday or Thursday. The last thing you want on television is a hangover. Believe me, red-ringed Wogan eyes are not a pretty sight!

'On a weekday, I'm usually in bed by midnight although I'm not particularly tired. Soon Ol' Wogan is sleeping the sleep of the innocent. It's amazing what a glass or two of BBC Hostility wine will do.'

One of Terry's greatest admirers is 'nice guy' Val Doonican. When Eamonn Andrews in the late 'seventies ran a *This Is Your Life* on Terry, Val was invited on the show.

'I think the reason was because I was Irish,' mused Doonican.

It was more than that. Terry and he became firm friends in the late 'sixties and have remained so ever since. Val is in no way surprised by the Wogan Phenomenon. As he explained: 'Terry's a bright guy, a marvellous wit and a formidable personality. He has had lots of television exposure, but has managed to last the pace and that's not easy. I guess he has the virtue of durability. Furthermore, he knows how to cope with difficult situations. He's a wonderful performer; I know it, I have done shows for twenty-three years on television and know the pitfalls performers face.'

Val was seventeen years in showbiz before his overnight success at the Palladium. 'Then,' he recalls, 'the press were suddenly asking about me. The irony of course was that I was doing the same work up to then and no one took any notice. That's show business. In a way I'm not unlike Terry. He had done his stint in broadcasting in Ireland and England before he hit the popularity polls. Terry's a natural; he has maintained high standards. The reason for this I think is because there is nothing contrived about his performances; he comes across as himself. That's not at all easy to do. He doesn't rely on gimmicks to make an effect. His chat shows are friendly chats, entertaining and often amusing.'

In 1986 Val had completed more than forty years in show business. He shares with Terry not only a love for golf but a characteristic charm. His show-business motto has remained: 'Don't forget why they liked you in the first place.'

Eamonn Andrews is also quick to acknowledge Terry Wogan's success as a broadcaster. When the BBC was working on plans for the Wogan show to run thrice weekly, Andrews was asked if he thought it would be a success.

'I think it will be a great success,' he commented. 'I mean Terry is a great success already. I don't know how much they're spending. If they're spending as much as they say at the opening, it seems a lot of dough. But I suppose they want to establish Terry as chat-show host.'

Andrews himself ran a chat show on ITV late at night in the mid-sixties, after he left the BBC.

'I was overproduced then and given the wrong kind of research, he reflects, 'but I was worried about using all the research I got. Now I know you don't use it at all. You just have it or you don't have a question line in your head before you sit down. It's too rigid. I now know that my work suffered from that, but we got nearly every one we wanted for the show.'

Eamonn Andrews has been labelled 'Mr Unflappable', although he asserts the label is misleading. 'I still get nervous before every live show, and I am deeply vulnerable to criticism. Some remarks can hurt a great deal, especially when you believe that they are unfair criticism.'

Terry's sensitivity to press criticism is well known. Friends claim he takes some of the criticism needlessly to heart. Perhaps he should take note of David Coleman's words on the same subject: 'Memories are short, telly-personalities are sitting ducks and satirists have a living to earn.'

Coleman has been a constant target of *Spitting Image* and *Private Eye*, but he remarked he was rather pleased with the *Spitting Image* puppet. 'It's the only one which is better looking than the real thing.'

Terry's attitude to Fleet Street can be summed up in his own words: 'I am only on the front pages to sell newspapers. There are about three or four on-going stories in Fleet Street that sell newspapers, stories like Lady Di of course. Recently it was Princess Michael, and whenever they can, they come up with a Wogan story – irrespective of how true it is.'

In a profession that has been described as 'mean, hostile and envious', few will deny that Terry has collected less criticism than most of his colleagues. On-screen, he remains plausibly nice, cheery, sociable. 'It's easy to forget that what you're looking at, every time, is a highly professional performance,' commented one critic.

One of the continuing fascinations of *Wogan* is the number of contrasting characters invited to face its star host. They may be as different as Vanessa Redgrave and Michael Caine, or Mick Jagger and Lord Gerry Fitt. Not all the shows run smoothly. There are some obvious risks to be faced. On Wednesday, July 9, 1986, Terry chatted to Prince Philip for more than twenty minutes almost entirely about the boring subject of carriage-racing championships. Desperately Terry tried to steer the conversation away to the royal wedding between Prince Andrew and Sarah Ferguson.

'If we may talk about one of the subjects that . . .' Terry began, but Philip retorted: 'No, I have already talked about it.'

When the producer held up a cue card off-screen, prompting Terry to ask more royal wedding questions, the eagle-eyed Duke made a joke of it saying: 'Why don't you hold it up for the audience to look at?'

More tiresome chat followed about carriage racing and the viewers were treated to film clips of actual races. Terry persevered in his efforts to break the stranglehold.

'You have been quoted as saying of late that as you grow older you have become a little bit cynical about life and about the society in which we live. Does that still hold good?'

Philip laughed sardonically. 'Well, as it was only about a fortnight ago that I said it, I suppose . . . why do you want a second-hand interview?'

Terry tried to end the chat by wishing him well with the new addition to the family. 'Not yet,' exclaimed Philip startled. 'In due course. Oh, I see you mean my daughter-in-law.'

The following day Terry was reported to 'be nonplussed after the verbal mauling'. The interview underlined in a most embarrassing way that serious restrictions must never be placed on a chat-show host, otherwise, as in this case, the conversation comes across as appallingly stilted. Undeniably, Terry's experience carried him through an uneasy situation, during which at times he appeared unusually ruffled. One of the funny lines to emerge from the interview was: 'Horses are great levellers.' Terry agreed with tongue in cheek. It was plain to the viewers that his interest in carriage racing, indeed horses, was negligible.

Curiously, Fleet Street was inclined to take Terry's side in the débâcle and thought that the Duke was somewhat unkind to the host. On the same evening the show was saved by the appearance of the likeable Michael Caine, who told some delightful stories about his years in Hollywood and why he had returned to live in England. He said his daughter was educated at a Catholic school 'because I'm Protestant, my wife is Muslim and her god parents are Jewish'. By the time Mr Caine had finished it was noticeable that Terry had fully regained his composure and could look any horse, royal or otherwise, in the face.

It was inevitable that Terry Wogan's performances would attract the attention of perhaps the most outstanding television critic of recent years, Clive James, whose pen is at once both witty and caustic. Sydney-born James, with the shoulders and neck of a rugby forward, first came to admire

Terry's morning radio programme, which at one time he described as the best of its kind in the land.

He was less complimentary about Terry's appearance as presenter on *Come Dancing* and the *Eurovision Song Contest*. In June 1976 he told readers in his *Observer* column that 'the bionic man is already with us, not just in fictional but factual form. What else is Terry Wogan, for example, but a Six-Million-Dollar Man with a shamrock in his buttonhole'.

When Terry began to present *A Song for Europe*, James observed in 1980: 'There was a time when this would have suited him down to the ground, but lately he has been cultivating, not entirely without success, a new reputation for spontaneous intelligence. To sustain this new image in the context of the programme under discussion, he would have to, after each number, either fall to the ground floor racked with spasms of mocking laughter or else shoot the perpetrator miraculously through the head.'

Was James, who has spared few television personalities with his wickedly amusing pen, really suggesting perhaps that Terry Wogan was too intelligent to be wasting his talents on programmes such as *Come Dancing* and *A Song for Europe?* There are those who would probably agree with him. James did concede though that Terry had brought 'spontaneous intelligence' to *Wogan*, an accurate enough description. One of the *Wogan* team put it another way: 'The man flies by the seat of his pants. Nobody else would do it live at that pace.' Someone else observed: 'The special ingredient is the way Wogan uses his talent for beguiling nonsense to knit it all together'.

Terry, despite the ups and downs of the show, welcomes the challenge of live television: 'The essence of my job is to take risks. I've never minded things going wrong, because I can usually turn them to my advantage.' And he is in no doubt about the source of his skills: 'When people are kind enough to compliment me, I remember the stark terror of television in Ireland. Anyone who survived that can survive anything.'

What next for Terry? He has hinted that he would like to

try America. Irish actor Jim Norton, discussing the Wogan Phenomenon, remarked to me in Dublin in June 1986: 'I am convinced that Terry should give America a bash. That is where the real big money is to be found. In Hollywood I heard his name mentioned numerous times by stars who had been interviewed on *Wogan* and everybody liked his style. I feel he would go down big there. He has after all done what he had wanted to do in British television. What is there for him new?'

Friends and admirers suggest that after the run of *Wogan* ends, and in the event of his deciding to give America a miss, Terry should tackle an *avant-garde* solo show, a kind of way-out chat for his television audience. The possibilities are endless. It could be a little of Dave Allen, Clive James and Bob Monkhouse rolled into one. Something wildly Woganesque.

Terry's popularity continues unabated. Awards come thick and fast. In February 1986, he even topped an opinion poll making him the man most women in Britain wanted to spend St Valentine's Day with. For nine consecutive years he has been voted TV Personality of the year. He received an award from the Broadcasting Press Guild for best screen performance for a non-acting role in 1982 for *Blankety Blank*. He built up an audience of twenty million for that show. Among the many awards Terry has received are Best Dressed Man in 1983.

One of the off-screen highlights of Terry's career arrived in 1982 when show-business stars from all over the world gathered to pay tribute to him at the special lunch in his honour. Sponsored by the Variety Club of Great Britain, the celebrities included the then BBC Director-General, Alasdair Milne. Six hundred and fifty guests paid £20 a head, plus wine, for lunch, the cash going to charity.

Millions of words have been written about Terry, most of them complimentary, some bizarre, others banal. 'You can't be loved by everybody,' sighs Terry philosophically. Yet many have found the private Terry a replica of the public image, which is no mean boast in these testy times. Because he is successful and reckoned a 'nice guy', he poses a problem for the newspaper and magazine people who seek him out for interview. Doubtless he is often amused by what is written about him, sometimes alarmed, and occasionally perturbed.

There was the priest-columnist from Ireland who visited his dressing-room at the BBC Television Theatre in Shepherd's Bush and tackled Terry in the nicest way imaginable about the state of his religious beliefs in 1986. Few, if any of the Fleet Street people, had thought of that, although one audacious lady did try to equate his popularity with Jesus Christ's. The irony in this particular case was that the priest would be published in an Irish Sunday tabloid that more resembled the *Sun* than the *Universe*. Terry, the priest noted, was 'embarrassed by his question'. 'He gave a nervous little laugh. It was obviously a question he hoped I wouldn't ask.'

But Terry, who is never lost for words, confessed that he was brought up in a good Irish Catholic family. 'I have difficulty in believing in the existence of God and I'm not a terrific supporter of religion. That doesn't mean I'm against religion or that I have no religion.'

As they talked, it struck the priest that Terry had rejected an image of God rather than rejecting God. 'There is too much goodness, too much decency in the man to call him irreligious.'

Terry's confession wasn't finished: 'When I was growing up, we were always told that faith meant you had an unquestioning belief. I have never accepted that kind of faith since I was about sixteen years old. I still find it hard to think of myself as a non-believer and yet I know I am not a believer in any accepted sense. I'm at best an agnostic.

'My mother is a wonderful Catholic. She always was and always will be. Helen, my wife, is a terrific person. She really does have a wonderful faith. She goes to Mass. And so do my children go to Mass. And illogical as it may seem I often go to Mass myself. I'm sure all that seems strange to you. I'm different from most others in that the thing that constantly makes me believe in God is mankind. I tend to have a great faith in people. Maybe I'm naive. But I always expect people to do the right things. I don't expect people to cheat or to lie. I go through life in blissful euphoria. I'm not expecting anyone in the BBC to stab me in the back. I don't expect anyone to do anything nasty to me. I treat people in a certain dignified way and I expect them to treat me in the same way.'

When Irish-born actress/journalist Jeananne Crowley met the great man she came away convinced that she had found the answer to the mystery of his popularity. 'Many minds greater than mine have puzzled sorely over the secret of Wogan's success. As far as I can see he's paid simply for being Irish or at least fulfilling the Great English Public's expectations of what an Irishman really ought to be. A sublimely modest chap – the description he suggests – is obviously a clever ploy to fool those of us who, listening to him on radio, have come to the conclusion that broadcasting is as easy as falling off the proverbial log.'

Miss Crowley summed up: 'Mr Wogan never loses the run of himself, so to speak.'

By now Terry had adopted the motto (once adopted by millionaire fashion designer Diane Von Furstenberg): 'Everyone is talking about me, so I figured why don't I?' He did not share the Paul Theroux concept that 'humorists are often unhappy and satirists downright miserable'. He was cheerful and responsible whenever he was confronted by the press and continued to give three or four interviews every week. Some of the writers went away disappointed; they had sought to find chinks in the Wogan armour, instead they discovered few flaws.

He wasn't, as far as they could discern a hypochondriac, insomniac, hell-raiser, bisexual, drug addict, cynic, manic depressive, woman-fancier, or a cheat. Nor did he possess those self-destructive characteristics that made Brendan Behan notorious. The guy was simply normal. Happily married he regarded his glamorous career as just another job. He liked a drink but wouldn't run a mile for a bottle of stout; he liked good food and good wine but swore to all and sundry he wasn't a glutton.

There was a story told in Fleet Street that a hardened news editor of a tabloid was furious with a young woman reporter who came back from an interview with Terry and said she could not find warts on Terry. 'Ridiculous!' boomed the news editor, 'there must be warts on the fellow. Everybody's got warts somewhere. Don't tell me Wogan is an exception.'

'There are none,' reiterated the reporter.

'Ask his wife, ask his doctor,' bellowed the news editor, 'I tell you there must be warts.'

By the end of the unreasonable set-to the young reporter was inclined to take her boss literally, a fatal thing to do where Wogan is concerned, for he doesn't always see things in the literal sense; far from it. He has been known to send reporters up the wrong path in the most amusing way possible. But warts? Nobody so far has discovered any serious blemishes in the great man.

Curiously, the literary pilgrims from Ireland who visit the Wogan shrine at Shepherd's Bush tend to search for Terry's more serious side, as though suffering from the delusion that all Irishmen are serious-minded, which of course is a myth.

Author Ulick O'Connor made the pilgrimage from Dublin to meet his fellow countryman. They met in the convivial atmosphere of a small Italian restaurant. It had been five years since their last meeting, and in the meantime O'Connor had written plays and books and sporting pieces for *The Sunday Times*. He shared with Terry an interest in rugby. He wasn't long seated in the restaurant before he discovered 'the magic side of Terry'. He observed: 'The Wogan magic they call it. I know the voice of course, a seductive, well-bred Dublin burr, dwelling lovingly on the long vowels, with a Limerick under-tow. But television demands more than a voice.'

Clearly Terry was under intense scrutiny. How he

responded to the O'Connor technique I can only imagine. Anyway, O'Connor found 'his smile a winner. But you notice something that hasn't been commented on before – the eyes are a special shade of green, emerald. Yes, actually emerald eyes.' Only an Irish author could have observed those green eyes.

'Those nostrils,' continued O'Connor, 'if they flared any more would turn the nose into a snout but, as it is, there's a suggestion of a faun. That's of course until you see the tum, for who ever heard of a fat faun! – Wogan's fight-the-flab days are over.'

At the interview Terry 'wore a herring-bone sports coat, flannel pants and was very relaxed'. He assured Ulick O'Connor that 'he didn't feel any pressure. He had an empire inside the BBC, virtually a whole floor working on his show. He left them to handle everything so that he could have the time to handle himself. He admitted he was like a quivering jelly before he went on but he had to work to conquer it.'

Dublin journalist Deirdre Purcell went to Broadcasting House in London to meet him. Her verdict: 'Terry's person-ality is more contained than expected but genuinely affable. If he has agreed to talk to you for an hour, the hour is yours.'

The English magazine journalists tend to concentrate more on *Wogan*. Talking about the show, the girl from *My Weekly* summed up: 'There's a lot of Irish blarney in Terry's style but he is a real "pro", although he plays down the sugges-tion that he has any particular talent and says "Any eejit could do it". However, as some of his stand-ins have disco-vered, it seems deceptively easy.'

It is not often that one finds Terry's name in the *News of the World*. But on Sunday, February 16, 1986, he was back at his whimsical best (after those thoughtful interviews with his Irish friends) as he talked with Ivan Waterman about how 'the leggy lovelies on the TV show turned him on'. Then he made (for him) the startling revelation: 'I'm not a boobs man, I'm a legs man! The truth is I just adore beautiful

legs. Just take Selina Scott and Joanna Lumley. Both dyna-
mite, aren't they? Great legs. Very much my kind of
women.'

Asked about the women on *Wogan*, he mused: 'There's
Samantha Fox – she's like a doll, something you put on a
shelf and admire, but don't touch. We've had real idols on
the show, like Sophia Loren, Gina Lollobrigida. They're
fabulous ladies as well. But perhaps the only time I was
starstruck was when we had on the veteran star of Hollywood musicals June Allyson. I've always had a terrific crush
on her. I used to go and see her movies two or three nights
a week'.

Terry sometimes likes to chat with journalists in the dressing-room of BBC's Television Theatre at Shepherd's Bush.
This is the number one dressing-room and it has on the
door the rather formal 'Mr Terence Wogan'. He shares his
five-star dressing room with the Esther Rantzen show, *That's
Life*, which is also televised from this theatre.

Normally Terry sees the press bang on time. He locks the
door on the inside, promises an hour only, and then may
run over by a few minutes. There are knocks on the door
at regular intervals and outside people utter breathlessly:
'Terry, are you nearly finished?' If it happens to be a
beautiful woman he is talking to, he'll probably quip: 'I'm
having a lovely conversation with this gorgeous woman.'
More often than not, Terry will have a BBC staffer standing
by in the room near him taking down everything he has
been saying in shorthand.

When Vicki Woods, from *The Observer*, met Terry in his
dressing-room, she asked bluntly: 'Don't you hate being
interviewed?'

He pulled a solemn face and raised his eyebrows, as he
replied: 'Sometimes I bore myself.'

'Do you like the BBC?' he was then queried.

Terry looked surprised. 'That's rather like asking "Do you
like the Vatican?" I've never actually disliked it or failed to
get on.'

Miss Woods seemed to discover 'a dominant ego' in

Terry's make-up, but at the same time she described him as 'a very BBC sort of person'. She explained: 'He manages to mix a deep vein of organisation-man seriousness with the naughty bits that make him so much fun to be with.'

Terry reminded her of what Eamonn Andrews had told him three years before: 'I remember Eamonn saying there are only three ways to get the elbow (as a performer) from the BBC. One: the public tires of you. Two: you tire of what you're doing. Three: the people at the top – the mandarins, the senior management – tire of you. The last of course is the most final. And for *Wogan*, I'd say the least likely.'

More bangings on the dressing-room door. Terry exclaims: 'What is it? be off wid ye.' Then he opens the door and cries: 'For the last time . . .' but promises in the same breath that he wouldn't be long.

There are those who believe that the BBC thinks that Terry walks on water. One of them is Miss Vicki Woods who says: 'They indulge him and kowtow to him in their distinctive way and some people even claim that he has them running.'

Terry joked: 'No man is a hero to his valet. The kowtowing that goes on here is balanced by the family at home. It's a bit of a cross for the family the way I'm treated here.'

Journalists who have met him in his dressing-room have invariably remarked on his 'ordinariness'. When this was mentioned to Terry, he said: 'I'm trying to eschew artificiality. On my gravestone I'd like them to say: "He looked as if he didn't know what he was doing.".'

Women reporters like to discuss love and romance with Terry, believing him to be a great romantic at heart. But they find that when it comes to romance Terry can be painfully shy. 'I still don't understand the way some fellows can approach women,' he laments. 'Because of my crippling shyness, I was never able to chat up women. I just had to accept that women were going to be my one big stumbling-block in life'. As a young man working in Dublin he had a very simple attitude to the opposite sex. 'Women,' he recalls, 'always had to come to me. At a dance I'd just sit there and wait for someone ugly to come and invite me on to the floor.'

Terry, although aware of what he calls 'the menace of the press', realises he has got to live with them. He cannot hope to become the Monk of Shepherd's Bush, nor does he particularly want that label. It is enough to be known as the Bard of Shepherd's Bush. He will be happy to play along with the press, one imagines, as long as they are not nasty to him.

Most certainly all his achievements are really the culmination of his twenty-five years in broadcasting in Ireland and England. It has been a long slog.

He entered broadcasting, as we shall see, almost by accident. Soon he was to bring to his new career a highly original approach. He was to prove a born innovator. His individual style was recognised by the experts in his field but, ironic as it may seem, the crucial transformation in his career did not take place until he arrived at the BBC. Why this was so we shall examine later, for it was this happening that led to the Wogan Phenomenon and created the Wogan Industry.

It was the most remarkable happening of his life as a broadcaster.

PART TWO

BANKER TO BROADCASTER

What is the good of friendship if one cannot say exactly what one means?

—OSCAR WILDE

6   *Nuns and Jesuits*

Limerick is a leisurely three-hour car journey south-west of Dublin and meets Bernard Levin's three essentials for the picturesque city: water, spires and heart. Nestling snugly by the river Shannon, it has a plethora of church spires, and the heart of Limerick is to be found in the gaiety of its people, their mischievous humour, and their love of sport, particularly rugby football.

Limerick has been the birthplace of poets, novelists and at least one film star, Richard Harris. Its best-known novelist was Kate O'Brien, who settled in the English countryside, and decades ago the operatic world acknowledged the outstanding merits of Limerick-born tenor Joseph O'Mara and diva Catherine Hayes.

It was here in a quiet, unobtrusive terraced house, 18 Elm Park, that Michael Terence Wogan was born on August 3, 1938. No church bells pealed out over the city to mark the occasion. Nor did his name appear in the births columns of the national or local newspapers. Like other babies born in Limerick on that day, he arrived unheralded and unsung. He was the first child born to Michael and Rose Wogan and his arrival brought great joy to his parents, his father in particular being thrilled that the baby was a boy.

Elm Park is a respectable middle-class area situated a mile or two from the city centre and skirting the main road to Shannon Airport. Two rows of modern two-storey houses face each other in the terrace and near by are the Limerick Tennis Club grounds. Terry's father worked as manager of a city grocery store, Leverett & Fry, but couldn't afford a car, so he cycled to work.

Michael Wogan had come from Dublin and in a short time he ran the neatest shop in the street. Customers remarked on it, also on Michael's cultured accent and agreeable manner. He was regarded as a good businessman and ran a successful store. His wife, Rose, a Dublin woman, made no secret of the fact that she found it extremely difficult to settle in Limerick, but gradually she came to terms with her new surroundings and the strange people.

'Once I got to know them I came to like them,' she recalls. 'The trouble was, all my relatives and friends were in Dublin.'

Young Wogan was born into a world that already was seeing the dark shadows of war creep ominously over Europe. Nazism, with Hitler at its head, was sweeping Germany, while Mussolini's Fascists had control of Italy. The Spanish Civil War was coming to a close with victory in sight for General Franco. Newspaper headlines highlighted the conflict between Russia and Japan, as Soviet bombers hit targets in that country. War correspondents were already discussing the likelihood of outright war. The United States President, Franklin Roosevelt, fearing the growing threat of war in Europe, called for a moral quarantine against aggressor nations.

But in Ireland the threat of war seemed remote. In Dublin on this sunny August day the crowds flocked to the Royal Dublin Horse Show and, being the season of high fashion, the ladies responded in style. More than twelve thousand people attended the show and saw some 'thrilling jumping'. In contrast, life in Limerick was relatively quiet. On the previous day, August 2, there had been car races around the streets, otherwise the citizens were more concerned about holidays. Traditionally, it is a month when thousands of Limerick people go to the County Clare seaside resort of Kilkee for two weeks' vacation, turning the resort into a miniature Limerick. The more well-off Limerick people have

their summer houses there. Because of the birth of their first
child, the Wogans decided to take no holidays that month.

They had already decided to call their son Michael
Terence. He was a healthy baby and caused his mother little
trouble. Each morning a proud Michael Wogan senior cycled
to the city centre to open his grocery store, which was
making a reasonable profit. When young Wogan was six
years old a second child was born and he was named Brian.
By now Michael Terence was attending the school run by
Salesian nuns. He wore a navy blue uniform and was
accompanied by his mother to school each morning.

The nuns remembered the little boy by 'his jet-black hair
and glowing red complexion and shy nature'. It was a
private convent school and his parents paid an annual fee.
There were between twenty and thirty boys and girls in
each class and the subjeccts taught included Irish, English,
Religious Knowledge and Maths.

'Young Wogan was always very well behaved,' remembered Sister Lynch. 'I taught him Irish and found him quick
on the pick--up, intelligent and interested in what he was
doing. I think he looked in some ways like his mother. At
three o'clock each day Mrs Wogan called to take him home.'

Among young Wogan's pals at the school were Jim Sexton
and Finbar Sheehan. Like him, they were good at reading
English and in this respect were considered a little ahead of
the other boys and girls. They were by now in senior infants.
When a boy did something wrong he was told to sit beside
a girl in the class. Some little boys cried or sulked and
resented the practice, regarding it as 'humiliation'. Young
Wogan was liked by the nuns and they don't recall him
suffering the 'humiliation' or 'disgrace' like the other boys.

Young Terry and his pals were for the most part oblivious
of the war devastating Europe and elsewhere, although from
time to time Mrs Rose Wogan pointed out to her young son
the war photographs in the newspapers and told him how
lucky he was to be living in Ireland. The country was of
course neutral, so life continued in Limerickk undisturbed.
The period was known as the Emergency and a regular army

and reserve force stood by in case Winston Churchill decided he wanted the strategic Irish ports. But the Irish Prime Minister, Eamon de Valera, was adamant that Ireland must play no active part in the war.

At the age of seven young Terry's big day arrived. (To avoid confusion with his father's name, it had been decided to call him Terence, but that soon became abbreviated to Terry.) Dressed in a neat new suit, Terry received his First Communion with Jim Sexton and his pals. It was a joyful occasion, shared by parents and nuns. The children usually expected gifts or a little money from relatives and neighbours, and were rarely disappointed.

The Wogans were staunch Catholics but not in any fanatical sense. Theirs was a simple faith and often an unquestioning one. Mrs Rose Wogan ensured that Terry never missed Mass on Sundays. At the age of eight he was sent to Crescent College, which was then located in the city centre. The college catered for the sons of middle-class and professional people and was labelled 'snobbish' by some Limerick citizens who sent their sons to the Christian Brothers. The Crescent had a good academic reputation and a fine sports tradition. The Jesuits ran a strict school. They gave the boys 'lots to do and you were expected to do your homework efficiently and in time.'

Since boys were punished for misdemeanours and this punishment was carried out by the College prefect of studies who soon came to be feared by the boys. The punishment ranged from two slaps, or biffs as they were called, on the hand to six slaps, depending on the gravity of the offence. The prefect used a leather strap and this became a dark symbol in itself. However, Crescent College at this time was no different from other schools and colleges throughout the country, where corporal punishment was the norm. Like the other boys, Terry Wogan feared the leather strap. The prospect of visiting the prefect in his room on the second floor off the landing, near which stood a glass display-stand with sports trophies, did not appeal to him, nor to his great pal Jim Sexton. They vowed to avoid a visit there at all costs.

'There was a small queue of boys outside the prefect's room each day,' recalled Terry's classmates. Some of the boys were terrified of the punishment. 'The prefect at the time was a fair man,' recalled Jim Sexton. 'The punishment never exceeded the offence.' After Fifth Year in secondary school the punishment ceased for fear of revolt among the bigger and more rugged boys, a highly unlikely happening at the time.

Young Wogan was studious and invariably had his home-work ready for inspection each day. Classmates can't remember seeing him in the punishment queue or in serious trouble with the priests. He was regarded as more advanced academically and better read than some of his classmates. By now Terry had taken up rugby and being a strong healthy boy he was reckoned to be a good prospect.

In class he continued to show his innate flair for the English language with the result that his essays were always amongst the best. The priests looked upon him as 'shy', something with which Terry himself agreed. Some parents claimed that the education at Crescent College was 'imprac-tical' and mainly catered for boys going into the professions, but other parents argued that it was adequate and fitted their sons well for life after school. It was also accepted that the Jesuits were adept at placing their ex-pupils in jobs and in this way showed they cared about the boys who went through the college.

Both Michael and Rose Wogan were satisfied with the progress made by young Terry at school. His examination results were favourable and they had received few, if any, complaints about his general behaviour. Occasionally the Jesuits visited their house in Elm Park and talked to them about Terry. This pleased the Wogans. As the good-natured Mrs Rose Wogan would say: 'The priests cared about my son's education and his future.'

Limerick in the late thirties and forties was an ideal place for boys to grow up. Outside of school Terry and his pals enjoyed life tremendously. In summer they played tennis, fished and indulged in a variety of games. Their parents brought them to Kilkee, although by now Terry, an independent boy, was spending holidays with his grandmother in Dublin and was becoming acquainted with Nelson's Pillar, the Zoo and other metropolitan landmarks. Recalled Jim Sexton: 'Limerick had everything we wanted. One day Terry's father brought home a selection of soldiers' caps and helmets and distributed them among us. We revelled in our new-found military status and played at war with great gusto. We played hard but we learned to take the knocks and come up for more'.

Girls did not figure in their zestful world. If boys under the age of sixteen paid attention to girls they were considered 'sissies and unmanly'. 'Being seen with a girl, however pretty,' remembers Jim Sexton, 'was a mark of unmanliness so the boys avoided them like the plague. We had so much else to do that we couldn't stand around talking to girls.'

The truth was of course that in those days sex was only a word in the dictionary, remote and incomprehensible to most boys. It was unthinkable in most cases for parents to discuss sexuality with their sons and daughters; in time they hoped their children would mature, get a job and marry. The Wogan home was no different from the rest. What mattered most in all these middle-class, respectable homes was a boy's good social behaviour, school record and attendance at Mass on Sundays.

One of the most popular pastimes with Terry and his pals was the playing of table soccer in the Wogan home. The boys had their favourite English League teams and stars, Terry's being Blackpool. Soon the boys noticed that Terry was commentating on the games, giving the mechanical players on the board real names.

'Terry could carry on the commentary right through a game and make it exciting,' said Jim Sexton. 'We all loved sport and knew the names of every big star and league team.'

They found Terry's home friendly and the atmosphere hospitable, just as in their own homes. 'Terry's home was happy and we were always sure of a warm welcome,' recalled one of his classmates. None of the boys at that time would think of disobeying his father, least of all Jim Sexton or Terry himself. He remained the figure of authority and expected to be listened to and to have his wishes carried out.

Each house had its radio, or wireless as it was known at the time, and on big sports occasions the boys would listen to commentaries; other times it was music. Once Jim Sexton came round the back of the Wogan house and found Terry doing an imaginary commentary on a big soccer match. It confirmed his own view that his friend was interested in radio and would love to be part of it.

Occasionally the boys were brought to the cinema in the city. This was reckoned a 'real treat' and the boys loved it. They had their dreams and fantasies of becoming football stars or film stars, anything you like to mention. His pals found Terry good-humoured, very loyal, generous and eager to help when called upon in various ventures. They swapped books and comics. All the time the Catholic faith remained an essential and inescapable part of their young lives.

'We certainly wouldn't talk seriously about our faith,' said Jim Sexton. 'Obedience was the strong commandment in those days. Yet to some of us – I think Terry Wogan too – God was a remote and rather severe figure. You had this feeling of remoteness and fear of striking up a personal relationship, but our faith was an essential part of our upbringing, a living thing. Most of us had good relations with the priests who taught us. I don't think either Terry or myself was actually afraid of going to school. We tried to do the best we could. We played rugby but hadn't a passionate interest in the game. Terry had the makings of a good front row forward if he took the game seriously. Looking back, I believe that the bond between us was a love of reading and sport. We loved words, new words fascinated us. We played with words. I remember for instance, that, some original phrases turned up in Terry's English essays.'

The boys had little money. As one boy later recalled: 'Our pocket money consisted of tuppence or sixpence a week. But we weren't money-conscious. Money wasn't an important factor in our lives. Any money we got we spent on comics and sweets. None of us smoked. Our parents would not have tolerated it. Alcohol was for grown-ups and tough rugby players. We enjoyed living, that's all we ever thought of.'

Today, Terry recalls with a certain pleasure those early days of his life in Limerick: 'It was a very happy fifteen years. I was glad I experienced it, very glad I was born in Limerick, because the city has a kind of individuality. I suppose anyone who comes from a small place thinks it has. 'I liked Limerick. I made a lot of nice friends there. They were important years for me, the formative years of my life. I liked Crescent College.'

Discussing the Jesuits and their influence, if any, on his early life, he reflected: 'I don't think they made a lasting impression on me. I never found them to be particularly impressive or indeed to live up to the reputation they had with some people. Perhaps it was an advantage for me being at a day school where we hadn't them all the time. However, I found the Jesuits good teachers and I did like my particular teachers. My early life was, I suppose, made up of sport and education. My parents made sacrifices to educate me. They hadn't much money. My father was after all only the manager of a grocery store, but then neither had my friends' parents much money. Like Richard Harris and his family, we also went to Kilkee on summer holidays, but I also loved going to Dublin to stay with my grandmother. I became orientated towards city life and that was important for the future.'

Occasionally Mrs Rose Wogan recalls with affection those days in Limerick: 'Terry, I remember, didn't want to be called Michael from the first moment he spoke a word. He didn't like being confused with his father. So we called him Terence and later just Terry. As a boy he had two passions –

reading and sport. He spent a lot of time reading *Just William* books; which he borrowed from his school library at Crescent College. He was absolutely mad on sport, but I wasn't surprised because all his pals were the same. They were full of energy and vigour, real outdoor types. I also remember Terry listening to the radio a lot. He used to play around pretending to be a radio interviewer. At times he could be a solitary boy; he was shy by nature. I never spoiled him.'

Terry was extremely close to his parents, respecting their wishes, yet from an early age he had a mind of his own. It was more than stubbornness. He remembers his father as a 'really hard-working man who often brought office papers home in the evenings and worked on Sundays. He was subsequently rewarded by being made a director of the company. My mother tells me I was very shy as a kid. I ran home the first day she took me to school. I was the type of child who'd lock the back gate to keep out the other kids. At the same time I was never put upon because I was a big fellow for my age. I remember the avenue bully having a go at me one day, so I hit him. There were no problems after that. I was never off a bike in Limerick and every Sunday in the summer I'd go fishing with my father or with friends. I wasn't particularly good at school mainly because I was too lazy, but one thing I did enjoy was debating, for which I won a number of prizes. I was greatly encouraged by Malachy Martin, a remarkable man whom I believe is now regarded as a wild-cat theologian.'

Today, his former classmates remember Terry as an articulate and forceful debater. Once in a debate for Crescent against Mungret College he was partnered by Desmond O'Malley, now a prominent Irish politician, and they 'demolished' the opposition. The subject under discussion was that rural Ireland contributed more to the prosperity of the country than did cities.

That young Wogan was an unusually observant and imaginative boy was underlined when he travelled from Limerick to Dublin in the fifties for his first rugby international match at Lansdowne Road, when the participants were Ireland and England. Accompanying him on the excursion train were two friends. Later he recalled the occasion: 'On arrival in the city I went straight to the Granny's in Drumcondra where I murdered a huge lunch. The strongest memory I have of the day is the smell of stout. It seemed to be everywhere, except the Granny's. The train, the tram, the terraces, the powerful whiff of Guinness permeated everything. I've never smelt it as strongly since then, except perhaps on one occasion when I travelled with the might of Old Belvedere Seconds to play a country-town side in the wilds of Westmeath. That first scrum-down! Several strong men had to be helped from the field, overcome by the fumes before a ball was even kicked.

'I always think that lunch *before* the game is a mistake, whether you're a player or spectator. Just have a surreptitious gander at that eejit beside you on the terrace: the flushed cheeks, the glazed eyes. He might as well be at Dalymount, or Dollymount, if it comes to that. And wait until Ireland score! He'll be all over you, in more ways than one. I hope you will not be wearing your good coat.'

On that fateful day in Lansdowne Road Terry saw Ireland's diminutive-sized President, Seán T. Ó Ceállaigh (O'Kelly), the first President he had ever laid eyes on. He hadn't seem him immediately because the President arrived at the far end of the ground from where he was sitting.

'He was not the kind of man you saw immediately, even in the kind of coat that he was wearing, which was a camel-coloured crombie number, and worn under a homburg. Though great of heart, Seán T. Ó Ceállaigh was small of stature. *Nobody* saw him immediately. But when they *did*, a full-throated roar rang around Lansdowne Road. Even at my then tender age, I was moved by what I thought to be a loyal greeting, the crowd's approbation of their leader. Then I realised what it was they were shouting, as one mighty voice: "Cut the grass!" "Cut the grass"!

'Ireland has neither the time nor the place for persons of

power and position. No wonder the High Kings didn't last. Probably jeered out of it . . .'

Back in Limerick Terry's friends laughed when he told them this story. To Jim Sexton, it contained the witty detail he had come to expect, the comic observation. Jim believed there was a 'journalist in Terry waiting to get out'. Mrs Rose Wogan and her husband Michael also thought that one day he might become a power in Fleet Street. At this time Terry had no idea what he wanted to be. Soon he would be leaving Limerick because Michael Wogan Senior was going to Dublin to take up a promotion. Terry had completed his Intermediate Examination and he was now nearly fifteen years of age.

Leaving his friends, he realised, would be a wrench for him, but his teachers told him there would be greater opportunities career-wise for him in Dublin and he was thankful for that. For then, in the mid-fifties, emigration was one of the main talking-points, jobs being very hard to find.

The Wogans were further relieved that Terry would be going to a Jesuit school in Dublin – Belvedere College.

7   Belvedere Boy

James Joyce and Belvedere College are synonymous. Terry
Wogan and Belvedere are not universally linked, although
many Dubliners know of the connection and Terry himself
has always spoken proudly of his *alma mater*.

Belvedere has long been classed as one of the great
educational establishments of Dublin, a college fit for a
James Joyce, Tony O'Reilly (now chairman of Heinz in
America) and Garret FitzGerald, former premier of Ireland.

'By the time I arrived at Belvedere,' recalls Terry Wogan,
'my early life had already been shaped by the Jesuits at
Crescent College, Limerick. I think what Belvedere College
gave me was a feeling that you were as good as anyone else
and that there were no limits to what you could achieve. I
never heard any teacher, lay or Jesuit, tell me this, but it
seemed to be inherent in the attitude of the college. Belved-
erians have a good estimation of themselves – I don't mean
in any arrogant manner, but in a self-confident way and it
shows in the kind of individual the school continues to
produce.'

When Terry entered by its main door for the first time in
the mid fifties, he was stepping into a building that was once
the stately town house of Lord Belvedere. In the nineteenth
century people in the area of Great Denmark Street, mostly
the poor, stared in awe at the stream of horse-drawn
carriages, the comings and goings of fashionable society,
and appreciated the pageantry which could be had so
cheaply.

James Joyce, the college's most famous past-pupil,

attended Belvedere from 1893 to 1898. A frail boy, he was
known to all as Jim Joyce; he was an exceedingly pious boy,
being head of the sodality. Joyce was a remarkable young
actor and his English essays were superb. However, by the
time Terry Wogan entered the college, Joyce's name was
unmentionable; he was regarded as 'the blasphemous, sex-
obsessed defiler of the Church he had betrayed.' Joyce had
done the unforgivable – he had denigrated his old school in
A Portrait of the Artist as a Young Man, particularly stressing
the corporal punishment aspect.

Whenever Terry Wogan was asked about Joyce and
Belvedere, he would remark good-humouredly: 'They don't
talk much about Joyce. They think he let the side down.'

But distinguished historian Owen Dudley-Edwards, a
proud Belvederian, argues: 'Joyce is a faithful son of
Belvedere. The Jesuits gave him a European sense which
was to be one of his most distinguishing characteristics and
he was genuinely affected by the classical atmosphere of the
place.'

Terry Wogan joined a college that continued to turn out
scholars, patriots and sportsmen. It prided itself in its
forward thinking. For Terry, at the age of fifteen, the change
to Belvedere was a challenging experience and he took a
little time to adjust to his new surroundings. Being familiar
with Dublin was a help to him. Soon he was playing rugby
and performing in the college plays and musicals. The
atmosphere appealed to his independent spirit; he found the
discipline less stringent than in Crescent College, Limerick.

Terry's teachers found him attentive to his studies; his
general school behaviour was good and he possessed a likeable personality. 'He was an average boy, very normal and
not at all outstanding,' said Tom Mahon, one of Terry's
teachers. 'He was a very bright lad but he wasn't exactly a
hard worker. I think all the teachers had the feeling that he
didn't really know what he wanted to do.'

William Ward taught for fifty years in the college and
remembers thousands of pupils passing through his classes,
including Terry Wogan. 'In the academic sense young

Wogan wasn't exceptional in any way,' he recalls. 'I mean he did not stand out. Like many other students in the college, he was bright and intelligent and worked fairly hard. The last thing I expected was that this ordinary boy would become a great success in broadcasting, but when I see him now on television I am proud of him. He is excellent, a real entertainer who knows how to get the best out of people.'

Charlie Morgan, who taught Terry English and history, is not at all surprised by his achievements. He remembers his outstanding performances in Gilbert and Sullivan musicals. 'Terry was a very good character-actor, most convincing in comedy parts. He had a fairly good voice and spoke very clearly, appearing quite at home on the stage.

He was a burly lad and also excelled at rugby. He was popular with the other boys, and I felt he was happy at the college.'

'Today, Terry says that he had a rather undistinguished academic career at Belvedere ('Any teacher will tell you that'). 'I know that I did well at college musicals and also at rugby, and doing well in those things gave me a good feeling of achievement.'

Classmates of Terry's found that he wasn't an obvious extrovert. But he was very humorous and a tremendous personality. He was also a good talker and story-teller. He was interested in girls to the extent that most boys were, but girls never fitted much into their lives at this stage.

As a contemporary Belvederian recalled: 'We were surrounded by girls' schools but it never went further than a bit of dalliance after school. It was pretty harmless. There wasn't much money around and none of us could afford to take a girl out. With strict parents, pocket money was in short supply.'

Anyway, sex didn't figure large in the lives of Belvedere students of the time. Sexual stirrings were matters for the confessional, recalled a scholarly past pupil. 'On the role of sex it was impossible to speak with any certainty. The Jesuits normally practised a very careful agnosticism as to what took place outside school hours and school events, although they often surprised students by knowing more about their backgrounds than they imagined.'

Reminiscing about his days at Belvedere, Terry says: 'I suppose it took me a little time to adjust after Crescent College. Adjusting to a new school is never easy. During my time at Belvedere when I should have been studying I was building social bridges, as it were. It's important that you make friends and all the rest of it, so whatever academic ability I had went into this, so I didn't do as well as I should. I was in the honours class and did Greek and Latin. Languages have always been my strong point. In those days classics and the arts got priority because the priests felt they would make a priest out of one. The dumb ones took science, but I hear it's all changed now – science has come into its own!'

Terry's humour invariably surfaces in any conversation. On the question of a priestly vocation, he quipped: 'I prayed that I wouldn't get a vocation. Apart from that, I made very good friends in the college and enjoyed their company. I remember one of the best things to happen to me around this time was when I went to a retreat in the Jesuit House in Rathfarnham in County Dublin and one of the priests told us: "It's virtually impossible to commit a mortal sin." I wish somebody had told me that when I was about seven or eight years of age because we were always under the threat of this sin and had irredeemably black marks on our souls for virtually every peccadillo. That priest really lifted the shutters for me. It was as if a great weight was lifted from my shoulders. I remember it so clearly. I loved the life in Belvedere because it was relaxed and you enjoyed a certain freedom.'

Terry sat for the Leaving Certificate at the age of seventeen, which was considered young to be finishing secondary school. That summer he went on holiday to Kilkee, County Clare, and contracted viral pneumonia. The illness set him back some months. However, he had no intention of enrol-

ling at university. 'I felt my parents had spent enough
money on my education. I was anxious to go out and earn
a living.'

Because he had a year to spare, he decided to enrol in
the philosophy course at Belvedere, a course which was
considered 'very useful to boys'. It was conducted by Francis
Schrenk, SJ, a studious priest with the welfare of the senior
boys very much at heart. He was convinced that the boys
should take the course in order to prepare them for the
demands of the world, also to shape their young lives. The
course was usually taken by students too young to enrol at
university, and the class was small – between seven and
ten.

At the outset of the first term, Father Schrenk would tell
the class: 'I look upon this course you're embarking on as a
serious preparation for whatever career you happen to take
up later.' It was a practical study of philosophy, dealing
with the principles of ethics, and gave the boys some insight
into the minds of the philosophers themselves. Father
Schrenk always considered Belvedere a step ahead of other
colleges in Dublin. 'We were ahead, I think, in training
students for life and providing them with a challenging
academic atmosphere. I encouraged students to ask questions. I wanted them to be able to think for themselves, to
be able to make decisions, to have moral values.'

To the quietly-spoken Jesuit with the ascetic appearance,
young Terry Wogan was 'just another pupil'. He recalls: 'I
remember he asked plenty of questions, just like the others.
All of them were intelligent and did not accept without
question my philosophical ideas. As the course progressed,
I knew they were enjoying it; it was something new and I
was treating them in a mature way.'

Later Terry would say: 'This course gave me a whole new
dimension on life, formed in me new attitudes and for the
first time I looked at myself in a different way. We were
regarded as a sort of élite by the rest of the college.'

Although people came to Belvedere to advise on careers,
he was still undecided on what to do after the philosophy

course. He thought of being an actor but had no idea of how to go about getting into the business.

'I wasn't a great one for knocking on doors. I was still shy and in no way pushy.'

He loved reading books and enjoyed getting new ones. He was also a voracious radio listener and regularly tuned into the BBC Light Programme. The zany humour of Hancock, Sellers and Milligan tickled his fancy and he reckoned it helped his own sense of humour.

The late fifties was a bad time for finding jobs. They were years of economic depression in Ireland. 'If you hadn't a priestly vocation you were on your own,' Terry recalls. 'Many young people emigrated to Britain and the United States. If my father had been a doctor, I would probably have studied medicine, or if he was an architect I would have taken up architecture. Luckily, as it turned out, he wasn't in either of these professions. But he did finish up as a managing director of a chain of groceries – and full marks to him. He worked hard for whatever he got.'

One day the Rector of Belvedere College called on Michael Wogan Senior and told him that the Royal Bank of Ireland was looking for 'fellows to do their clerking' and he suggested that Terry apply. Shortly afterwards Terry sat the bank examination with about seventy others. 'I can't recall how the exam itself went for me, but the interview was good. I suppose a certain amount of native cunning was involved.'

He got the job and the first bank he was assigned to was the Cornmarket, which was centrally based in Dublin.

'I'll never forget my first day as long as I live,' he recalls. 'They taught me how to separate two-and-sixpence's from two-bob bits! And how to count notes with the left hand rather than the right. I got very good at this in the end.'

Although he had begun on eight pounds a week, he was determined to make the most of his opportunities. He began to study for his bank exams. Eventually he was transferred to the Phibsboro branch on the outskirts of Dublin. Soon he

found that the 'snug banker' was on twenty pounds a week
and that the 'ideal man' was the snug man in the bank.
Promotion, he learned, would be painfully slow, but this
didn't worry him; he had a job and that was all that
mattered. There were some other ex-Belvederians who were
finding it hard to get jobs. He knew that a lot of people
regarded banking as a 'boring, dead-pan type of job', but if
they had joined him in the Phibsboro branch they would
have quickly revised their opinions. Sometimes he found
the experience quite hilarious.

The bank was unusual in that it catered for large numbers
of cattlemen and wealthy farmers who attended the nearby
mart. A lot of money passed through their hands. It was a
very eccentric bank. Being close to the cattle market, the
smell was terrible. 'There was one old farmer we hated
dealing with, who really stank', Terry remembers. 'When
he came into the bank, it was heads down and we all disappeared behind the counter till he walked out again. Always
it was the same. Whenever this solitary individual looked
for someone to take his deposit or cash his cheque, he was
met with stony silence. Then there was the cattleman who
came in one day stoned out of his mind and chased the
manager into the lavatory, where he locked himself in. The
chief cashier had to rush out and call the police to get him
out!'

The staff at Phibsboro, he found, were no angels. He
might be chatting politely to a customer when a sponge
would fly across the bank and hit him in the face. Or he
might suddenly feel the office mop in a most uncomfortable
place while he was chatting up a pretty girl. But he was
having fun all the same and making good friends. He found
that the customers weren't the only characters around. 'Our
porter, who constantly told me it was not his job to cook
anyone's meals, had been virtually forced by the manager
to cook his lunch. I remember he took great satisfaction in
buying a piece of steak, kicking it around the room half a
dozen times and jumping up and down on it, before serving
it on a nice clean plate!

'The porter used to accompany me on the top of the number 19 bus to head office in Forest Place with £5,000 in old notes to have them changed for new ones. He'd often say to me: "What would you do if someone came up to us and said: Hand over that money? I know what I'd do," he said, "I'd tell them to take the bloody money and go." '

The social side of life was always important to Terry. He seldom neglected it. His friends said he tried to maintain a happy balance between his social and working life. He admitted that at times banking could be slightly repetitive and a little boring, so he deliberately cultivated an enjoyable lifestyle by joining the best amateur musical group in Dublin – the Rathmines and Rathgar Musical Society, better known as the R & R. Among his friends in the chorus was Bryan Kelly, a tall sturdy young man who sang in choirs and worked in the family business. He had been educated at Rockwell College in County Tipperary.

'Terry wasn't a marvellous singer,' Bryan recalls, 'but he had a sweet baritone voice. He was very supportive to beginners in the chorus and went out of his way to help them. This generosity was a trait of his. While he was casual and good-humoured off-stage, he took his chorus work seriously. Usually the R & R brought in experts in voice training and production from London and one learned a good deal. The R & R was reckoned to be a good training ground. We learned the rudiments of dance. Some of the principals went on to the professional stage and did well.'

Sometimes Bryan Kelly visited the Wogan home and brought along with him his old Grundig tape-recorder. 'We both loved the Goons,' he says, 'and Terry and I would interview each other. I could see that Terry was interested in radio, Tony Hancock and Peter Sellers in particular. He responded to their humour. I felt that he wanted to get into radio, or some form of show business.

Bryan was always struck by the warmth of the Wogan home and Terry's respect for his parents. He believes that his father was a big influence on him. 'I admired Michael Wogan a lot. He was a very intelligent man and in the grocery and wine business he was ahead of his time. I remember he used to talk about the delicatessen in the context of food shops of the future and the scope it would provide.'

During the winter months Terry continued to play rugby with Belvedere Seconds, but he was unlikely to establish himself in the first team. A cartilage operation did not help.

'I don't think he took rugby seriously,' says an old team-mate.

Terry also joined the Dublin Grand Opera Society, but he never expressed any ambition of reaching the Royal Opera House, Covent Garden or La Scala in Milan. He vividly remembers walking on in Verdi's *Aida* carrying spears. 'The whole idea was to see the opera for nothing. One evening we refused to put on the muck – cocoa or something. Two of the most consumptive slaves you ever saw marched onto the Gaiety stage that night.

'We used to drink in the Green Room at the Gaiety. I remember on another occasion we were supposed to take part in the Easter Hymn Parade in *Cavalleria Rusticana*. The Italian producer of the opera – blue in the face – suddenly appeared in the Green Room while we were in the middle of a drink. "OK, so you like to drink your beer," he bellowed. "Drink it! The procession is over. You can all go home." '

Back in the bank, Terry was passing his examinations.

'I think he would have made a good banker,' recalls Noel Curran, one of his bank managers. 'He knew how to deal with money.'

However, at heart Terry knew he would not make a businessman. It wasn't his forte, he told himself. But he does possess affectionate memories of his time in banking: 'I enjoyed myself and banking gave me a lot of pleasure. I think I grew up in the bank. I learned how to relate with people, how to get on with people and also to take orders and, in the midst of it all, I preserved my sense of humour. I suppose I lived from weekend to weekend, work to pleasure. I had dates with girlfriends, a drink or two. The social side was good. I wasn't very pushy, although I must have been ambitious. I was never really unhappy in the bank. I realised though that I was drifting and I had still no clear idea what I would like to do. In those days you had a secure job and that's what mattered most.'

One day he spotted an advertisement in the newspaper that Radio Telefis Eireann was looking for a trainee announcer. He decided to apply, although he knew that hundreds would be doing the same thing. Terry thought the job looked interesting and had good potential. He applied and was called for interview. After five years it looked as though he was soon to leave the world of banking for broadcasting. Suddenly the prospect excited him.

'The bank let me off for an hour – they thought to see the dentist – when I went for the audition. I was given six weeks' training while still with the bank, but I was really looking forward to making a full-time career out of broadcasting.'

8 *Radio Announcer*

In November 1961, at the age of twenty-three, Terry Wogan became a full-time broadcaster, exchanging the bank's staid offices in Grafton Street for rooms in the General Post Office (the GPO) in Dublin's main thoroughfare, O'Connell Street.

Terry had by now almost forgotten what his bank manager had said to him: 'I think you have a good future here if you care to stay.' Terry thanked him politely. He welcomed, however, the freedom associated with broadcasting and the opportunities it provided. He was determined to give it all he got.

'He was very enthusiastic about his new job,' recalls Mrs Wogan. 'I couldn't see him failing to do well.' She had been surprised by his decision to go into broadcasting. 'I thought he had settled in the bank. It was a solid job and I remember saying to myself: "That's him fixed for life." When he told me he was considering the move I wondered what was coming next. Terry was of course always surprising me and I never knew what next to expect.'

Some years before, a gangling Eamonn Andrews had entered the same building, as he later recalled: 'The atmosphere was unbelievable and as far removed from my romantic ideas of broadcasting as Mountjoy Jail from Malibu Beach. It was grey, cold, unwelcoming. Unmarked doors with frosted-glass panes punctuated whole tiles stretching from one end of the corridor to another. It was a vision that persuaded Larry Morrow to describe Radio Eireann as "the largest public lavatory in the world".'

But Terry Wogan wasn't too concerned about the chilly,

old-world atmosphere or the 'unmarked doors'; he saw his future there, and he didn't mind that he had joined the ranks of Irish broadcasters for a 'mere pittance'.

Looking back, he says today: 'I don't know how I got into broadcasting, in fact I don't know how I passed the audition because my Irish wasn't all that good. They must have seen something or heard something. I was really very lucky. Radio Eireann's Denis Meehan was really the master man who brought me on. For the audition you sat in front of a microphone and read something in Irish and English. I couldn't believe my luck when I was appointed.'

The ebullient Wogan was an unlikely candidate for the dull Civil Service atmosphere that permeated Irish broadcasting. Would his bubbling personality be crushed by the system? wondered one aging Civil Servant, who had watched Eamonn Andrews battle with frustration until he was on the verge of despair. Eamonn would say of the system: 'The place seemed to be ruled by Civil Servants who sat hunched over desks reading paragraphs and sub-paragraphs or rules that gave reasons why everything was impossible.'

Terry was to see the more bizarre side of the place. He decided that in order to preserve his sanity it was imperative to look at the lighter side. Usually he parked his Morris Minor on the pavement of the lane opposite, crossed the top of Henry Street by Galligan's outfitters, through the side entrance of the GPO and took the lift.

'Three floors full of unseen Civil Servants sped by, the doors opened, and there it was – Radio Eireann Reception,' he recalls. 'The reception had a young woman, a messenger, two phones and a plain-clothes Special Branch man asleep in a chair. To the right as you came out of the lift was a glass-doored corridor with most of the studios off it. To the left, another longer, darker corridor which housed the programme offices, administration, engineering, the gramophone library, the continuity suite and the main engineering control room.

'And it wasn't that long a corridor . . . but then, it wasn't that big a radio station. Big enough to be the summit of my worldly ambitions, though, in 1961.'

Terry's job of radio announcer could be described as the catch-all in broadcasting in Ireland. It combined continuity (linking programmes, covering breakdowns, filling gaps between taped programmes by promoting later shows, etc.), news-reading, compiling request programmes for the hospitalised and for troops on United Nations peace-keeping duties, introducing symphony concerts, setting the scene for listeners at the beginning of radio plays – the list of the functions of a radio announcer at that time was almost endless.

One of the ironies of the job was that everybody thought he or she could do it standing on their heads. As news announcer, Maurice O'Doherty would say: 'The announcer always gives the impression that though the folk group about to go on the air may be too drunk to sit down, never mind stand, nevertheless all is serene in the studio, and the fact that the whole station is falling about one's head is a tiny hitch in the works which will be put right within a few seconds.'

The man paid to hire announcers, Denis Meehan, was round-faced, authoritative and quick-witted. His philosophy was simple. He would tell trainees: 'You are not paid what is laughingly called your salary to sit serenely on your fundament while everything goes smoothly. You are paid to be able to deal with the occasions when things go wrong and, what's more, to convince the listeners that what we have is just a little difficulty, not the end of civilisation as we know it.'

Terry Wogan and the young trainees found Meehan a remarkable person. As an active announcer, despite the fact that he possessed a light tenor voice of ordinary though pleasant quality, he always conveyed the mood of calm urbanity that convinced listeners that all was well in the best of all possible worlds. At the time when he was appointed studio supervisor (a bureaucratic title) all announcers were women, or, in the case of males, light tenors (not to be confused with counter-tenors!). It appears that the engineers had a theory that a high-pitched voice was more easily understood by listeners. But when Denis Meehan came to have a say in who went on the air as an announcer, he kicked this quaint notion out the window. Baritone voices, including Terry Wogan's light baritone, were accepted; even a bass or two came into his own. Meehan's reputation grew with the years. Maurice O'Doherty observed: 'If you measured up to his standards you could be reasonably sure that you had a future in broadcasting. The fact that he offered a post of full-time announcer to Terry Wogan convinced me that the young Limerickman was on his way to success.'

Terry admits that he was 'hooked line and sinker' after his first broadcast. He thought: 'Me and the microphone will be never separated again.' That first broadcast took place in one of the old studios – 'up a rickety staircase to a dark felt-lined room with a table, a chair, and the kind of microphone Edward VII used for his abdication speech; dry-mouthed, clutching the closing prices on the Dublin Stock Exchange, and the Cattle Market Report, there's nobody there but me, not even a dozing engineer for support. The cue-light and the microphone are being controlled from the main control room.

'Green! Go! Claustrophobia sets in almost immediately. The roof seems to be pressing down on my head and shoulders. I'm losing control of my breathing. I'll never make it to the finish! I do, my cheeks flushed, my eyes popping and my head swimming from lack of oxygen. I've made it!'

Terry's personality was set to create an impression in the quaint corridors of the GPO where laughter was sometimes suppressed for fear of attracting unnecessary attention. Usually tranquillity reigned, but the atmosphere was deceptive. It struck some colleagues that Terry took life easy and wasn't easily ruffled. He arrived at his desk well dressed and usually wore a tie. As one woman announcer said: 'He was well groomed and didn't seem to model himself on anyone in particular. And he was always himself, easy-going and cheerful.'

It wasn't all work and no play among the staff in those days. Enjoyable parties attracted plenty of eligible men and not a few handsome ladies. Terry was invariably popular at these functions, for he was a good singer and story-teller. Denis Meehan, whom some Radio Eireann people regarded as a Jekyll and Hyde, was also a popular performer and he and Terry seemed to hit it off well together.

Andy O'Mahony, a stocky figure with more than a hint of the academic, joined Radio Eireann in the same year as Terry Wogan. He too had left the bank for broadcasting. Among the trainees with him was Gay Byrne, and they were trained by Denis Meehan. Andy remembers Meehan asking Gay Byrne: 'What do you think is the most important quality in a broadcaster or announcer?' Gay replied: 'To be relaxed.' Andy could not think of a suitable reply. Meehan commented: 'To be pleasant.' He didn't see the need for university education to make it in broadcasting in those days. What was needed in his opinion was a pleasant voice and to be able to read the news in Irish and English.

Andy O'Mahony had never met Terry Wogan up to then. Now they worked together in the same room at the end of a long corridor. He quickly formed the impression that Terry possessed obvious broadcasting talent; his voice was agreeable, relaxed, and Terry always struck him as a person he liked to be with. Terry had a gift of relating to people and he made you feel good, the kind of colleague you looked forward to meeting next morning.

Broadcasting then ceased at ten o'clock in the morning and did not resume until about one o'clock. 'During these extended intervals,' recalls O'Mahony, 'I would accompany Terry on long walks when we'd chat about our bank experiences and what we hoped to do in broadcasting. Terry used to say that he wasn't destined to remain in the bank. I felt that broadcasting suited his personality and he was optimistic about the future. I remember he was already planning documentaries we might attempt.'

At the heart of Terry's wit was perceptiveness, he decided.
'I think his humour was largely his way of looking at the
world. He wasn't a gag man. He never told gags. He was a
good psychologist and a shrewd observer of people. He
became popular with most of the staff.'

Maurice O'Doherty saw another side of Terry: 'When I
first met him it was his irreverent sense of humour that
stood out. It was more than irreverent in a way, it was
sardonic. It is humour typical of Limerick people in general;
most conversations in Limerick are tinged with irony, which
is all very well if all the participants are from that area, but
outsiders are inclined to get the wrong impression from the
sarcastic banter in the taverns and tea-houses of Limerick.
It is easy to come to the opinion that the whole population
of the place is a seething collection of frustrated malcontents.
People who come from parts of the country where humour
is somewhat less robust are, it must be admitted, inclined
to the view that Limerick people are grossly unhappy in any
activity in which they participate, particularly work. This is
not true. Shannonsiders are as serious about their work as
anybody else, but the cynical element in their make-up gives
them a healthy disregard for bumph. They can wax bitter
about the complex maze of regulations that beset the path
of anyone who works for the Government.'

Terry as usual was inclined to see the humorous side of
situations. He remembers Andy O'Mahony stopping a
record because it was interfering with their philosophical
discussion and plunging the plain people of Ireland into
puzzled silence for some minutes before he realised what
he'd done . . . and Denis Meehan with his uncanny ante-
nnae for broadcasting talent, his pullovers (through which
his braces poked cheekily) and his two cars, which hadn't
a headlight or a charged battery between them . . .'

Terry was not above the odd outrageous act, something
that was bound to echo through the corridors of the historic
GPO — as, for instance, when he unbuttoned a lady
announcer's blouse as she read a long ponderous introduction to an orchestral concert; or set fire to another

announcer's script and watched his face as the flames devoured his very words; or when he got a nose bleed in the middle of the one o'clock news.

Around this time the Dubliners, the popular folk group led by Ronnie Drew, had issued a single called *Seven Drunken Nights*. Because the lyrics were deemed 'obscene' the song was banned from the Irish airwaves. The action underlined the deep conservatism of the radio chiefs. It was something that disappointed Terry Wogan, who was always inclined to defy convention, provided it was within good taste. He saw nothing wrong with the ribald song, in fact he rated it rather comic.

One of THE most popular radio programmes at the time was *Hospital Requests*, which was transmitted every Wednesday afternoon between 1.00 and 2.30. Andy O'Mahony believes that it was as presenter of this programme that Terry made his first impact in broadcasting. 'Terry was the first broadcaster in Ireland to talk directly to listeners. This is an art in itself and he carried it off effortlessly. His success really brought him into the limelight. He was able to communicate with people in a friendly voice and in a humorous way. What might have been a dull programme turned out to be an entertaining one for listeners.'

On one occasion Terry was presenting the programme as Maurice O'Doherty 'sat serenely' in the continuity studio below him, reading the first edition of one of the evening newspapers. 'And now for the Clancy Brothers,' announced Terry briskly. On came the record. The title of the song was 'Isn't it Grand, Boys?' The subject of the song is a corpse from whom all life has not yet departed as he lies on the bier. In his own mind, he passes ironic comments on the mourners ranged around him. His reflections go like this:

> Look at the mourners,
> Bloody great hypocrites,
> Isn't it grand, boys,
> To be bloody well dead?

Let's not have a sniffle,
Let's have a bloody good cry,
And always remember the longer you live,
the sooner you'll bloody well die.

Look at the widow,
Bloody great female,
Isn't it grand, boys,
To be bloody well dead?

The record played, Terry went on to the next batch of
requests. Downstairs, however, all hell had broken loose.
Maurice O'Doherty saw the phone in continuity light up
and it stayed lit up for the next three-quarters of an hour.
In fact, so many calls were received objecting to the song
that O'Doherty had to ask a few colleagues to help out by
fielding some of the complaints, otherwise he would have
been on the phone all afternoon.

He shot off to the studio where Terry was broadcasting
to tell him to make some remark about the record. Terry
expressed some surprise about the public reaction, and
when he resumed on the air he 'waffled a bit about how
sorry he was to have ruffled so many feathers, but that
really he couldn't see what all the fuss was about'.

Maurice O'Doherty realised that Terry's words utterly
failed to cool the situation. The angry callers turned their
attentions from the ballad and instead showered abuse on
Terry, some demanding his 'immediate resignation'. The
widespread   reaction   proved   that   the   programme
commanded a large listenership; it also showed how sensitive many listeners were to anything remotely irregular.
Terry was prevailed upon privately to admit that perhaps
after all the lyrics of the ballad 'weren't entirely suitable for
transmission on a programme devoted to bringing a little
cheer into the lives of people who were sick'.

'The fuss didn't bother Terry in the least,' recalls
O'Doherty. 'That evening he went off to play golf as though
nothing unusual had happened. The plain fact is that the

ironical attitude displayed in the lyrics of "Isn't it grand?" appealed to his quirky sense of humour, but in extenuation he was like the rest of young people, and the young aren't renowned for their sensitivity in certain situations.'

Terry and Maurice worked for some years together on Mondays and Tuesdays. In the mid-sixties there was an extension of broadcasting hours. Up to then the radio station came on the air at eight o'clock in the morning and closed soon after ten until one o'clock. It was decided to close this gap and in future the staff announcers would fill the hour from ten to eleven o'clock with a slot hilariously called *Rogha na mBan*, which literally means 'Ladies' Choice', a programme of requests for housewives, much the same as the BBC had been presenting for many years.

Denis Meehan had just appointed Terry Wogan senior announcer, and so Terry produced the slot on Mondays, which Maurice presented. 'By some bureaucratic sleight of hand,' says Maurice, 'I, in turn, produced on Tuesday and Terry presented. At least that was the theory. but on Mondays the producer didn't appear in the studio until a couple of minutes before eleven. When the programme came off the air, we both adjourned to the nearby Tower Bar for coffee. Similarly, on Tuesdays, when I was "producer", I saw no reason to turn up until eleven either. The Tower Bar was one of several hostelries in both Henry Street and the famous Moore Street that were much frequented by the staff of the radio station. There were eleven studios in the radio station itself. If anyone of importance happened to be looking for someone, it was usually a fair bet that the person being sought was taking a little light refreshment in the Tower Bar, which of course could lead to disciplinary action if one was supposed to be working. Therefore, the Tower Bar was known as Studio 12. Rumour had it that there was an extension from the Radio Eireann switchboard to the bar.'

By now Irish television (RTE) was successfully in operation; to be precise it had started transmitting its first programmes in December 1961, a month after Terry Wogan joined Radio Eireann. It afforded welcome new opportunities for announcers, and Terry was among those who would soon be on the box. He began, like Andy O'Mahony, reading the news.

O'Mahony remembers that the atmosphere became very competitive with the advent of television. 'We were all eager to get a chance to prove ourselves.' It was also a time of change in broadcasting itself. A new Broadcasting Authority, under the chairmanship of Eamonn Andrews, had taken over the running of radio and television, but it was only a part-time body. In November 1960 the Authority, with the consent of the Minister, appointed an American, Edward J. Roth Junior, to be its first Director-General. Already a contract had been signed for new broadcasting buildings at Montrose in the city suburbs. The result was that radio and TV staffers were no longer bound by Civil Service conditions and regulations. To everyone's relief the long corridor leading past offices to studios was brightened considerably when the Post Office tiles that lined it were boarded over, and it became quite luxurious when a carpet was laid on the floor. The office stationery became more presentable. Eamonn Andrews would have approved of the changes, but he had already left for London.

Terry Wogan, like his colleagues, was relieved that broadcasting was moving forward. There were more opportunities. To television producer Adrian Cronin, Terry was a good news-reader on television. 'Anybody who could read without fluffing lines was, in my opinion, a good news-reader. Viewers for some reason or other idolised the people who read the news; they became stars in their own right. Terry possessed a good voice and looked relaxed.'

Off screen, he was much taken by Terry's 'puckish humour'.

In those days the news was rehearsed. 'On one occasion,' recalls Cronin, 'Terry Wogan was scheduled to read the news. Before it was the programme, *The Danny Kaye Show*, in which Danny did impressions of a German officer. Terry was rehearsing the news and at the same time taking off Kaye, pulling faces and being so good that he set us all laughing. He was very funny, so funny that the cameramen found it hard to concentrate. I suddenly became worried that he might unwittingly pull some faces as he read the news bulletin. Terry was completely unmoved by my anxiety. He was a professional and, of course, knew where to draw the line. He was a very witty man and an extremely easy-going person and talented. I didn't find him ambitious.'

In terms of sequence for the presentation of *The World This Week*, a television anthology of the week's news, Andy O'Mahony came before Terry Wogan. When Terry was given his chance he was regarded as a great success. At one point O'Mahony feared that he would lose the programme to Terry. 'I was prepared to lose it after I heard that the editor of the programme had discreetly asked Terry to take over. But Terry insisted that we continue to share the programme and he had his way. At a time when others would have grabbed at the chance, Terry showed a complete lack of ruthlessness. The truth was he couldn't hurt people. He was thoughtful, he didn't need to be ruthless. I considered his gesture characteristic and something I would have expected from him.'

9 Jackpot

Terry Wogan's first major break in television came his way unexpectedly. Already a familiar face to news viewers, he realised he would not become a real personality until he presented his own show. The darling of the box in the early 'sixties was Gay Byrne, a dapper young broadcaster with a smooth style and rare gifts. Gay had been presenting the very popular *Late, Late Show* since 1962, and the first home-grown Irish quiz game, *Jackpot*. Now with his new commitments at Granada Television in Manchester, he decided to resign as presenter of *Jackpot*.

Terry was chosen to take his place. *Jackpot* was a simple quiz game. The attractive Miss Olive White introduced the guests and also spun the wheel to get a category, then the presenter would proceed to ask the contestants three questions and they could get a bonus question with a prize of £25.

While presenting the quiz game itself would pose no problem to Terry Wogan, he admitted to friends that he was aware of the dangers of taking over a show Gay Byrne had just left. 'Gay has the polish and the experience. As a calculated risk I have accepted the offer, but I am dead scared of making a mess of it. As a TV news-reader it is hard to go wrong. Presenting a show like *Jackpot* is something else.'

Television producer Adrian Cronin was of the opinion that Gay would be a difficult act to follow. But he had faith in Terry's ability and was convinced he had the requirements for such a show – charm, good looks and an effortless style.

He had suspected for some time that Terry was only using news-reading as a stepping-stone and that he didn't intend to stay with it. 'I think that he wanted to become a star in television like the other young men in the station at the time.'

Cronin felt that RTE might have profited by giving Terry a show more suited to his talents than *Jackpot*, where there was scant scope for self-expression or originality. To Cronin, Terry was witty, a gifted ad-libber, and someone capable of imposing his personality on a show.

It was the technical aspect of television that worried Terry. He was a novice and he hoped his lack of experience would not be a great handicap. RTE itself was only finding its way and some of the new producers had yet to master the subtle technicalities. Otherwise, Terry was confident and this confidence had grown since he had begun with radio.

In the early days, though, Andy O'Mahony noticed Terry's lack of self-assurance and thought that the building of confidence in his case came slowly. 'Terry knew he was good in radio, for instance, but he didn't realise how good he was or his own true potential.' Although he knew that Terry had a 'striking appearance' on television, he was convinced that radio was his medium and he communicated superbly to listeners.

It was a good time in Ireland for budding talent. RTE chiefs were anxious to discover successful television presenters and personalities. They had been accused of 'aping the Americans for too long', but, as Adrian Cronin would point out, the enormous success of the *Late, Late Show* encouraged people to think in terms of Irish-made programmes. 'We began to attract qualified Irish people from Britain and Canada and a few Irish discoveries were coming along, including Terry Wogan.'

By now the station's own magazine, the *RTE Guide* was being published every week and selling to a wide public. For Terry's launch on *Jackpot*, space was devoted to his background, his Belvedere days, his R & R activities, and his own thoughts about television. It was Terry's first taste of publicity and he enjoyed the experience, and was seldom lost for words.

Off-screen Terry, as a chief announcer, helped to coach trainees as radio announcers. Among them was Brendan Balfe, a sharp-faced, ambitious young man with a profusion of dark hair and deep-set eyes. Balfe enjoyed the six-weeks' course with Terry and regarded him as an able communicator. On the morning he was to make his first broadcast from Henry Street he arrived in the studio with about an hour to spare. Shortly afterwards Terry came bounding into the room. 'Don't be nervous,' he exclaimed. 'Don't be conscious either that half a million listeners will be tuned in and that if you make a mistake-'

At that moment Brendan nervously interrupted him: 'Go away, leave me alone, Terry. I don't want you around me.'

Terry smiled. 'Don't worry about me. I'll stay in case anything goes wrong.'

'I tell you I don't want you here, Terry.'

But Terry was determined – and stayed in the studio. As Brendan began to go through his official station words, first in Irish, then in English, he suddenly felt something cold and wet trickling down the back of his neck. He managed to get through the news bulletin, then he looked around at Terry who was smiling whimsically.

He held a jug in his hand. Brendan realised it was water that Terry had poured down his neck.

'Why the water, Terry?'

Terry pulled a face of feigned innocence. 'Did no one tell you?'

'Tell me what?' Brendan queried.

Terry explained: 'That's the initiation rite every announcer has to go through here, I thought you'd heard?'

'So that's why you stayed here in the first place!' Brendan chuckled. He had grown to like Terry during the training course. He regarded him as a totally natural broadcaster. As a person, he felt he had an irreverent, even mischievous

The author, Gus Smith, outside the house in Limerick in which Terry Wogan was born.

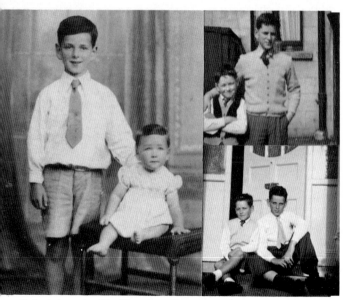

Early photographs of the Wogan boys, Terry and his younger brother, Brian.

Terry's hard-working grocer father, Michael.

Jerry's love of rugby began on the pitch at an early age. Here he is lining up (above) with Crescent College in Limerick (standing at far right) and (below) with the Belvedere College Senior Cup Team of 1957 (fourth from left in back row).

A very suave looking young Terry in an RTE publicity photo from the 1960s.

The bride and groom.

Demonstrating how much game-show hostesses – and sets – have changed since Ireland the 1960s, Terry presents *Jackpot,* his first break in television.

The BBC Radio One team from 1970. Terry is third from the left.

Mark White, who recognised something special in Terry's voice and started him on his career with the BBC.

aching Terry's level of success involves the inevitable photographs at Heathrow Airport.

Frances Whitaker, Terry's first producer of the *Wogan* show.

sense of humour. Conventions didn't worry him, least of all breaking them. 'The guy's incorrigible,' Brendan decided.

There was another occasion that he had cause to remember. The Cattle Market Report was read before *Farmers' Forum* in the same studio. The *Forum* consisted of about four experts directed by a chairman discussing topical matters of farming interest. Brendan would come into the studio where the *Forum* panel was seated and begin to read the Cattle Market Report. Usually it was typed on a sheet of paper and referred to ewes, heifers and fat bullocks.

Terry had warned him: 'When you get to the word bullocks, don't use the *other* version.'

Brendan knew that Terry was using this to test his ability as a reader. The result was that Brendan kept thinking of the word bullocks for fear of forgetting it. As he proceeded to read the report, with the *Forum* panel casting curious glances across the table, he suddenly came to the word fat then panic stations. . . . Terry had so confused him that he was now on the point of uttering the *other* version. Suddenly he got a fit of the giggles and the *Forum* panellists began to laugh with him, so he continued to read the report in mild hysterics. Afterwards, Terry said: 'That was well done, Brendan!'

'Never do that to me again, Terry!' remarked Brendan, wiping away the beads of perspiration from his forehead.

If Henry Street studios were deemed inadequate for broadcasters, they were seldom short of laughs. Every morning, for instance, a large amount of mail was delivered to the announcers' room. If Terry Wogan arrived early he would have it sorted out and the next day's *Hospital Requests* prepared; this burst of energy meant that he had the rest of the day to himself, which he often enjoyed on the golf course. Maurice O'Doherty remembers that at this time they had a correspondent who wrote his letters from a mental hospital and every week without fail addressed them to the 'Lady Announcers'. In addition to graphic details of the activity he would like to engage in with the ladies concerned, he requested them to send him certain items of underwear.

It was all quite harmless and a little sad. The staff came to recognise the handwriting and automatically threw the letters into the waste paper basket.

One Monday morning, Terry opened one of the letters and in addition to the usual contents, there was a red-coloured ten shilling note to assist in the buying of the underwear. Since it was unlikely that the ladies would accede to the man's request, it seemed to them that the 'knickers loot', as Terry Wogan called it, would buy quite a few sandwiches in the Tower Bar. It did, but only for a few weeks; one of the senior executives in the station contacted the police in the area of the mental hospital and arranged to have the letters stopped.

Maurice O'Doherty was convinced that Terry wanted to get away from news-reading. He recalled him saying once that 'news-reading held little appeal for him'. Maurice felt that since Terry was 'highly individualistic' it could be assumed that the strict discipline of news-reading would not appeal to him as much as an area where he could exercise control over what he was doing.

Party-going continued to be a popular pastime with people in the station. They were familiar with each other's party pieces, yet Brendan Balfe never failed to be intrigued by Terry Wogan's impromptu performances, or for that matter Denis Meehan's. 'It was a fantastic experience,' he remembers. 'Just when the party happened to be sagging or drawing to a close Terry and Denis would start their word games. They made conversation virtually out of nothing – a fly on the wall was sometimes enough to set them off. Or Terry might say: "Where does that leave the Dalai Lama?" This would inspire Denis to fantasise about the subject. The party-goers would be reeling about the floor with laughter. Again Terry might begin: "Take two nouns, Denis . . ." This was enough to keep the fun going. They went off in different directions, plunging into wild fantasies, verbally bouncing off one another. Usually they'd be nursing their drinks, but weren't drunk.

'The whole business reminded me of Flann O'Brien, or as

he was called in Dublin at the time, Myles na gCopaleen. I mean, there was a hint of Myles in Terry saying: "The Son of Pharaoh's daughter was the daughter of Pharaoh's son. Know that old one?" It was marvellous fun and kept the party alive for hours. I think because they shared a love of this kind of humour that Terry and Denis were good friends and played golf together. Denis appreciated Terry's wit, even if others didn't, which was rare. Their presence at parties was always looked forward to.'

Curiously, the only time Brendan Balfe ever saw Terry crestfallen was when he complained to him of rumours 'going the rounds' suggesting that he (Terry) was a philanderer, Terry resented the fact that some people were trying to link his name with certain pretty women when he wasn't really interested in them. Brendan was surprised. He wondered why Terry took the rumours to heart. It was something he and his colleagues in the station would laugh over. To Brendan, the episode revealed a sensitive, perhaps even vulnerable, side to the man. To Andy O'Mahony, Terry possessed a serious side. 'He could be reflective, realistic too. He concealed his knowledge. He carried it lightly.'

Terry was the first to admit that all was not well with his performance on *Jackpot*. From the opening show the portents weren't reassuring. He remembers: 'On the first *Jackpot* programme I had a very charming producer, but unfortunately he must have forgotten to make sure that everything was in place. At the end of each game, contestants were given the chance of deleting a letter or dipping into a box for a prize. The first woman on the show chose to dip, so I told her to put her hand into the box. She stuck her hand in and after fumbling around for a few seconds said to me: "There's nothing here!" And there wasn't. Someone had forgotten to put the bloody prizes in. Still we managed to get out of that one with a little bit of patter. If I'd been a newcomer to television, they'd have thrown me out.'

Adrian Cronin had to admit that Terry wasn't as successful as he might be on *Jackpot*, mainly because viewers identified the show with Gay Byrne and for some inexplicable reason Terry was failing to get to the Irish public. Perhaps it was his puckish humour, for as a natural performer there was no reason why he shouldn't have shone, reasoned Cronin.

To Andy O'Mahony, Terry was ahead of his time in the sense that he 'sent up *Jackpot*'. He took the rules of the quiz game and all that it implied for granted; the problem was that the viewers expected you to get it right. It was one thing to do a straight quiz show, but to send it up was a bit risky, particularly in Terry's case since he wasn't an established star.

'I suppose the real trouble was that *Jackpot* was a simple show,' says O'Mahony, 'but Terry approached it in a highly sophisticated way and it didn't come off because viewers weren't prepared for it.'

Maurice O'Doherty studied Terry's performance carefully and concluded that he had approached the show without any real preparation, presumably believing that it was unnecessary since Gay Byrne had made the show look so easy. Some viewers got the impression that Terry had never seen the show transmitted, for when a bell indicated that it was coming to an end, he thought it was the signal for a commercial break, and the floor manager had to remind him audibly that the show was over.

'I felt that the plain people of Ireland did not care a lot for Terry as a presenter; Gay Byrne was more their man. It was the early days of television and Terry's impish sense of humour was inclined to alienate members of the public who interpreted his mockery as somewhat hurtful. Ironic Limerick humour was not well known to people from other areas of the country, and they just didn't like it.'

Willowy blonde Suzanne McDougald replaced Olive White as the hostess and spinner of the wheel on *Jackpot*. She looked stunning on screen. Suzanne worked at modelling but was now attracted to a career in television. She found Terry quiet, even shy, someone who took his work seriously. Soon she told herself *Jackpot* was limited in scope and would scarcely extend his talent. 'Terry was good with people,' Suzanne recalls. 'But the show wasn't clever or sophisticated enough to provide him with a chance to be witty.'

She was taken aback at first, but later amused, to learn that people were linking her romantically with Terry. 'It was nonsense. The trouble was that the rumours spread and it actually proved embarrassing for me. I knew that Terry was dating a girl called Helen Joyce, one of my modelling friends. She was tall and beautiful and had these remarkable green eyes and a lovely soft voice. Just the girl for Terry, I thought. When I told Helen about the rumours, she laughed. I didn't know how serious they were about their romance. The other models I knew were talking about them. Helen was very popular.'

Jackpot enjoyed good TAM ratings and not everyone believed that Terry Wogan was struggling as presenter. After his first-night experience on *Jackpot* he admitted it affected his confidence. 'It was the most traumatic experience of my life. Nonetheless, I was greatly encouraged by the flood of letters from viewers saying that I would go on to be a success.'

Talking to me later about the show, he said: 'One way of doing a show like *Jackpot* is to give oneself a smooth synthetic gloss – like a Hughie Green, able to cope with any situation. Another way – my way – is to try to be human and natural and sincere. I can't do the quick-fire stuff. I'm introspective, I suppose. Maybe it's the boy-philosopher coming out in me. It's impossible to be truly yourself. If you concentrate on being yourself you're just not. Experience gives me confidence, nothing else really.'

One critic observed: 'On screen Terry is amiable, boyishly fumbling on occasions, every mother's ideal man, every teenager's Big Boy Wonderful. He heads the answers to *Jackpot* questions with an air of pleasurable surprise. Contestants and viewers feel at ease. His job is to help fill the cup of human happiness and he's willing to give a lot of thought and work and worry to doing just that.'

Reassuring words, but the tyranny of television is that the viewers have the last word and in this case too many of them were missing Gay Byrne. Perhaps in the final analysis Suzanne McDougald had the answer: 'The trouble was that Terry's inexperience as a television performer came through.'

Terry has never been reluctant to talk about his experience on *Jackpot*, principally because it shook his confidence. 'I don't think I ever did myself justice in television in Ireland.' And he touched on the real reason for his failure on *Jackpot*, when he observed: 'It was a nightmare experience. I just couldn't cope with the technology. I had come from the more intimate medium of radio, where there were only me in the studio and a producer and two soundmen working with me, to this huge television studio with what seemed hundreds of technicians and those enormous cameras looking at me.'

Jackpot was Terry's first failure in television. The memory would stay with him for a number of years. But there were other more pressing things in his mind, something that was likely to divert his thoughts from *Jackpot*. It was a little matter of romance.

10   *Terry in Love*

Every Irishman is a great lover at heart. Terry Wogan never classed himself as a Rudolph Valentino – he was too shy to don that mantle – but he saw himself as an ardent lover and Irish-style romantic. In the mid-sixties in Dublin he was regarded as one of Ireland's most eligible bachelors and more – he was a heart-throb, much in demand in the marriage stakes, and every mother's idea of her ideal son-in-law. Eligibility was measured by a steady job, genuine prospects, good looks, charm, personality, ambition, manliness, wit, age. Terry at twenty-six was the ideal age, and it was clear he would never have to resort to a secret visit to Lisdoonvarna in County Clare, where match-makers abound. Moreover, he was a media man, a face on television, and Ireland in the 'sixties regarded television stars in the same way as a generation of Irish before had regarded film stars – as idols. Terry had his admirers.

In the corridors of RTE rumours began to circulate that Wogan was in love. Colleagues, who dined with Terry and Helen Joyce immediately saw how relaxed and happy he appeared to be. 'Terry's a new man,' remarked one colleague. In those days relationships developed slowly, often from casual meetings, and Terry was in no hurry. It was hinted in RTE that it was a case of love at first sight, but he likes to say that from the beginning he got on well with Helen and gradually they had a firm understanding.

They met at a party given by the Russells, Paul and his Belfast-born wife, Grace, who was one of the top models of the time. Another was Helen Joyce. 'I had seen Terry read

119

the news on television and thought he was rather nice,' she recalls. 'When I was introduced to him at the party this impression was enhanced. He was pleasant but not pushy or outgoing. In fact, I considered him somewhat shy. This rather appealed to me. Up to then I believed that people on television were pushy, even abrasive. That night Terry saw me home and said he would telephone me in a few days. Men had sometimes said the same thing to me and hadn't always kept their word, but Terry did. He said that his parents had bought tickets for a musical at the Gaiety Theatre but found they couldn't go. "Will you come?" he asked me. "That would be nice," I said. On the night we found to our disappointment that we were sitting behind a pillar. It was later that he told me he had purchased the tickets in the hope that I would go to the theatre with him.'

After that they continued to see each other a few times a week, sometimes going to friends' parties and the occasional dress dance. The relationship gradually developed, says Helen, but it was nearly six months, even longer, before she gave any serious thought to any permanent relationship. In the early 'sixties it was not unusual for couples to go out together for a year or two before they even thought of getting engaged. Helen found she and Terry had disagreements and arguments and she attributed this to frustration, probably being so close and yet so apart. It was almost unheard of at the time for couples to go on holiday together abroad and share the same bedroom, or indeed share an apartment in Dublin. In traditional Irish circles it wasn't considered the 'proper' thing to do.

Helen Joyce was attached to the Miriam Woodbyrne Model Agency. Fashion correspondent Ita Hynes remembers Helen for her 'striking colouring, high-cheeked beauty and creamy skin, her superb figure, her charm and personality'. Miss Woodbyrne, who drew few distinctions between her models, regarded Helen Joyce as 'attractive and determined'. She could say the same thing about most of her girls. They were in a competitive business and were expected to be 'ambitious and go-ahead'.

This did not mean that Helen was making lots of money. Like the other top models, she had to work on provincial fashion shows, department-store shows and in the back-breaking job of showroom model to balance the books. Like the other models, Helen made some of her own clothes. Ita Hynes recalls that 'right through the 'sixties the models were like a family: they socialised together, shared their problems – and often their clothes and accessories. And in the background hovered Miriam Woodbyrne, at once their mentor, mother-figure, confessor and friend. She trained the chosen girls with the discipline of a sergeant-major, laid down the law on how they behaved in their private lives as well as on the ramp, negotiated rates of pay, and generally acted as a benevolent duenna.

Interest in fashion and modelling was at its peak. Mammoth fashion shows drew large crowds. The star models were Helen Joyce, Adrienne Ring, Winnie Butler, Terry O'Donnell, Hilary Freyne and Maeve King. At this time, 1964, the Miriam Woodbyrne models were finding work abroad. Helen Joyce, Rosemary Scully and Maura Boylan were working with Pierre Balmain in Paris. Adrienne Ring was working in Hollywood. When the international model manager Eileen Ford visited Dublin she was impre-ssed by the Woodbyrne models and offered some of them work abroad.

Miss Woodbyrne encouraged socialising between her girls. She arranged that a table be reserved each week at the Saturday night dance at DUBLIN's Gresham Hotel for the models and their escorts – with a free ticket for each girl and her escort – and one for Miriam. The girls brought steady boyfriends and acquaintances. It was very much a 'boy-meets-girl' situation, typical of the era. Inevitably, the fashion models and the rising stars of television met each other both at the Gresham dances and at each other's parties.

Terry Wogan became a popular figure at the dances, where he was regarded by the girls as witty company. Usually the girls drank Club Orange and the men bottles of

Guinness. This was paid for by having each male escort contribute £1 to a drinks fund for the evening. It was the way Miriam Woodbyrne wanted it.

Ita Hynes remembers that at this time 'fashion models were remote, stately and almost disdainful creatures. They glided along the ramp as though on wheels and, when being photograped, tended to pose like statues. However, Miriam Woodbyrne sensing the change in the style of modelling, revamped her training classes to include contemporary dance. She also realised that the coming of commercial television to Ireland would probably create more work and that they would need to be trained for photography with a little acting and a more relaxed style. In this respect Helen Joyce was ahead of some of her colleagues. She had been a member of an amateur dramatic society and was considered an able actress.'

At this time she and the other models were paid ten shillings and sixpence a day, and two guineas for a fashion show, no matter where in Ireland it took place. But it was reckoned a glamorous job and attracted lots of pretty girls. Already Helen Joyce's thoughts were on romance and she knew she would have to make a choice between modelling and marriage. To Miriam Woodbyrne and her models, Terry seemed the ideal partner for Helen and they knew that she was 'very much in love with him'. Miriam had no doubt in her mind that Helen would choose marriage.

Terry was paying the price of being a television personality. Not that it was a threat to his romance. 'For a while it made me somewhat anti-social,' he recalls. 'I couldn't get used to people staring at me wherever I went, so I sometimes kept away from places I would like to have gone – particular parties and so on, and stayed much to myself, except when I went out alone with Helen or the Meehans. If I went into a pub the chances were I'd have some fellow come straight up to me, tell me how much he enjoyed my programme and then spend a quarter of an hour telling me how much better he could do it. This happened all the time. I suppose it's an Irish trait. Because my face was becoming well known on the box I was attracting quite a lot of fan mail and phone calls. Most of the fan mail was complimentary, I'm glad to say, so were the calls – even though they occasionally sailed close to the wind.

'I remember one young woman with a sexy voice used to ring regularly and say: "Terry, mummy and daddy have gone out for the night. I'm all alone here with a bottle of gin!" I didn't accept. Then at any party I'd go to alone I'd usually have to steer clear of trouble, particularly from fellows if their birds happened to fancy me. I'd find myself saying: "Look, just leave me alone. Go and enjoy yourself. I'm not interested." For a long time it became such a bind I just didn't bother going out to parties. I remember one fellow with a few jars on him who insisted that I took a few puffs of a cigar that he was smoking. I didn't want to smoke his bloody cigar and although I told him so politely several times he persisted. Finally, I told him if he didn't leave me alone I'd thump him. That got rid of him. Someone came up to me a few minutes later and asked what had happened. I told her and she said: "Oh, my God, it's just as well you didn't hit him, he's got a terrible heart condition." '

But there was one place where Terry could relax and that was in the Creole Restaurant in Dun Laoghaire, a seaside spot renowned for its yachting clubs and impressive pier. Running the Creole was Roger Lewis, a heavily built, genial individual who liked meeting people. The restaurant, which accommodated sixty people, was located in the basement; Roger lived in rooms upstairs. He was both owner and chef. When he purchased it in the early 'sixties it was in his opinion 'too up-market' so he brought it down a peg to suit the pockets of his clientele. His motto was: value for money.

Roger got to know Terry and his father Michael quite well. 'Michael used to advise me on the wines to buy and the different selections I should have. He was most helpful.' He noticed that Terry liked veal and sole. He would remark to Roger: 'I've enough steaks at home. I'll have the fish'. Soon Roger knew the kind of dishes all his regular clients liked.

In the case of Terry, it was usually fish with well-creamed potatoes. 'Terry,' he recalls, 'was very particular about the creamed potatoes. I had to have them right for him. Funnily, if he had been watching his figure he wouldn't have touched them, so I concluded he hadn't a weight problem. He was most times a one-course man and only took a starter or dessert in certain company. Denis Meehan often dined with him; Denis loved my lobster bisque with a dash of cream.'

Some nights Helen would join Terry at the Creole, along with Denis Meehan and his wife, Sylvia. If Terry and Denis happened to be working late the women would go early to the Creole and wait for them. Last orders were at 12.30. If Terry and Denis came together without Helen and Sylvia they would stay on until after two o'clock, chatting about anything from golf to musicals. Occasionally, Terry might pop his head into the kitchen and ask Roger to prepare something for them. Roger found them very good company and might even join them for a short time at their table. 'If they were talking business I would never go near them. But I could see they were relaxing after work and enjoying themselves.'

In the Creole there was an alcove off the kitchen and this was popular with certain individuals who wanted privacy. Sometimes if Terry arrived alone early in the evening he would dine there. On other occasions film stars booked it. Suzannah York, Ursula Andress, Eamonn Andrews, Milo O'Shea and Peter O'Toole were patrons of the restaurant.

On September 23, 1964, the newspapers announced that 'television's most eligible bachelor Terry Wogan has become engaged to Miss Helen Joyce of 132 Leinster Road, Dublin', and the columnist added; 'Long regarded as television's heart-throb, he ended all rumours about his romance with Miss Joyce when he told me today that he had just become engaged.'

'We probably drifted into the engagement,' remembers Helen. 'I can't recall Terry getting down on bended knees and asking me to marry him. I know I didn't pressurise him in any way to get engaged or to marry. A few months before this he produced a selection of engagement rings but none of them fitted my finger. Terry said: "We'll leave it for a while." I don't think he wanted to get caught so soon!'

It was in the sitting-room of Helen's home that Terry arrived one lunchtime and handed her the engagement ring, a large diamond cluster that he had bought in Dublin. 'I could see he was excited about the occasion,' says Helen. 'I never regarded him as a great lover or a Don Juan, but he can be very romantic about birthdays and anniversaries. That evening we went out together and celebrated.'

Their engagement brought special joy to Terry's mother, Rose. 'I'm delighted he's settling down,' she said. 'He has picked a lovely girl.' Already the happy pair had decided to live in a flat after their marriage. Helen told friends she had no hesitation giving up modelling for marriage. She was looking forward to her marriage the following year.

Terry had no doubt he had made the perfect choice. He was still, though, surprised that Helen had decided to have him. Today he says: 'She was one of the most beautiful girls in Ireland and she could have had anyone. But why me? All I can say is that it was the luckiest moment in my life when she said: "Yes, Terry I'll marry you." We liked each other from the start. But if I hadn't left the bank and been "someone in television" I'd never have had the nerve to approach her in a million years. I started to send her flowers, and I still bring her flowers. You have to do that. What the blazes do you get married for if you're prepared to let the romance in your life disappear.'

During their courtship days he remembers that they argued a great deal. 'That was probably all down to sexual frustration,' he reasons, 'because of the inhibited kind of lifestyle in Ireland at the time'.

Dubliners, starved of colour and pageantry, found fashionable white weddings of film or television stars a welcome relief from drabness. As expected, big crowds waited outside the Church of Refuge in the Dublin suburbs of Rathmines on the morning of Saturday, April 24, 1965, to cheer the newly married Wogans. Smiling, and linked arm in arm, Terry and Helen walked into the light rain. At that moment the crowd surged forward and nearly swept them off their feet. Confetti showered on the happy couple as they struggled to get to the waiting car for the wedding breakfast in Portmarnock on the north side of the city.

More than 160 guests had attended the church ceremony, among them television personalities Olive White (now Mrs Christian Browning) and Suzanne McDougald. Helen Wogan looked radiant in her Veronica Jaye full-length gown of ribbon lace and cummerbund of wild silk. She carried white roses and orchids.

'I was quite nervous about the occasion,' Helen says today, 'but I did arrive at the church on time! I remember it as a very happy day, one that stands out in my memory.'

Her three attendants, Mirian her sister, model Maida Cooney, and Mrs Liz Burrowes, wore Empire-line dresses in shell-pink satin with embroidered satin bodices. Brian Wogan, Terry's brother, was best man. That Saturday evening they flew to Spain for their honeymoon.

In the subsequent months Terry and Helen lived happily in a city flat while they looked around for a house in surburban Dublin. Terry was extremely busy with radio programmes such as *Terry Awhile* and *Children's Forum*. It was a tribute to his success that Radio Telefis Eireann decided to break with tradition and call a programme after him. But Terry wasn't overjoyed with the name *Terry Awhile*. 'There's RTE for you again! They never go the whole way and make it a name programme show. Take mine. Why not the *Terry Wogan Show*? Why not the *Gay Byrne Show* instead of the *Late, Late Show*?'

Otherwise, the programme appealed to him. It gave him scope to chat to listeners, play records and between the music pass on greetings, add his own mildly irreverent but always light-hearted and inoffensive comments.

He was elated when Helen told him she was pregnant. The prospect of being a father for the first time tickled his fancy and he looked forward to the birth with growing anticipation.

A busy writer as well as broadcaster, Terry contributed to magazines and newspapers. Once he compiled an amusing guide to broadcasting terminology, when he described an announcer as a 'a rare avis indeed, who requires the looks of an Adonis, the voice of Gielgud, the taste of a Da Vinci, the wit of a Wilde, the dress sense of a Brummel, the eloquence of a MacLiammoir, and a good hairdresser. The fact that none of RE and TE's announcers ever approximates to any of these qualifications is a tribute to their indomitable egos.'

When queried at this time about his earnings, Terry's reply invariably was: 'I'm making good money at the moment – about £7,000 a year – but I work hard for it.' When it appeared that everything was rosy and the future bright, tragedy struck. Their first child, a daughter they christened Vanessa, suffered from a heart condition and died only three weeks after birth. It was a shattering blow to both Terry and Helen. Both had been excited about the prospect of parenthood for the first time. 'I remember I had everything ready – clothes, the nursery,' says Helen. 'It was quite a trauma. I think a tragedy like this leaves its mark for a very long time, maybe for ever.'

Terry could not disguise his feelings. He would say: 'The poor little thing just wasn't strong enough. We didn't really have long enough to get to know her.' Helen's doctor told her: 'You'll not get over it until you have another child. I suggest you get pregnant again.' The experience left them frightened that the same thing might happen again, but they decided to try for another child. 'I am sure the personal loss of Vanessa strengthened the bond between Terry and me,' recalls Helen. 'I know I felt closer to him than ever before.'

Being busy eased Terry's grief. Presenting *Terry Awhile* gave him an opportunity to ad lib and be himself. As he sat in the studio he had in front of him a typed sheet listing the titles and singers on the records he introduced; otherwise he could ad lib and strive to be original. 'I did not regard myself as a disc jockey,' he says. 'I preferred to be known as a compère or communicator. For some reason people used the term disc jockey in a degrading manner . . . looking down their nose at you, kind of thing. I was proud of my work. I regarded myself as a professional.'

Around this time ambitious young broadcasters in RTE were sending tapes of their shows to the BBC, hoping to be noticed. Realising that he was 'a big fish in a small pond', Terry decided to wrap up one of his tapes and mailed it across channel. He made no secret of the fact that he was sending it, although he entertained no great hopes that he would be noticed. He told himself that there were scores of disc jockeys trying to get work in the BBC and he could not see Irish applicants standing much chance of making it.

11   Mark's Discovery

Mark White, the assistant head of the BBC gramophone department, sat upright at his desk in a room on the third floor of Egton House, alongside Broadcasting House in London. He was one of the staff who would adjudicate on tapes coming into the office 'like rain' from aspiring disc jockeys and 'pirate' DJs.

'Each week,' Mark recalls,' dozens of tapes were being received, so I decided to appoint a young producer to sift through them and chuck aside those he considered a waste of time. I asked him to make a small pile of the tapes he reckoned had some potential. These would be shortlisted for final adjudication by me, and another senior producer.'

Mark White rose from his seat to check files; he stood well over six feet tall, was slim and athletic-looking, and walked with a military bearing. By now he had been over twenty-five years in broadcasting and show business. He first joined the BBC in 1942 as an assistant in the recorded programmes department. 'I thought I'd applied for a job in the gramophone record department. It wasn't until I'd been interviewed and offered the post that I found out my assumption was wrong. As I had a job in advertising at the time I politely turned down the BBC job. But they persuaded me to change my mind, and I've always been grateful to them.'

Mark was born in Harpenden in Hertfordshire in 1916; his father was a consultant engineer by profession, and his grandfather was the author Mark Rutherford (William Hale White); his mother was Irish and was regarded as 'a character' – perhaps one of the last eccentric matriarchs.

Mark volunteered for the Dorset Regiment in 1939 but was invalided out in 1940.

In the middle and late 'forties in the BBC he was specialising in what were called 'dance music shows', or what is now known as popular music. His overall boss was the legendary John Watt. Among his first productions were *Write a Tune for a £1,000* (it nearly didn't get on the air because it smacked of commercialism), *Jazz Club* and *Band Parade*. Among the people he worked with were Ivor Novello, Margaret Lockwood, Ted Heath, Charlie Chester and Henry Hall.

In 1949, he left the BBC and went to work for impresario Claude Langdon. He became Langdon's production manager at the Empress Hall, Earl's Court, a venue that in the 'fifties became as famous as the London Palladium. Its prime function was presenting ice shows. Among the non-ice shows were the Markova-Dolin ballet and Sunday concerts featuring Sir Thomas Beecham.

After five years Mark left the Empress Hall and became a freelance broadcasting producer. The BBC offered him quite a few radio shows and he also freelanced in commercial television. This started with the production of the *Jack Jackson Show* for ATV.

Now in his new post as assistant head of the BBC gramophone department, Mark White was heavily involved in the setting up of Radio 1. Soon he would be responsible for signing up a number of ex-pirate-radio disc jockeys such as Tony Blackburn, Kenny Everett, Dave Lee Travis and 'Emperor' Rosko.

As he resumed his seat at his desk in Egton House he was interrupted by a young producer who stuck his head around the door and said: 'I thought you'd like to see this tape before I chuck it in the bin.'

Mark saw that the young man was holding in his hand a flat spool of the old-fashioned kind of tape. The producer said: 'This tape is wound back to front. Looks like the chap was in a hurry, don't you think?'

Mark said nothing as the other continued, 'Anybody who sends a tape like that, we really can't be bothered with'.

As he turned to go, Mark said quickly: 'Hang on a minute before you chuck it in the bin.' Suddenly he himself was fascinated by the kind of person who would submit a tape like that. He asked the young producer to put it back the proper way so that he could hear it.

What he eventually heard pleased him. 'Here was a bright, cheerful and absolutely natural-sounding voice,' Mark recalls. 'There was no trace of pretension. It sounded as if it liked the music it was playing and talking to people. It was the complete opposite to many tapes we were receiving. These other disc jockeys were desperately trying to impress you. Radio 1 had just been launched and everyone wanted jobs as disc jockeys.'

Something else intrigued him. He noticed the sender of the tape was Terry Wogan from Dublin. 'The name's brilliant,' he thought. Shortly afterwards he phoned Terry and was a little surprised to learn that he was working full-time for Radio Telefis Eireann. At the time BBC had a series called *Midday Spin* in which they used various new people as a kind of try-out. Mark decided to offer Terry a chance on the programme. It was agreed that Terry could broadcast it from Dublin. 'I went to this trouble because I thought there was potential there,' Mark says. 'Why was I impressed? I don't know. Maybe it was just instinct born of experience in broadcasting. The same thing happened when I first heard Tony Blackburn's voice. I also decided to take him on. In the case of Terry Wogan I remember saying to myself: "There's something there. I think that person's very good." '

Eventually, when they met, Mark found Terry very enthusiastic: 'He said he was keen to come over and work for the BBC and I said we would like to have him.' Terry was offered an opportunity on the new *Late Night Extra* programme, which would run five nights a week on Radios 1 and 2. He was the only Irishman on the team of compères. It meant that he had to fly to London every Wednesday from October 4, 1967, to compère his programme in the series. It ran from 10.00 pm to midnight and consisted of pop records and interviews with people of various interests.

In December of that year Terry decided to resign as senior announcer from Radio Telefis Eireann and go freelance. Working for the BBC meant he had to spend two days each week in London and, with additional work in the pipeline, he felt he could no longer give RTE his full-time commitment. There was also another reason. As Terry explains: 'After doing a few programmes they called me over for a press photograph with the other Radio 1 disc jockeys. Since I was still under contract with RTE, I said to Robin Scott, who was head of Radio 1: "For goodness sake, clear this with the Director-General of RTE first." He said he would but of course he forgot.

'The next thing I knew was that the photograph appeared in a Dublin evening newspaper and Kevin McCourt, then Director-General, had a canary when he saw it. Even though I explained the situation he still wasn't too pleased with me, although he did say I could do six weeks of *Late Night Extra*. That was one of the major decisions I had to take in my life – to do the six weeks and then say no to the BBC and return to my steady job as announcer, still doing light entertainment, television commercials and so on. I thought: "To hell with it, I'll take the chance." So I made my decision to resign, something I should have done years before. Since my future now seemed to lie with the BBC I suppose I had no compunction about resigning. In another way I was trying to prove to myself that I could perform on a bigger stage than RTE's.'

The flying was also getting to Terry. For *Late Night Extra* he was paid £35 a night; his plane ticket and hotel cost him more. He was also taking on more commercials in Ireland, so there was little time for relaxation. There was one special moment of joy in 1968 when Helen gave birth to a baby boy whom they named Alan.

Forgotten for a while was the tragedy of little Vanessa. Terry was thrilled with his first son.

*

In the summer of 1969 Terry was invited to stand in for Jimmy Young and made such an impression that BBC chiefs offered him the plum afternoon two to four spot on Radios 1 and 2. As one Irish newspaper put it: 'This is the biggest break an Irish broadcaster has got since Eamonn Andrews went off to chair the *Ignorance is Bliss* show in the early 'fifties.'

Speculation centred around his position in Ireland. He decided to give up *Terry Awhile*. He admitted he was thinking of going to live in London. 'I'm not looking forward to another winter in the air. I've a premonition about spending Christmas in the Outer Hebrides or some God-forsaken place.' It was clear his mind was made up. He was thinking beyond radio: 'I have to think in terms of exposure in both media. Naturally I'm thinking of television in Britain. You need that kind of exposure but it's very hard to get it.'

Terry's decision to throw in his lot with the BBC did not surprise his colleagues at RTE. Gay Byrne felt that he was doing the right thing. Meeting Terry one afternoon after recording a sponsored programme, Gay said to him: 'Give it a try, Terry. Go and live in London.' Although he had never been a pal of Terry's, he knew that he had made a breakthrough at RTE by having *Terry Awhile* named after him. 'Before that,' said Gay, 'announcers were merely voices and anonymous people.' Gay was of the opinion that Terry had no other option but to go. 'I felt he was living in the shadow of other people in Ireland. I think he didn't see enough opportunity in broadcasting for him here.'

To producer Adrian Cronin, it was inevitable that young broadcasters should look for opportunities in London and elsewhere. 'I remember that Gay Byrne was getting work in Britain, so was Arthur Murphy. Eamonn Andrews had set the example years before. I really believe that Terry didn't always get the breaks in Irish broadcasting, especially in television, so it was no surprise to me that he should look across the channel.'

Andy O'Mahony, who remained one of Terry's close

friends, felt that he had found the framework he wanted in the BBC, which was freedom to experiment.

'I think Terry was right to take the gamble,' recalls Mark White, who had been watching his progress with more than passing interest. 'He was getting the big opportunity'. But Mark realised that by today's standards Terry had been paid 'peanuts' for presenting *Midday Spin* and *Late Night Extra*, but he was 'in' and gaining experience, that was important.

It was an opportune time for Terry to uproot himself. Mark White was conscious of the 'quiet revolution' taking place in the BBC, where four new networks had been launched. Terry would have more opportunity. 'We were moving in the direction of American radio,' reflected Mark, 'where you pressed a button and you had pop music and you pressed another and you had Frank Sinatra. At the time the Beeb was a very happy ship and everyone was looking towards the future.'

Today Mark White lives in retirement with his wife, Stella, in the Isle of Man, writing books and travelling. Whenever in London he calls on Terry. Looking back on the crucial year in the life of the young Irish broadcaster, he says: 'I think it was an achievement for Terry to get into the BBC in the first place. At the time many people were trying to do the same thing; I mean, all the best pirate-radio disc jockeys. So Terry's was a real achievement.'

At thirty-one years of age, Terry decided to leave Ireland and try his luck in London. In the early 'fifties he remembered that Eamonn Andrews had left to go to the BBC out of a sense of frustration, but in his own case it was for other reasons. 'I had reached a point in Ireland where I felt I had done all I could do in broadcasting. I wanted a new challenge. I was confident about the change, yet I told myself it was a hell of a risk to take to uproot my family. During my stint in London I had found more freedom than at RTE. I found there were fewer restrictions on me as a broadcaster. The BBC suited my individualistic style.'

For Helen, who was three months pregnant, it was an important decision. It meant finding a house in London and trusting that everything went well for Terry. But if that was what he wanted, that was it. She knew he needed to broaden his horizons and she wouldn't discourage him. *Jackpot* hadn't done him justice; he had been thrown in at the deep end and at a time when television was relatively new in the country.

Although confident that he would succeed at the BBC, she did entertain a slight apprehension about the change. Fortunately she had a very good friend in Olive White (Terry had stayed with Olive and her husband Christian Bernard when doing *Late Night Extra*).

Curiously, Terry himself was assailed by some uneasiness about the change. 'I was a bit apprehensive about it but not terribly worried. I knew what I could do. I had confidence in myself.'

Brendan Balfe had no doubt that Terry should take the risk and told him so. 'I told him he had nothing to lose and an awful lot to gain if things turned out right. I imagine the BBC said to him: "You will have to be available for work in Britain – or else the deal is off" It was a great opportunity for Terry, one in a lifetime.'

Success came quickly to Terry in his afternoon radio programme. Inside a few months millions of listeners were tuning in. Terry admitted that it was a simple gimmick that helped to launch it nation-wide. 'I was looking for a gimmick and we came up with the keep-fit thing and it certainly seemed to work.'

At four o'clock every weekday, millions of housewives, secretaries and factory girls battled against bulging waist-lines and heavy hips. Leading them in the fight was Terry with his slimming hints. So popular did the exercises become that he had letters of complaint from irate factory managers about girls stopping work to touch their toes and swing their arms, but he also received letters from happy ladies who had lost inches in the right places.

Terry was jubilant with his new-found popularity. 'I got some women writing every day,' he recalls. 'For them it was just a release. Some of them lived in a fantasy world, though, and I got the sort of letter that said: "When are you coming to see me, darling?" If I played a request for a wedding I got bits of wedding cake, for instance. But some of them were really eccentric.'

His dose of exercises made such an impact on female listeners that the BBC considered publishing a Terry Wogan Keep Fit Book. By the autumn of 1970 the programme had become so popular that BBC chiefs handed Terry a contract until the end of the year. Only two other disc jockeys had long-term contracts – Tony Blackburn and Jimmy Young.

Terry had aimed from the beginning to make the show personal for listeners. He was concerned with communicating with his audience through his own personality rather than the music. 'The show itself was ad lib,' he recalls. 'I didn't choose the records, the programme editor did that. I didn't involve myself with it because I was relating to the listener.'

Terry was convinced by now that he was making a success of his career in Britain. His contract was renewed and the future looked bright. Yet he remembers some BBC producers advising him to stick with Ireland. 'In the long run,' one producer told him,' you'll have a better standard of living in Ireland.' Terry brushed such curious advice aside. He was young and he didn't mind taking risks. 'I had no fear of failure. I was determined to make a success of my career. The BBC offered plenty of scope and I liked the people I was working with. I decided to stay at all costs. Helen, my wife, backed me all the way. She felt I wanted this new challenge. I had done what I wanted to do in Ireland.'

By now Terry had joined the Harold Davison Organisation, one of the leading agencies in the entertainment world. Having establised himself quickly as a radio personality, he began to reap the benefits – personal appearances and the possibility of a television show. Discussing his afternoon show, he attributed part of his success to his accent. 'I'm lucky I've a classless accent. In England they judge you by your accent, but the Irish can't be categorised. I say things a bit differently. I don't write scripts. It's all spontaneous. Sometimes it works, sometimes it doesn't. I occasionally say something and afterwards wish I hadn't said it but there's nothing you can do about it.'

In November came the first of Terry's awards. He was placed third in the Reveille award, which was presented to the top disc jockeys of the year. Terry came third in the section for best disc jockeys on Radio 1. Tony Blackburn was first and Jimmy Saville second. There were twenty-five competitors in this section, and Terry beat DJs like Emperor Rosko, Dave Cash and Johnny Walker. 'I just can't believe it,' was his first reaction. 'I never really expected to win, because last year I wasn't even with the BBC.'

But exactly a year later he went one better when he was placed second when the BBC's top DJs were named at Tiffany's Club, London. Tony Blackburn was named top DJ on Radio 1 and Tony Brandon on Radio 2. To Mark White, Terry's success was no surprise. By now Mark was the first boss of Radio 1.

12 Breakfast Show

Mark White was appointed head of BBC Radio 2 in 1972 with a special brief to develop the network in the same successful manner as Radio 1. 'When I took over, Radio 2 was still staggering under the dead weight of the remains of the old Light Programme,' he remembers, 'and had been denuded of most of its money and needletime, which I had to fight to get back.'

He knew he needed a star name to ensure a big new audience. Terry Wogan, he assured himself, was the natural person to fill this spot. He approached him privately and asked him if he would be available to host a new breakfast show on Radio 2. 'I'll be delighted to do it, Mark,' Terry told him.

At this point Mark had to persuade the radio chiefs to agree to let him have Terry. 'What I was really doing was pinching him from Radio 1. I thought they would kick up hell about the move. I asked them bluntly: "Do I get your backing?" The answer was: "You do". I knew I was already half-way to success by getting Terry.'

First he had discussions with Terry about the music to be played on the programme. With Radio 1 playing pop, Radio 3 classical, it was left to Radio 2 to provide middle-of-the-road music, such as songs by Andy Williams, Frank Sinatra and Ella Fitzgerald. The producer of the show would choose the records. After a few weeks, Mark White had no doubt that the *Breakfast Show* was a success. It was lively and spontaneous with plenty of scope for Terry to ad lib. He came up with lines like: 'Mother, what do you think you're doing?' and 'Come on, kids, let's get up and go.' Mark had utter faith in Terry not to go overboard. 'I had no fears about him in the way I had about Tony Blackburn. The idea of Terry doing something out of line was remote. At times, perhaps, he said something that might have been better left unsaid, but it was within good taste. It was funny.'

By now the Wogans had settled happily into their new house by the Thames. They had two children, Mark and Alan, and a third on the way. Entertaining friends to lunch or dinner was a custom that had begun in Dublin and was now being kept up. One Sunday they had Mark White and his wife, Stella, to lunch. Stella, a smart and intelligent woman, recalls: 'The lunch went on and on and became a whole day. Helen was a good hostess, very meticulous. Everything was just right. She went out of her way to make it all enjoyable for us. I could see she was a good cook. If it was a roast that was on the table, it was Terry who usually carved it. Terry was the boss. Helen let him be the celebrity.'

At dinner on another occasion Stella noticed how much in love they were. 'Standing together in the drawing room, I noticed how they held hands or looked into each other's eyes; it was their touching way of showing affection. It was charming. The Wogan home was a happy one. I thought that Terry was strict with the children. Helen was a very good mother. When her second child was born I remember the ward was full of flowers and cards.'

It struck Stella when she first met Terry that he was slightly unsure of himself. 'When he came to London and began to work with Mark, he said to me: "I have taken on all this, let's hope it all goes well for me." I reassured him. I told him not worry. I felt that nothing could go wrong. I think he thought he might have made a mistake in bringing Helen over to live in London. I suppose it was understandable. He could have fallen on his face. But when I first met him I knew he would be a success. I had no doubt about it. He valued Mark's opinions a lot. I think his happy marriage was a big factor in his career. Helen was very supportive from the beginning.'

To Stella, Terry had the intelligence of his father, Michael, and the wit and charm of his mother, Rose. 'I think Terry resembles his mother more than his father,' says Helen Wogan. 'Mrs Wogan has the same sense of humour as Terry.'

Terry liked to spend as much time as possible at home, although his favourite occupation there was 'sitting around doing nothing'. This extended to the boat he bought and moored at the bottom of the garden, but he admitted he wasn't an outdoor person. The *Breakfast Show* meant a change in his schedule. In the morning the bedside telephone shrieked and the voice of a BBC commissionaire announced: 'Hello, Mr Wogan, it's half-past-five.' That's when he got up. Luckily, he never had a problem waking up. 'My wife hardly stirred,' he recalls. 'I was in the kitchen by six. I would have a cooked breakfast – bacon and eggs with orange juice and coffee. I think it made a difference: I didn't fall down with hunger in mid-morning.'

Over breakfast he leafed through the previous day's newspapers – the *Daily Mail* and the *Guardian*. At 6.27 he climbed into his mustard E-type Jaguar and was quickly on the motorway. In half an hour he had covered the twenty-eight miles to the BBC studios in the heart of London. Around 7.10 he pulled into the car park, then headed for the main control room, where he picked up the box of records for the coming day.

The *Breakfast Show* went out from a continuity studio overlooking Portland Place. It was a dingy place where the atmosphere in summer was clammy. At 7.32½ Terry was on the air. He had no preconceived ideas about what he was going to say. He had no script, just a music running order and certain fixed spots like the 8.15 traffic and 8.27 racing bulletins, and the news.

Terry's eight million listeners were mostly mums and dads. 'I think a whole generation of children grew up with an abiding hatred of me because they were forced to listen to Radio 2 when they would have rather listened to Radio 1.

The show quickly evolved its own style – one of trading insults with his listeners, or irreverent introductions to records and fellow DJs – a constant stream of good-natured badinage and 'calumny'. Often bordering on the outrageous and rude, Terry admitted that he walked a tightrope. 'I never knew what I was going to say until I turned on the microphone.'

The BBC chiefs were aware that not everybody welcomed Terry's relaxed formula, but he quipped: 'I've brainwashed them all . . . The constant dripping, wearing away the stone, or should I say drivelling. My relationship with listeners is one of mutual recrimination. I do the talking, but I try to establish a dialogue by getting them to write in. The great thing about a daily show is that you can continually refer back to the day or the week before.'

He created a fantasy about the view over the roof tops across Broadcasting House. He talked of the tennis courts, the swimming pools and the cattle browsing across the acres of green. Or he might be tempted to give a running commentary on the BBC's Director-General emerging from his flat in a hideous Chinese dressing-gown to pick up the milk or going for a jog with Lord Longford or Tony Benn. Some listeners, it was rumoured in the corridors of Broadcasting House, found Terry's fantasies too much and refrained from tuning in; others regarded them as a morning tonic in a grim world. His former colleagues at Radio Telefis Eireann smiled among themselves because they recognised their origins. 'It was the same kind that Terry used to do at parties with Denis Meehan,' says Brendan Balfe, 'except that now he was fantasising on radio and British listeners were having a ball.'

The critics' reaction ranged from 'brilliant' to 'irritating'. Too much talk, said one. An irritant so early in the morning, said another. They complained that the Wogan bonhomie didn't translate from afternoon to morning and that the records played were a load of rubbish. Terry wasn't worried: 'As far as I'm concerned the programme's working out for me very well.' He insisted that his choice of music was not a lot of rubbish. 'The records I play are vastly different to those on Radio 1. I play Sinatra, Bennett, Como – singers like that.'

By now Terry had become a well-known face on British television. After his setback with *Jackpot* on Irish television, he knew it would take some time for his full confidence to return. He compered the Miss World Contest, which attracted twenty-four million viewers. Although he was happy to do the show, he said he did not wish to be identified solely with beauty contests. He had his own lunchtime programme *Come Dancing* and *They Sold a Million* on BBC 2. He reckoned that this was too much television exposure: 'I took the work because I just wanted to establish a face to tie in with the voice'.

But Terry is one of those people who invariably sees the funny side of things, even though he admits he can be frustrated or bored like the next man. He resented criticism of the Miss World Contest: 'I don't care what anyone says about finding more beautiful girls walking down High Street. I've never seen fifty more beautiful girls in one place in all my life. And they're not stupid. People think that girls who enter contests are all thick as two short planks. If anyone is asked to be interviewed for thirty seconds in front of a television camera and asked banal questions, they are going to come across as banal and look a bit ridiculous. I realise the questions I have to ask are banal – but what else can anyone do in thirty seconds? I know what the women-libbers say, but the fact remains that almost twenty-five million people watch the programme every year – the women maybe to criticise, the men simply to look at fifty beautiful girls. It's not a cattle market – certainly the girls don't think so, otherwise presumably they would not do it.'

Backstage fascinated Terry. He found it a frightening time for the girls. Interviewing them he noticed they were paralysed with fear. 'They may be beautiful girls but they've perspiration over their upper lip and they're twitching.' When the tension built up in the rehearsal room before the contest he was surprised to find that the girls in order to ease the pressure broke into song together.

Terry's first experience of beauty contests began in Ireland, often in village halls where the important thing was to pick the local girl, otherwise he would be lucky to get away with his life! Once he was asked to adjudicate in the Irish Midlands, in a marquee. He discovered he was the only judge and compere. The place was full of drunken fellows 'who'd beat you up for tuppence, particularly if their wife or girlfriend happened to like you on television!'

To interview the girls he was led to a caravan without a light in it and which the girls had to enter one at a time. All he could see was the whites of their eyes and their teeth flashing! 'And I was supposed to judge these unfortunate girls,' he recalls, 'for poise, personality and charm. That was one of the times I picked the local girl, took the money and ran!'

On another occasion he was asked to pick the Queen of the Festival in his native Limerick. The prize was a trip to Paris. He had to question them on general knowledge in front of the French Consul. The first girl was brought in and he asked her, 'Do you read the papers?' She replied that she did and added: 'I always read the papers from cover to cover.'

'What page do you read first?'

The girl looked at him. 'I always read the news first, then the woman's page.'

'As a matter of interest, you know what the prize is?'

She looked quizzically at him. Terry said: 'What's the capital of France?'

'God, I don't know that one.'

She hurried out, with the French Consul staring after her.

The second contestant came in. Terry went through the same routine. She didn't know the capital of France, which was ironic since the prize was a trip to Paris.

By now he was getting desperate as the French Consul sat uneasily beside him. When the third girl entered briskly and informed him that she read everything from the stock exchange to the sports pages he felt reasonably confident. But when he asked her the all-important question she put her hand to her chin and, looking extremely puzzled, muttered: 'Oh, it's on the tip of my tongue'.

As a last resort, Terry said: 'It begins with P. Is that any help to you?'

She smiled triumphantly and said: 'Ah, didn't I know it was Portugal all along!'

For a few years Terry was a popular compere of the Rose of Tralee Festival. One evening he was with his wife, Helen, and some friends in the Festival Club, where a dance was in progress. A big fellow, probably a farmer thought Terry, approached Helen and said to her: 'Miss, would you care to dance?'

'No, thanks very much,' Helen said politely, 'but I'm with friends.' The big fellow was incredulous, couldn't believe he had been refused a dance. It was never done in the country. He continued to look her up and down for a few seconds, then said with an imperious grin: 'Ah, sure, you're too ould for me anyway!'

In the early seventies Terry was aware of the anti-Irish joke in Britain but he tolerated it. However, he made no excuses for being Irish. He didn't pretend to be anything else. He had no time for what has been described as the 'stage Irishman' and he could be critical of fellow Irishmen in Britain who possessed the ghetto mentality and were reluctant to mix with other nationalities, especially the English.

It was not a particularly good time to be Irish in Britain. The IRA had commenced their bombing campaign. Mark White became slightly worried about possible British reaction to Irish broadcasters, especially to Terry Wogan. He felt there might be complaints from listeners. 'But I do not remember a single complaint to the BBC,' he recalls. 'No one asked why we were employing this fellow Wogan from the South of Ireland.'

Terry kept clear of politics. If he had found a gimmick to make his afternoon programme popular with listeners, he now found that 'Wogan's Winner' had caught on in a big way. His racing tips were eagerly looked forward to, even though some of his predictions left the punters seething with anger and with empty pockets. Once he decided to bring will-power into it and asked the listeners to concentrate on Miss Penny in the 3.35 at Warwick. It won at seven to one! The next day he had a letter saying: 'I was walking along the High Street at 3.35 today when I was impelled by a tremendous force and me and my shopping trolley were shot down the street.' The letter was from a Mrs Penny!

At ten o'clock in the morning he handed over to Jimmy Young. 'These handovers became hilarious,' Mark White recalls. 'I mean, you had the mischevious Terry trying to send up the more serious Jimmy Young. Jimmy is no fool, he's an experienced performer and knew how to handle Terry.' Mark realised that by now Terry had become larger than life. The feedback from the programme was excellent and he knew his faith in Terry was justified. In Ireland Terry's friends were puzzled by the transformation that had taken place. They had watched him go to Britain with a competent reputation as a broadcaster and become in a relatively short time one of the biggest names in the business. Was there an element of luck? Or was it because the BBC offered him more scope? Or, again, was it because Irish people had often failed to appreciate his puckish humour?

Today Terry explains: 'I had time on the *Breakfast Show* to develop my sense of humour. There was no comparable show in Irish radio so there was no scope for this kind of development. I could talk as I liked. I was doing what I liked doing. Spontaneity was and is my forte. It's as simple as that. I don't mean to say that everybody liked my breakfast show. I'm sure many didn't; there's always been a love-hate thing between me and my listeners – and viewers.'

Mark White attributed the transformation to Terry's imaginative mind and his bubbly personality; above all, as he says today, to Terry's friendly voice and his warmth as an individual.

Listeners often asked themselves how Terry could turn

on the charm and the humour so early in the morning, when others got up silently from their beds and didn't laugh or come to life until noon. Terry says: 'I found no problem being myself in the morning. I think it helped having no script. By ad libbing I was able to get on with it. In Irish radio we were bedevilled by old-fashioned practices. RTE didn't trust their broadcasters to ad lib. I was always encouraged by the BBC to ad lib, to be spontaneous. The BBC give you credit for intelligence and maturity. They give you the microphone and you're in control. You were in charge of what you were doing. I put no limit on my ad libbing, for instance. I let if flow.

'I was lucky it happened to me at the right time. I was over thirty years of age, I knew what I was doing and it appeared to me then that most people doing this disc jockey act hadn't really addressed the question of what they were doing. Anybody in my opinion can sit in front of a microphone and put on records and say who's singing on the record. I wanted my show to be a conversation. At that time disc jockeys usually read out complimentary letters they got. I read out the nasty letters mailed to me and sent up the writers.'

Back in Dublin news-reader Maurice O'Doherty followed Terry's career with keen interest, often wondering to himself how his old RTE colleague had broken down the sedate barriers that had for so long encircled broadcasting at the BBC. Maurice found Broadcasting House an austere and even forbidding place, a building that positively dripped with dignity, and gave one the impression that it was populated by workers of grave mien who constantly reminded themselves that they were the true embodiment of Public Service, dedicated to informing, and in second place entertaining, the great British public.

He reckoned it was a surprise for them when one of their broadcasters – in this case Terry Wogan – began to mention the fact that he was befriending the London pigeons. It was in O'Doherty's opinion the 'surrealist Wogan imagination taking off and people were being asked to believe that sheep and cows were grazing in the window-boxes of Broadcasting House. The truth was that the British people almost believed him.

O'Doherty was convinced that Terry's jokes about senior staff in the BBC actually made the British public realise that behind the cloak of dignity that shrouded anybody with a 'big job' there lurked a real human being with human problems just like everybody else. Even the Director-General seemed to enjoy the ribbing he received, as did his wife, who actually telephoned the studio one morning to ask Terry to play a request for the DG's birthday.

On a cool October morning in 1973 Maeve Binchy, the London correspondent of *The Irish Times*, dropped in on Terry's morning programme, which she considered was aimed at the 30–plus group. She was particularly curious about the money Terry was earning. She found him in whimsical mood: 'A totally ridiculous amount of money, absolutely enormous, quite ludicrous!'

She wondered about 'Wogan's Winners' and was told by Terry: 'Well, I make them up. I just look at the name of a horse and say that's it. I don't know one end of a horse from another any more than you do. If I did I would be in business.'

Terry played another record in the self-operating studio. Maeve enquired about his script.

'Are you mad?' chuckled Terry. 'I couldn't work with one. I just say what comes into my head. I know it's not great but they get the feeling I am talking, not reading, and I think that helps. I just keep letters on the desk in case I run out of something to say, or I lose the whole pile of records or something.'

Maeve was intrigued. 'Do you panic?'

'No, I don't panic. Actually it's time I had a bit of panic, now that you mention it. It makes the show livelier. I was going to have a panic there when I couldn't find the traffic report. I thought you were sitting on it.'

More chat, more music. Inevitably, she came round to the

Irish image and for the first time ruffled Terry by implying that he was stage Irish.

'Me?' he countered swiftly. 'Now why on God's earth do people say that sort of thing? They say it about everyone who made it, about Val Doonican, Eamonn Andrews, Milo O'Shea, Dave Allen, it's stupid. We are Irish, yes, and on the stage, yes, but not in a sense of being Uncle Toms. I suppose people say that because they know I have made my life here and don't particularly yearn to come back to Ireland just now. They would prefer me to be homesick. The kids are happy here, the two boys have just started school. Helen likes it, we have a lot of friends, and a lot of money. OK, a lot more money than we would have in Ireland, and I have a standard of living that I wasn't used to before but am very used to these days.'

After that gentle outburst, Terry switched on the charm and told Maeve: 'Well, listen, you are very good to have got up so early and come along. I hope you weren't bored out of your mind. I'll be delighted to read whatever you are going to say. I don't think I told you anything really, and I'm not going to tell you how much I earn so don't ask me a third time, will you?'

The next day Britain's first legal commercial pop station was to go on the air. The BBC became nervous that all its disc jockeys might to to Capital Radio, and so had tied up the best ones with long-term contracts.

Maeve Binchy decided that Terry Wogan was not moving from the BBC. With that 'ridiculous money', why should he? she asked, making her way out of Broadcasting House.

13   *'Court Jester'*

'Hello, I see the Director-General's not up yet; I can see his teeth in a glass on the window-sill.'

It was such morning flights of fancy that in 1975 brought a directive from the secretariat of the Director-General, warning Terry Wogan to lay off the D-G. His immediate response was to step up the frequency and outlandishness of his references. Colleagues genuinely feared he risked the ultimate sanction. No one in the Beeb had ever before gone so far. Terry's reply was: 'No, I have the ultimate sanction. I can walk out.'

Later, there was a story told in broadcasting circles that when he eventually 'eased off' he met the D-G's wife at a dinner-party and she remarked to him, puzzled: 'Oh, dear, why don't you mention my husband's name any longer, Terry?'

Half-apologetically, he told her: 'I thought he – '

'No, no,' she assured him. 'He rather likes – '

Terry understood. He has compared himself to a court jester of the Middle Ages waving his pig's bladder at the king. But he is wise enough to know how far he really can go. 'You've got to, otherwise you'll have your head chopped off,' he says. 'I'm a survivor. I've a professional nose for what I'm doing. To be truly subversive is not in the interests of survival.'

Ironically, when Sir Charles Curran retired as D-G, he asked about fifteen BBC staff he felt had served him particularly well to a small dinner-party. Terry was one of the first invited. His style on radio has always been fantastical,

149

allusive and mildly subversive. His commentary quite over-shadowed the records he played. But the *Breakfast Show* was making demands on him. Mark White thought that Terry could be 'edgy' occasionally if things weren't going his way. He suspected at one time that the relationship between Terry and his producer was strained. He knew that Terry was unhappy.

He talked to him about the problem. Mark decided that the only way around it was to change the producer, for if a presenter was asked to play music with which he was desperately unhappy it would have a detrimental effect on the show. The mood of the music must be suited to the show. The relationship between presenter and producer could be a tricky one.

Some months later, in 1976, Terry thought he had had enough of the breakfast programme. One day, over lunch with Mark White, he confided his views.

Mark remembers: 'Terry said to me, "When you offered me this job four years ago I was delighted to take it. But I wasn't sure how long I would be able to carry on. You know the demands on me – I mean getting up before dawn, I'm expected to be chirpy, cheerful. I don't know whether I can go on." I told Terry I couldn't answer his question. What I could tell him was that the BBC wanted him. Nobody wants to move you, Terry.'

They chatted about it and by the time they rose Terry seemed prepared to go on.

Mark recalled another occasion when Terry's contract was up for renewal and Harold Davison, his agent, astounded the BBC contracts people by saying: 'I don't want any more money for Terry.'

Everyone said: 'An agent not looking for more money!'

Davison explained: 'No, Terry is earning all the money he wants. There's only one thing we want to stipulate.'

The BBC man asked: 'What's that?'

Davison replied: 'Terry's fed up with driving to London in all kinds of weather. He wants to be collected every morning.'

The BBC contracts people realised it was a small price to pay for the most popular broadcasting voice in the country.

Mark White speaks proudly of his discovery of Terry Wogan and his introduction of the *Breakfast Show*, and 'his grabbing of the *Jimmy Young Show* from Radio 1 to Radio 2 and developing it into Radio 2's second most popular and successful show.

Terry Wogan talks affectionately of the *Breakfast Show*, but contrary to general opinion says he cared very much about how far he could go in the show. 'I always knew how far I could go,' he recalls.' I was being amusing without being offensive. When you are doing a long radio show like that you are bound to say something you shouldn't have said, but I don't believe I ever offended good taste. I think I enlivened the dull mornings for many listeners – so they tell me anyway. I am reminded of that morning show wherever I go. I loved doing the show; it was, I suppose, a form of therapy. I got everything off my mind. It was great fun.'

Terry greatly enjoyed the rapport he established between himself and Jimmy Young. For years it was to become the highpoint of the morning. 'It did really develop into something quite extraordinary,' he says. 'In the beginning we did it only as a little joke. It was never scripted. Jimmy is a great professional and very easy to work with. This banter between us as I handed over to the *Jimmy Young Show* was really the creation of word pictures and was something very peculiar to radio.'

Jimmy Young has acknowledged 'this special broadcasting relationship between himself and the leprechaun from Limerick, Terence Wogan'. As he recalls: 'Our names were first linked way back in 1969. It was in that year, and using my shoulders as a launching pad, that he first projected his portly personage towards stellar stardom. Yes, I'm afraid I must own up. The whole tragic story is my fault. It all seemed so innocent at the time. All that happened, all those years ago, was that I took a couple of weeks holiday and the Beeb decided to hire Wogan as a two-week holiday

replacement for me, and thirteen years later, we're still stuck
with him. Too late I realised what I had done.'

Jimmy says that when his own radio programme began
at 11.30 it wasn't too bad. He had the protection of a two-
and-a-half-hour gap between them. It was when he moved
to the ten o'clock slot that 'in a single moment of madness,
I doomed myself to daily-morning torture for the rest of my
contractual life.'

Later, he would write good-humouredly in his autobiography:

It happened on the very first morning. At about a quarter
past nine I walked, all unsuspectingly, into Studio Continuity 'D'. From behind my head – yes, he really does, as
he often tells you, spend these mornings looking at the
back of my head – came the dulcet Irish tones: 'Hello,
Jimbo,' he cried, 'why don't you pop into my studio a
little later on, say at about a quarter to ten, and trail what
you're going to be doing in your programme between ten
and twelve?'

Naive fool that I am, I thought: what a kindly Irish
gentleman he is to be sure, and I accepted. Had I know
him then as well as I know him now I would also have
known that kindliness was far from being the prime
motivating factor behind his thinking. Survival, more
likely. What I had not bargained for, of course, was that,
in very short order, he would succeed in dragging me
down to his level. That, however, is what happened.
Within a week we were discussing suspender belts. I was
surprised, as I turned up at the studio each morning, to
see him still sitting there. I quite thought that Lord Reith
would have struck him down personally with a thunder-
bolt. I needn't have worried. The luck of the Irish
prevailed, as I might have known it would.

Later, Jimmy Young would say that the listeners loved
the carry-on and each morning came to expect it. He agrees
with Terry that it started out of nothing but as time went

by it helped to boost both radio programmes. 'As far as I could see,' Jimmy reflects, 'the BBC bosses liked it and so did the Board of Governors. As I was to discover one morning in 1979, even Her Majesty the Queen loved it.'

At her home in Dublin, Terry's mother rarely, if ever, missed the *Breakfast Show*. 'I used to find it very funny,' she recalls. 'I'd wake up early and put on the radio and enjoy myself at Terry's expense. I found that many of my Irish friends also tuned in. Some of them wouldn't miss the show for the world. Sometimes he would refer to Ireland, even joke about things here. Today I miss him in the mornings.'

When Terry was not discussing the idiosyncrasies of the BBC's Director-General or the pigeons on the rooftop of Broadcasting House, he kept his millions of listeners up to date on the antics of the American soap-opera stars. Actor Larry Hagman, alias JR Ewing, the 'nasty' in *Dallas* came in for a lot of sardonic attention, so did other members of the Ewing family. So often did Terry refer to these characters that listeners, rightly or wrongly, assumed that he despised the lot.

'I did not,' asserts Terry today. 'I knew that people watched the soaps so I felt that if I talked about these characters it would be topical and listeners would immediately identify with what I was talking about. When you are ad libbing a two-and-a-half-hour programme like the *Breakfast Show*, you have to draw on a lot of material, otherwise you'd dry up.'

By 1987 Terry believed that both *Dallas* and *Dynasty* had long run their course. As he explained: 'By protracting the agony the producers tended to become desperate to keep the storyline anyway credible. It's absurd.' This desperation was illustrated when some Hollywood stars, including Liz Taylor, were offered millions of dollars to appear in new episodes.

On the strength of his remarkable achievement on the *Breakfast Show* Terry is sometimes reminded by friends that he was the first Irish-born broadcaster to achieve this kind of success in Britain. He disagrees with such a claim. 'Eamonn

Andrews was the first to make the breakthrough and that was nearly a decade before I arrived in London. His success in *This Is Your Life* was a popular one and I consider it an achievement. Eamonn was also a first-rate boxing commentator.'

It was inevitable that Eamonn Andrews would think of Terry in terms of *This Is Your Life*. Terry himself had sometimes wondered when Eamonn would get on his trail. When he eventually did it was, as usual, an elaborate *Life* operation, involving Terry's family in Ireland, Mark and Stella White in the Isle of Man, Helen Wogan and the children. Terry had not the faintest idea of what was going on over his head. Eamonn eventually sprung the surprise on Terry when he interrupted him half-way through his breakfast programme on the morning of April 19, 1978. 'This is *your* life!' exclaimed Eamonn, thrusting a microphone at him.

'Eamonn, I'll kill you!' retorted Terry, for once almost lost for words.

Terry went on to introduce the next record, which started: 'I never thought you'd be here standing close to me'. The two then got into a BBC radio taxi and Terry continued his show from there and later from the foyer of Thames Television. Since *Life* is shrouded in secrecy, Terry had no idea who was awaiting him. Helen had kept the secret from him, although she was terrified that the children might blurt it out.

Among the guests on *Life* were Mark and Stella White; they had been flown in from the Isle of Man. Stella recalls: 'Mark and I joined Terry's parents, Michael and Rose, at the same hotel. We were delighted to be asked on the show. I could see that Michael Wogan was thrilled; he was very proud of Terry. But we were all trying to conceal the Wogans' identity before the hotel staff in case they learned the truth. The Wogans were given a different name. However, once when a round of drinks arrived, Michael, who was in jolly mood, annouced: "This is my party. No one must pay except me." He proceeded to sign on the room account, but unwittingly put down "Michael Wogan". We had to bribe the waitress not to tell anyone that the Wogans were in the hotel.'

Val Doonican found the show 'moving and much fun', while Jimmy Young was 'delighted to be present'. Michael and Rose Wogan looked 'very proud of their Terry', but Stella White thought that 'Terry was embarrassed and speechless'. James Sexton, who had travelled from Limerick, reckoned that Terry hadn't changed at all from the days when they played together at soldiers around Elm Park. When the show was over, Terry insisted on seeing his friends away. 'I remember,' says Jim Sexton, 'seeing him stand on the pavement saying goodbye until the time came when I was moving off, but there was no car around for him. It was the considerate Terry again. He hadn't changed. He was always thinking of someone else, never himself.'

14   Blankety Blank

Jimmy Gilbert, Head of Light Entertainment in BBC TV, had watched Terry closely on *Come Dancing* and his other television shows. He felt that he had the potential to become a household name in television, which up to then he wasn't. One day in late 1978, he sent for him and discussed with him the possibility of doing a new game show. 'It will be the first of its kind on British television,' said Gilbert.

At the time there were at least two popular game shows abroad, *Blankety Blanks* in Australia and *The Match Game* in America. It was hoped to base the new game on one of these ideas. Alan Boyd, who would produce, wanted a tape of *The Match Game* run for Terry. When the boxes were brought into the studio the wrong tape was played. This was *Blankety Blanks* which Boyd already 'hated'. When Terry saw it, his reaction was instant: 'I won't to do a show like this.' Boyd had called the show 'tasteless'.

However, when *The Match Game* was run, Terry liked it. It was fun and everyone in the show seemed to be enjoying themselves. He told Jimmy Gilbert: 'I'll do it, Jimmy.' Alan Boyd decided to adapt the American game, with the emphasis on witty interplay between the star panellists. There would be no big prizes, just 'silly prizes'.

After the first pilot, Boyd wasn't satisfied. He considered that Terry was adopting the same pace as in his radio *Breakfast Show*. 'Rip into Terry, spar with him, bounce off one another,' he advised a comedian before they made a second pilot. It worked. Boyd felt the show suited Terry's style. 'It was a learning experience for him,' recalls Boyd.

However, the BBC's top brass frowned on the show and regarded it as 'trivial'. Alan Boyd suspected that if they could, they would have 'killed' it before it was screened. 'I think its lack of any intellectual content rather upset some of them.'

But Boyd was confident that it would succeed. Soon it was generating 'a wonderful party atmosphere' with people like Beryl Reid, Paul Daniels and Patrick Moore sparring brilliantly with Terry. As the ratings soared and it got into the Top Ten Boyd knew that *Blankety Blank* had become a national cult. The attitude of the top brass changed.

Marcus Plantin, the director, was convinced that *Blankety Blank* was really ahead of its time. But he appreciated why BBC's top brass disliked it at the beginning. 'For one thing, the studio set was in loud tones of grey and pink and the *Blankety Blank* jingles must have made them throw up their hands in horror. But I could see that Terry Wogan was enjoying the duels with the stars on the panel; the rapport between them was scintillating. Since the show wasn't scripted, it gave him scope to ad lib. Spontaneity has always been his forte, so *Blankety* was up his street.'

What greatly amused Plantin was the way Terry deprecated the 'awful prizes'. He remembers: 'Terry made a laugh of the crummy prizes, mocked them, but this became part of the fun. Terry is brilliant at the art of deprecation. In a funny way, he broke all the rules, with the result that *Blankety* was really a parody on the game show itself. Doing it helped his television career.'

Alan Boyd feels that in a short time Terry became a household name. 'I don't think he pushed his own personality,' he reflects. 'He gave a lot of scope to the celebrities around him. I wasn't surprised when it attracted millions of viewers.'

But the show also attracted severe criticism from some viewers. They regarded it as 'rubbish' and accused the BBC of lowering its standards. While Terry agreed that it wasn't exactly the thinking man's show, he had no doubt in his mind that within a few years it would be the forerunner of more television game shows.

As the presenter of *Blankety Blank*, he was enjoying himself enormously. It was a simple enough game to follow: Terry, as presenter, had seated before him six panellists. He would announce a word like 'cold' and ask for the blank to be filled in. Someone in the panel would hold up a card with the answer 'cream' or another panellist might give the answer 'feet', which would be the correct one. For the viewer looking for light entertainment, it was fun and sometimes provided lots of laughs. Terry revelled in it and bounced off his panellists, intent on keeping the right balance between presenter and panellist.

To Helen Wogan, *Blankety Bank* was yet another step along the way for Terry and she knew he was finding it fun. 'I could see his confidence returning and he was beginning to like television again. It wasn't a show, however, I would have liked to see him do indefinitely.'

Terry could be demanding on his panellists. 'The wrath of Wogan can swiftly fall on any star who fails to toe the line on *Blankety Blank*,' observed one critic. 'They get the order of the boot if they aren't up to scratch – and they don't come back. There have been plenty of big names quite unsuited to the show. I've seen the best "freeze" and "die", others panic.'

Terry was said to be angry with one comedian who tried to take over the show. He was the worse for drink and that was inexcusable to him. 'I like a quick one before I go in front of the cameras, but this chap was gone. I was so angry I refused to go to the hospitality suite in case I hit him. I couldn't trust myself. I'm not a violent person, but he really had me going. Sometimes I have to shut somebody up when they're going over the top or being plain boring. But there was no stopping him. He certainly didn't appear again.'

He wasn't slow to pay tribute to stars like Lorraine Chase, Freddie Starr and Kenny Everett and claimed they helped to make *Blankety Blank* the success it became. Once in the middle of a question Kenny produced a packet of Spanish peanuts called BUM. Everybody collapsed. Terry had his own views why the show was popular: 'The great thing about *Blankety* is that other quiz shows give away huge prizes and large amounts of money to secure their success. Our idea of a prize is something more like a weekend in Leningrad or a plastic bicycle. I don't want the prizes to be any good. That would mean us all having to concentrate.'

As the months went by he felt his confidence grow. Now he looked forward to television because he was a success. The ratings were growing. 'The trouble with *Come Dancing* was that I felt when I was presenting it I wasn't doing it any better than anyone else and I wasn't doing it any differently either, although the show was popular. If you are any good you've got to bring something different to what you're doing. I suppose, bring your own personality.'

Success was bringing with it awards. In April he was voted top radio personality at the Radio Industries Awards in London.

But he continued to puzzle some media people, who believed he should be doing something more profound than his *Breakfast Show* or *Blankety Blank*. One critic mused: 'Off the air, and even on it, it is clear that Wogan is a man of intelligence and natural wit. So why does he waste his talents purveying his inexhaustible fund of trivia?'

It wasn't the first time that Terry faced such criticism. On this occasion, he said: 'Nobody can be too intelligent for something. The essence of light entertainment is its triviality. There's no more to be said about it. I've read stronger criticism in the newspapers about *Blankety Blank* and some people were kind enough to suggest I was better than the show. But what effect does criticism have on a show like that? Absolutely none. I resist the urge to think that I have something deep and meaningful to say to the people of Britain. I'm very sanguine about things really. You must never believe your own publicity. It is all very transient. If some people like me, there will be as many who can't stand the sight of me. You've got to be able to take public disapproval as well as fame.'

He was the first to admit that since arriving in Britain he had enjoyed a good run. Despite the hundreds of thousands of words written about him, few seemed envious of the Wogan Phenomenon. By 1980 he had grown somewhat more cautious: 'Sometimes I figure I'm in line for a disaster anyway. The critics have been fairly kind to me until now. Maybe now it's my turn for the pack of wolves to turn on me, and jump up and down with cleated boots. Anyway I don't believe there is such a thing as a television superstar. Television isn't a big occasion. It is very ordinary. It's not like the movies, where people become godlike. A superstar is someone like Elvis Presley. When I am doing the washing up sometimes, I say to Helen, my wife: "I bet Frank Sinatra doesn't have to do this." It brings you down to earth.'

Later that year the Wogan family was deeply saddened by the death of Terry's father, Michael. Terry slipped out of London and flew to Dublin for the funeral and to comfort his mother. His parents had been to stay with him since he came to London and he went out of his way to make them welcome. They watched his television shows and listened to his breakfast programme. His own brother, Brian, and Brian's wife would also come and stay from time to time. It was a close-knit family, which was the way Terry wanted it. He had always admired his father, and the way he worked so hard; he regretted he had had to wait so long for his material rewards.

1982 was to prove one of the most important years for Terry in broadcasting. He had plenty to smile about, although there was something of a stir when it was revealed that Terry and his family had acquired 98 per cent of Jo Gurnett Personal Management Ltd, which to everybody's surprise was found to have his Irish rival Gloria Hunniford on its books. She had appeared on the *Blankety Blank* panel, while another Gurnett signing, Kenny Everett, had also been on the panel. Was Terry compromising his own position as presenter of the show?

A BBC spokesman was quick to explain: 'Artists are

booked way ahead of the recordings and Terry's not involved in the selection process. A programme adviser sits down and goes through all the people who are currently in the news and his team try to keep a balance between old favourites and new artists. It's a complicated business and quite scientific.'

But the explanation didn't stop one critic commenting: "Terry no doubt is laughing all the way to Blankety bank'. But the matter did not rest there. In August of that year the BBC made a statement that no disciplinary action was being contemplated against Terry for allegedly plugging Gloria Hunniford on his *Breakfast Show* when he referred to her as 'Grevious Bodily Hunniford'. The spokesman dismissed suggestions that there was a conflict of interest, pointing out that 'Mr Wogan often gives teasing mention on his early-morning programme to people like Ray Moore or Jimmy Young, who had no connection with Jo Gurnett Personal Management Agency. He further added that the BBC had no objections to their presenters' outside business interests so long as they were honest and legal and did not conflict with their work for the Corporation. The BBC understood that the agency was run by Mrs Jo Gurnett and that Mr Wogan was not involved in the day-to-day running of the agency, which was a highly reputable one.

What was clear, though, was that at this stage – and not surprisingly so – Terry was consolidating for the future. Often he had been quoted as saying that show business is ephemeral and one's popularity as a performer could wane in a short time. But there was little fear that Terry's popularity was fading. He was said to have turned down a £250,000 offer from a consortium in Ireland who wanted him to head a new commercial-radio venture. He wasn't interested in unsettling either himself or Helen and the children. The offer nevertheless left him 'flummoxed and flabbergasted'.

At forty-four years of age, he was at the pinnacle of his broadcasting career; he had collected the status symbols that go with fame and the future looked decidedly rosy. In

November '82, he was honoured by the Variety Club of Great Britain. During the celebrations it was announced that he would have a new series of thirteen chat shows with the BBC, starting the following January. Terry was overjoyed: 'It's something I have always wanted to do. But I'm not the new Parkinson. I'm the old Terry Wogan and I hope people will enjoy me and my guests on the show.

Among the guests at the Variety Club function at the Hilton Hotel were BBC's Director-General Alasdair Milne and BBC Controller Alan Hart. Milne told the gathering: 'Terry has become a household word – like sink-tidy or waste-disposal unit! He is nature's answer to insomnia.'

Bob Monkhouse, a personal friend of Terry's, summed up: 'I don't know how he does it. Listeners send him all the comedy material – *free*. Then he publishes it in book form and sells it back to them!'

Terry had a typical reply: 'This is a tribute lunch. I've never been more insulted in all my life!'

At this point Terry suspected that the arrival of TV AM, which Parkinson was helping to set up, would kill his radio audience, so he was anxious to develop in the direction of television. Parkinson's departure left a gap in the BBC schedules for a chat show. The BBC bosses tried out a number of different candidates to fill Parky's shoes, among them Terry, Tim Rice and Frank Delaney. It became clear that Terry had the winning formula.

It was reputed that the Saturday-night slot would be worth £5,000 a show. Overall his earnings from radio and television amounted to about £70,000 a year; add to that his highly lucrative income from advertising, TV voice-overs and radio spots, and the figure would not be far short of £130,000 a year. On top of that, Terry was able to command up to £1,000 for a public appearance. Alongside the Wogan Phenomenon the Wogan Industry was growing fast.

Terry made it clear that what he was seeking in his new TV show was a conversational style. He admitted that it had taken the best part of fifteen years to approach the degree of ease and relaxation on television that he had acquired very easily on radio. 'It's much harder to bend television the way you want it to go,' he explained. 'What you have to do is make it look easy. My job is to put viewers at their ease and make them feel you are not going to embarrass them or make them feel uneasy. I prefer the radio because for me it's an easier medium, and I am more confident than I am on television. I was a natural for radio.'

By now Terry had cultivated a very thoughtful attitude towards his work. He convinced the media people that success such as he had achieved 'doesn't arrive by accident'. The heart of his career was in his morning radio show. 'It is so important to me that when the predictable offers came in from Breakfast TV I decided instead to sign a new two-year contract with Radio 2.'

'Terry Wogan beats all his radio rivals,' remarked one critic, 'because listeners want to hear him and not his music. He has no script, no interviews, no gimmicks.' Someone else said: 'Wogan is bland,' another: 'Wogan is old-fashioned,' and yet another: 'His patter is witty without being arresting.' But everybody agreed that he was a phenomenon.

The ratings showed that his Saturday-night chat show was a success, but Terry was not completely happy. He knew it had elements that restricted it. For one thing, it wasn't a live show. 'Having one show a week is restrictive,' he would say, 'you are limited in the guests you can have by their availability on a particular night. So from early on, I wanted to have a show that would be more than once a week.' He preferred a chat show with elements of the unexpected, topical and up to the minute. His own show was taped on the Friday and 'all polished and honed' for screening on the Saturday night.

But he made it known that he was not happy doing the show. 'It was easy. Yet I felt that the show shouldn't be a once-a-week thing; a talk show should be more than that, it should have continuity. If you present it only once a week, it's kind of special. It means you have to have major stars; your audience expects the spectacular.'

Came 1983. He was rarely, if ever, out of the news. He was voted Favourite Male Personality on TV for the fifth year running by readers of the *TV Times*. To mark the honour, the magazine had put his picture on page one and given him a centre-page spread, complete with pictures of Helen and the children, and Jimmy Young. Terry quipped: 'So I am on the front cover! I only hope it doesn't put viewers off voting for me next year'.

In October 1984 it was announced that Terry was giving up his breakfast radio show. This was because he was soon to host a new BBC TV chat show three nights a week. Terry said: 'I shall be extremely sorry to give up my *Breakfast Show* after twelve years, but that is probably long enough to be getting up at 5.30 am. It's my choice to leave because I feel the public should be given the chance to enjoy their mornings.' He hadn't forgotten Jimmy Young: 'It will be a wrench to say goodbye to the old gentleman after all these years. He used to think our little chat spoiled the start of his show, but I always felt they spoiled the end of mine. Without me to care for his bodily needs, how will he manage? He could get stuck in the corridor for weeks, months even.'

Since Terry had by now become an institution the press copiously noted his departure from his morning radio slot. One columnist wondered if the Queen would include him in the New Year's Honours List. His last programme on the Friday was typical of all that had gone before – he shot at anyone who came within firing range. At the special BBC reception to mark the end of the programme, Terry was a little tearful: 'I'm sorry to be leaving the show.' But soon he was back to his old self: 'I'll just have to get used to looking at the missus over the breakfast table again, that's if the kids can stand seeing me.'

Jimmy Young was inspired to write an open letter to Terry and this was published in a Fleet Street morning newspaper. In it, Jimmy said: 'I never thought I'd be paying my old sparring partner any sort of compliment, but I'm going to miss your cheerful face, your Irish insults! Who'll bring me my tea now? Some young whippersnapper half your age, I suppose. It's a sorrowful nation that faces the prospect of waking up without their morning dose of Wogan.

'Many a time on my way from Broadcasting House, I've been loath to admit that the lad from Limerick is the best thing to be stuck with in a traffic jam. How I and your other radio listeners – an old lady, living somewhere in Luton, Audience Research tells me – will miss your whimsical references to Grevious Bodily Hunniford, Burly Shassy and Julio Double-glazing. And there are those who will even suffer withdrawal symptoms without their daily dose of *Dallas* and *Dysentery*.'

Jimmy concluded: 'You and I are as different as chalk and cheese. But in our morning sparring matches, there's been a chemistry that worked between us. So now orft you jolly well go to your new job on the telly. And as you yourself might express it: Merciful time will heal the savage wound. The best of British. I'll be thinking of you.'

Monday night, February 18, 1985 . . . Terry was pacing the floor of his dressing-room in the BBC Television Theatre, Shepherd's Bush awaiting the first of his new thrice-weekly *Wogan* shows. He was smoking a large cigar and telling those around him: 'I'm not thinking about it. I'm not nervous.'

It was Bill Cotton, Head of Light Entertainment, who first suggested that the show be thrice weekly. Terry was in full agreement. As Terry explained: 'This is a risk show. That's what gives it frisson. The one thing we don't want, ever, is for the show to look as if it's been recorded.'

Watching the first *Wogan* was Terry's mother, 74–year-old Rose at her home in Dublin. Afterwards she talked about it: 'I laughed my way through the show. I'd watch any old rubbish Terry's on, even *Blankety Blank*. I think he's taking a risk doing it three nights a week, but I'm confident he'll be a success. I watch him all the time, but I miss him on the radio in the mornings. Now I switch on to Gay Byrne on Irish radio.'

Mrs Wogan was intensely proud of the Wogan Phenomenon. Yet she reflected: 'Terry may be a superstar in England but back home he is still "our Terry". He hasn't changed a bit. I am pleased he is popular. He comes home quite often to see me. Ten days ago he was here with Helen and one of the boys, Mark. They came specially, because he won't have a chance with the show running for so many weeks. I am very lucky with my daughters-in-law. They are very good to me now that I'm not that spritely.'

Today, at seventy-five, Rose continues to live most of the year in a purpose-built extension of the Woggan family home in Dublin with her younger son, Brian, his wife and family. Each September she joins Terry for a five-month stay but has not been to Shepherd's Bush to see *Wogan* because of her painful rheumatoid arthritis. 'She is very slow-moving and would be embarrassed coming to the theatre,' Terry says. 'But she is able to do most things for her own sense of dignity. At seventy-five she is entitled to . . . what you hate to see is the constant pain.

Terry has always been reticent about those he loves, so it was a surprise when he talked about his mum. True, they have always been close and her constant pain has cast a shadow over his life. In a quiet voice, he will say: 'It is awful for me to watch her in pain, the extraordinary pain I know she suffers. She has been in and out of hospital pretty consistently, two or three times a year, for the past five years. She's had operations on her hands, her arms, her knees and her eye – it makes people blind as well. The sad thing is that she's had no period of remission. Around fifty-five, it really began to hurt and it got progressively worse.'

Helen Wogan knew that Terry had been nervous at the start of the new series. She shared his anxiety, but as the weeks went by she suddenly was able to say to herself: 'He's a success. He's made it.'

The first *Wogan* got off to a dramatic start when Terry slipped and nearly fell on his face. But he recovered to ensure that the show continued at a brisk and entertaining pace, with Elton John particularly effective. The recipe of relaxed chat and topicality seemed to be a successful blend. Terry, looking more confident than ever before, struck up a friendly rapport with his audience in the Shepherd's Bush Theatre. All that mattered in the future was whether he would be able to get enough interesting and glamorous guests to make *Wogan* a continuous success. Next day Terry said he foresaw no problems with guests; in a moment of rare enthusiasm he even referred to the possibility of *Wogan* five nights a week. The critics weren't so sure. 'Wait and see' was their sober reaction. Not all of them were completely satisfied with *Wogan*. One critic thought the format wasn't completely right. Another forecast that within a few weeks it would be the most talked about light entertainment show in Britain.

By April the show was climbing higher and higher in the ratings. Michael Grade, Controller of BBC 1 and an ardent champion of Terry's, announced that 'Terry was the BBC's greatest asset'. No one argued with him. But in the midst of the excitement Terry kept his head. He was never one to be carried away.

He found time on April 24 to remember his twentieth wedding anniversary. He booked a place at a quiet little restaurant and after *Wogan* had finished on Wednesday night, he kept the rendezvous with the woman he likes to call 'Hel'. Terry has always been sentimental about anniversaries and never forgets them, but they are very private affairs and are kept secret from his admirers and fans. Earlier, before going to Shepherd's Bush, Terry had given Helen a bunch of roses and three cards. One card was romantic. Another – attached to the new Merc – said: 'Hope you like surprises.' The third was a joke card saying: 'Happy anniversary to a wonderful person who has not changed since our wedding day. Iron your face and I'll take you out on the town. Love Ter.'

What was even more important to Helen, as she prepared to keep that rendezvous in the little restaurant, was the success of their own lives. 'It's trust,' she thought to herself. Nothing had changed between them after twenty years of marriage. Even the success of *Wogan* wouldn't alter things. She felt so proud of Terry.

At his home on the Isle of Man that night, Mark White watched the show. He admits he is not a television chat show person. 'I only watched it because Terry was presenting it,' he said later. 'He was super.'

Mark agreed that *Wogan* would continue to be a success because Terry had imposed his own personality on the show, just as he had years before on his breakfast radio show.

PART THREE

WOGAN AND GUESTS

I have never been able to see how the duties of a critic, which consist in making painful remarks in public about the most sensitive of his fellow-creatures, can be reconciled with the manners of a gentleman.

—BERNARD SHAW

15   'Over-exposed'

'Terry Wogan's a bore.'

'Terry Wogan's peaked.'

These were some of the newspaper headlines that greeted Terry on the cold early mornings of January 1986. No one had ever dared before to call him a bore, although they had labelled him 'a chatterbox' and 'a prima donna'. Could it be that he was losing his charisma, that his show was becoming tiresome, played out. Did the viewers share his critics' opinion? Terry, who up to then had seemed infallible, was now, it appeared, proving a source of exasperation to some viewers.

The headline that sparked off the controversy was published in the *Daily Mail*. It screamed in large, bold type: 'IS THIS MAN TV'S BIGGEST BORE?'

The article by Shaun Usher, which would be described by his Fleet Street colleagues as 'constructive', stressed that Wogan was 'the victim of gross exposure by the BBC, being thrown into the ratings battle at every opportunity, so that his undoubted gifts of repartee and bonhomie were stretched to the limit and tending towards the tedious'.

The criticism was inspired, it seemed, by a Christmas show devised by Terry, in which he interviewed actors from the cast of *Dynasty* as though they were real people. One critic summed up most reviewers' reactions by describing the programme as 'creepy'. Another commented: 'Wogan's BBC nightmare is now developing a surrealistic dimension that draws one compulsively to it. An unknown actress

170

follows an obscure magician. Wogan lurches on with the crazed determination of the truly desperate.'

It was the first time I can recall Terry described as 'desperate', an accusation that would perhaps amuse him. The critics were already wildly over-reacting to a show that Terry had always regarded as light entertainment and not to be taken too seriously.

Terry understands better than most how harrowing it is to be constantly in the spotlight. 'I suppose I come second to the Royal Family in terms of exposure,' he sighs, with a faint smile. 'That's where I am. There are numerous disadvantages to being famous and visible. I'm hurt when I'm criticised, but I'm resilient – or I wouldn't be in the business – and my faith is restored every so often. While I continue to win polls as the most popular person on television, the criticisms are irrelevant. Usually they are just sensationalist attempts to provoke a news story or reaction from readers.'

However, the controversy, as Terry predicted, dragged on in the newspapers. Television critic Mary Kenny summed up: 'Perhaps he is over-exposed, as they say, perhaps he has peaked as a performer. But I wouldn't bet on it.'

The main reason why Miss Kenny would not bet on it was that in 1978 when she interviewed Terry and gave her report to a newspaper editor, it was turned down because the editor felt nobody would be interested in Terry. He told her: 'Terry Wogan has peaked. He has gone about as far as he will go in show business. Anyway, he's over-exposed.'

That was eight years previously. Inside a few years Terry was to get his own chat show, which would attract millions of viewers. Mary Kenny analysed Terry's performance and concluded: 'As a television performer his strength lies in his sheer nerve. He has brought the telling pause to a fine art, which is a daring accomplishment on TV, where the pressure from the director's gallery is to keep the action moving relentlessly.

'The aspect of Wogan's radio personality that television has not allowed him to deploy is the fey, wry, surrealistic

dimensions of puns, word play, and the imaginary characters that had become part of his radio act. Perhaps Wogan's
need for fantasy now seeks expression through *Dynasty* and
the like, rather than through his own inventiveness.'

But his critics reckoned without the BBC's support for
Terry. The Corporation's light entertainment boss Michael
Grade (whose motto is: 'If at first you don't succeed . . .
you're fired') believes that Terry can do no wrong. As Mary
Kenny pointed out: 'Wogan could dress in cap and bells or
recite the Albanian telephone directory as far as Michael
Grade is concerned. Because Wogan brings in the viewers.'

There was a surprise when the venerable political pundit
Sir Robin Day added his voice to the criticism of Terry's
Christmas visit to the *Dynasty* set. He described the show
as 'appalling and BBC's most humiliating moment'.

'I couldn't believe it,' he reflected. 'Terry Wogan was
talking to people as characters. He was speaking to fictional
people who don't exist as if they were real. It was appalling.
Awful! Terry Wogan is more boring than me.'

Sir Robin, the presenter of *Question Time*, made his
comments at the celebration of the programme's 200th
edition. He was asked why he thought six million viewers
watched the programme: 'I don't know why it has become
popular. It began in the BBC as something of an illegitimate
baby. It appeals to academics, professors and politicians. I
could never be over-exposed like Terry Wogan. After all I'm
only on thirty weeks a year and then only once a week.'

Terry's colleagues in show business were not slow to come
to his defence. They hit back at Sir Robin's claim that the
Wogan Christmas special with the cast of *Dynasty* was the
BBC's 'most humiliating moment'. Michael Parkinson said:
'Sir Robin's copping the British disease in knocking the
successful. I'm disappointed that Robin Day appears to have
joined in. That is unforgiveable.' Ronnie Corbett felt: 'It is
irresponsible and impolite to criticise one's own.' And Bob
Monkhouse praised the Irishman for his 'effortless style and
great skill' and added: 'The only problem with Terry is that
he is a bigger star than most of his guests.'

Terry wasn't in bleak Britain to participate for long in the stormy debate. He was sunning his much criticised person on the sands of the Caribbean island of Antigua. With him were Helen and his children, Alan, eighteen, Mark, fifteen, and thirteen-year-old Katherine. Interviewed at Heathrow airport before his departure, he said with a rather subdued smile: 'The critics have been saying I'm over-exposed since I started my chat show. You have to take the rough with the smooth, and it doesn't worry me too much. It's what the public thinks that matters.'

Few believed a Fleet Street comment that Terry was secretly devastated by Sir Robin Day's remarks. Few could visualise the great man devastated by anything. The question was now whether the critics were being too hasty in their judgment of what they themselves described as 'two spectacular flops'. If anyone was to blame, it was the BBC, for allowing Terry to be over-exposed, particularly in the light of their own assessment that he was one of their greatest single assets. But it was true that the Corporation identified Terry as a ratings weapon and did not worry about the problem of possible over-exposure.

As the controversy continued in newspapers and letters columns, it appeared that Sir Robin Day had had second thoughts. He intimated that his remarks about his BBC colleague Terry Wogan were not serious. They had been taken out of context. Speaking at the BBC before presenting the *World at One* programme on radio, Sir Robin stated: 'The remarks about Terry were all light-hearted and made over the lunch table.'

When Sir Robin's words reached Terry in sunny Antigua he said of the veteran broadcaster: 'I feel sorry for the fellow. I think it's very sad that someone has had to attack a colleague in this way. I don't want to have a go at him at all. All I can say is – poor old sod!'

No one could say for certain whether Terry was serious. His puckish humour tended to disguise his real feelings in the matter. For all his critics knew Terry may well have been treating the whole affair as a joke. He would say later: 'I'm always accused of being over-exposed, but that's impossible. If I were a comedian or a conjurer doing the same act continuously, there would be no argument, but I'm merely acting as a linkman between the viewer and the guest.'

On Friday, January 10, the Christmas ratings were published. One particular headline summed up the result: 'Wogan's a winner'. And the most ironic feature was that Wogan's Christmas Day interview with the cast of *Dynasty*, which had been panned, sneaked in at number 9 with a record sixteen million viewers.

Michael Grade was jubilant. 'Wogan is the most popular personality on British television,' he declared. Referring to Sir Robin Day's attack earlier when he had described the show as 'awful', Grade laughed and said: 'We are unlikely to be making Robin Head of Light Entertainment.'

As the suntanned Terry and Helen were preparing to dine with Prince and Princess Michael on Antigua in what was described as a 'secret dinner', he was telephoned by Grade who informed him about the ratings and the record numbers of viewers for a chat show.

By January 13, the BBC was even more enthusiastic about *Wogan*. They announced that they were prepared to put the show on five nights a week eventually. Michael Grade, speaking with the air of a football manager extolling the praises of his superstar, said Terry was one of their biggest assets. 'There is nothing wrong with a man who can get that sort of audience at Christmas. The notion there is any problem with Terry's show is a fantasy. He will stay on three nights a week but one day I would like to see him on five nights a week when we're ready.'

Grade seemed to be carried away. The risk of over-exposure did not worry him. He continued: 'Terry's show is not like the BBC's *Eastenders*. You don't have to be glued to the set, like you do for a serial. Terry's show is a rolling entertainment and you can dip out. If you miss a couple of programmes there is no problem. Twenty-five million viewers watch Terry's three shows each week. He is one of the BBC's successes and the show is going to be there for years.'

The critics continued to snipe at Terry. One Dublin critic had definite views on the question: 'So the great romance is waning at last. I speak of the long-running affair between Britain and the broth of a boy Terry Wogan. If the reaction in Fleet Street is any gauge, relations are definitely cooling, and while a complete break may not be imminent, it would seem that our hero no longer can do no wrong.'

But Terry had at least one pretty champion of the Wogan cause. Screen legend Sophia Loren said she could not understand television viewers being put off by three showings of *Wogan* each week. 'I like him,' she said. And Samantha Fox commented: 'Terry's proved he can do a brilliant job. If he's over-exposed let him be . . . people at the top always seem to get knocked'.

Frances Whitaker and the *Wogan* team on the seventh floor of BBC's Television Centre were not over concerned by the criticism of Terry. Like Michael Grade, they were satisfied from the ratings that *Wogan* was still as popular as ever. Frances Whitaker would say to me later: 'I could not imagine Terry being too concerned about it.'

Terry returned from Antigua bronzed and, by his own admission, eager to meet his audience and guests in the Television Theatre in Shepherd's Bush Green. As the show's principal celebrity, he had not only forged a unique familiarity with his television viewers but also with his friendly theatre audiences.

Terry still projected lots of charm and flair, but the first journalist to talk to him after his return found he was hurt by Sir Robin Day's remarks and the general flak he was taking from the press. 'Reporters,' he commented, 'ring me for interviews, then go away and print lies. It's happening more and more.'

But strangely, although he dislikes Fleet Street, he loves the publicity. What reassured him more than anything else was Michael Grade's utter confidence in him. Terry would say: 'I approve entirely of the ethos he's trying to create for the BBC. Television is chewing-gum for the eyes, a mild narcotic. It is an entertainment first and information medium second.

'Before I came along, the BBC had given in to competition from ITV. They had only three to four million watching in the early evening, now with me they get ten. If I get more serious in my approach, add more depth, how will it affect the public?'

Terry has long made it plain that 'his public' did not want serious chat. He explained: 'They don't want news of pretentious *South Bank Show* stuff. *Wogan* is a mass audience programme, like *Eastenders*. My talent, if any, is understanding what the viewers want and giving it to them.'

Ever since Sir Robin's caustic remarks about his Christmas show, viewers had wondered if and when the confrontation between the two would take place on *Wogan*. They are as different as chalk and cheese. Sir Robin is regarded as a heavyweight, Terry as a lightweight. Their individual approaches on the box are also different: Sir Robin achieves his results by a confident mixture of arrogance and skill, Terry relies mostly on wit and charm. When it was announced that the two would be facing each other on *Wogan* on the evening of January 20 it caused a stir. For Sir Robin, it meant his role was being reversed; instead of asking the questions he would have to find the answers. But he was known to be cagey, professional and not without a sardonic sense of humour.

The press had hinted that Wogan was angry over what Sir Robin had said about him, so viewers wondered what line the great man would take. Would he come bouncing from his corner and go straight into attack against an opponent older in years? Or would he adopt a gentle, humorous approach against the formidable Sir Robin, winner of many television battles against wily political opponents? It promised to be an intriguing confrontation, the type of thing that guarantees an audience for *Wogan*, although some critics regarded the whole exercise as 'too incestuous for words'.

After the signature tune, Terry immediately began his introductory remarks in his breezy, familiar style: 'Heaven, it's great to be back (*audience applauds loudly*). I've been in the Caribbean getting bronzed and fat, so that I would be ready and raring to go for another year of unmitigated *Wogan*. Three a week? Why not ten a week? I'll give you over-exposure! I spent sometime on holiday avoiding the better elements of the British press, who as far as I can gather want to know if I was taking over Westland Helicopters and Michael Heseltine was taking over the show. I hate to drive you berserk so early in the evening but I've a barrel full for you tonight . . . but first Sir Robin Day . . . (*lengthy applause*).

As Terry eased himself confidently into his chair on the stage of the BBC Television Theatre his mobile face betrayed neither anger nor resentment. He smiled broadly, pulled a comic face or two, and rolled those large eyes of his. Sir Robin, on the other hand, did not seem nearly as relaxed, but he still managed to look a heavyweight in television terms; neatly dressed with bow tie and matching shirt, he looked dapper and in flamboyant mood.

Sir Robin was the first to the punch: 'Can I welcome you back from your holiday, which you obviously needed so much?'

WOGAN: (*taken by surprise*) Et tu, Brute.

SIR ROBIN: I haven't been on holiday.

WOGAN: *Et tu, Brute*. I leave the country for a few weeks and you treat me to a tirade of abuse. What kind of . . .

SIR ROBIN: Can I just say this much, Terry – may I call you Terry?

WOGAN: Please do . . . No! I'm not so sure.

SIR ROBIN: I don't think we ought to have a slanging match.

WOGAN: Why not?

SIR ROBIN: I think we should set an example, otherwise people will think we are Cabinet Ministers.

WOGAN: You are not afraid of my acid tongue?

SIR ROBIN: I don't think we want people to think we are Heseltine and Brittan.

The interview was taking place during the controversy over Westland Helicopters that sparked off a crisis in the Government. Terry was holding his own and throwing punch for punch. The wily Sir Robin tried hard to turn the tables on his opponent and not without some success.

SIR ROBIN: I just want to congratulate you Terry. While you have been away you can't have known what was going on. Did you know for example that you won the *Private Eye* Bore of the Year Award (*prolonged applause from the audience who have warmed to the verbal battle*). I thought that was unfair. I could have thought of several other people who I might have put first.

WOGAN: So can I – you weren't nominated then?

SIR ROBIN: Not as far as I know.

WOGAN: (*Raising his voice as though for effect*) Why did you do it then?

SIR ROBIN: (*Surprised*) Do what?

WOGAN: Why did you stab me in the back?

Terry had made a direct hit. A look of relief swept over his face, as if he had rehearsed the punch and was delighted that he had made a perfect contact.

SIR ROBIN: (*Slightly apologetic*) I'll tell you exactly what happened –

WOGAN: You had a good lunch?

SIR ROBIN: I hadn't a good lunch at all.

Wogan tried to interrupt, but his opponent was having none of it.

SIR ROBIN: Can I be allowed to finish what I am –

WOGAN: I wish you would.

Laughter erupted from the audience. The contest was proving lively. It wasn't a mis-match after all.

SIR ROBIN: Now I am going to make my protest.

WOGAN: (*Almost gloating, sensing victory*) Make your point.

SIR ROBIN: (*In measured tone*) My protest is this – are you in charge of the dirty tricks department?

WOGAN: (*In a whisper*) Of this programme?

SIR ROBIN: For, before you came on, there was a warm-up man who told this audience (*applause for the first time for him*): 'I want you to help us and when he says Thank you, Sir Robin at the end of the interview you are to sit and snore. He said that will be our little joke.' So that is the kind of treatment I am going to be subjected to?

WOGAN: Nonsense, Sir Robin! Nothing was further from my mind. In fact, they are already asleep! (*Laughter followed by applause*)

SIR ROBIN: You asked me what happened. Well, I'll tell you. I woke up in the morning and saw the *Daily Mail*'s main feature and it asked: 'Is this man the biggest bore on television?' So I thought to myself: 'Oh dear, they're at it again.' You see, I have been on television for thirty years, much longer than you. I am an expert on boredom. I've been boring people every week for thirty years. When I read the article later in the day and saw it was you, I was pleased and relieved that it wasn't me. I told this story to three or four journalists with whom I was having a glass of wine when giving them a talk about *Question Time*, which is a programme that has just celebrated its 200th edition, while you were cavorting in the Caribbean and they took it all down. There is no one I like better than you, but your Christmas show was extremely awful. (*More laughter*)

WOGAN: (*fighting back*) Well, only sixteen million people seemed to enjoy it.

SIR ROBIN: What has that got to do with it? What else would they want?

WOGAN: There are plenty of things on television at Christmas time.

SIR ROBIN: (*Dismissively*) Not much, not much.

WOGAN: Why don't they have you at Christmas?

SIR ROBIN: They take me off like Rambo. I'm not fit for family viewing.

Sir Robin was ahead on points. His sardonic humour was proving a telling punch. Terry was too eager to counter attack and forgot his own forte – wit.

WOGAN: I read what you said when I came home. It nearly

spoiled my holiday. There I am lying in bed in Antigua. It is half five in the morning and the police have arrived. And one of these eagle-eyed Fleet Street news hounds phoned me and said: 'Have you read what Sir Robin has said about you in the papers? Well . . . ?'

SIR ROBIN: It's the sort of conversation where one has one's tongue in one's cheek, blarney if you like – you're an expert at it, except that you do it in public and I do it in private.

Terry tried to get a word in, but Sir Robin wanted to keep punching.

SIR ROBIN: Well, the Christmas programme did go wrong, didn't it?

Wogan broke into a short, whimsical laugh, as though dismissing the question from his mind.

SIR ROBIN: What were you doing there – selling vacuum cleaners?

WOGAN: Had you had a particularly good Christmas dinner?

SIR ROBIN: No, I watched it and I saw it and I understand that you were going to have dinner with these ridiculous *Dynasty* people. It was a great cock-up.

WOGAN: (*Boxing too defensively*) It was a joke.

SIR ROBIN: It wasn't very funny, was it?

WOGAN: Well, when I watch *Question Time* and you make your lumbering attempt at humour I sometimes think –

SIR ROBIN: Oh, no . . . !

WOGAN: I say that is not working either.

SIR ROBIN: Stick to the point. Yours was a big centrepoint Christmas night show. Be honest, Terry, you were rather disappointed in the whole thing, weren't you?

WOGAN: All I can say is that I am not here to defend my own programmes because there is no point doing that, otherwise I will turn around and start attacking your shows and you'll have to defend them.

SIR ROBIN: I will not have to defend them at all, for often they are not very good.

WOGAN: If you do 150 programmes a year as I have been

doing you can't expect them all to be towering works of genius.

There was a danger that the fire was going out of the fight and the audience at the ringside sensed it.

SIR ROBIN: You were sent off to interview these non-existent people.

WOGAN: Maybe you don't follow soap operas. Maybe you don't enjoy them?

SIR ROBIN: Yes, I do.

WOGAN: You know nothing about soap operas.

The audience laughed. Terry had turned the tables with a forceful punch.

SIR ROBIN: What's the difference? Bambozzle me with language.

WOGAN: Come along, how do you expect to react to criticism?

SIR ROBIN: Ever since I went on television I've been criticised day in day out. I've been impersonated and abused. Did you see yourself on *Spitting Image*?

WOGAN: I did, I hated it.

SIR ROBIN: I thought it was a frightfully good one of you.

WOGAN: I didn't think it was a bad image of me. (*Getting closer to his opponent*) Another Knight of Television . . . It never went to your head, did it?

SIR ROBIN: What . . . ?

WOGAN: Being knighted?

SIR ROBIN: Nothing has ever gone to my head. I'm just an ordinary chap who does his duty as he sees fit.

WOGAN: (*Swinging the big punch*) And knocking seven bells out of his fellow television performer!

SIR ROBIN: (*Wobbling*) No, no. no. I just said what everybody else thought – it was a bit of an awful programme and you weren't very pleased with it. All your programmes are bad.

WOGAN: (*Failing to nail him*) How nice of you!

SIR ROBIN: (*Following up with a lovely deft punch*) Would I have got on this programme if I hadn't said that Terry

Wogan was an awful bore? I didn't mean it to be taken down, I was there to do something else. I'm a simple bloke.

WOGAN: You're naive.

SIR ROBIN: Simple, not naive.

WOGAN: I think it shows naivety.

SIR ROBIN: Well you can think what you like. (*After brief pause*) Where did you get that extraordinary tie?

After another few moments the confrontation was over and Terry returned to his natural, beaming self and thanked Sir Robin for lasting the fight with him. It was a highly civilised ending with the referee bringing in a draw verdict. Yet it was not the type of show that brings the best out of Terry. At times he was boxing on his toes; he is better when he is more relaxed and throwing quick short punches. There was too much tension for his own good.

For the viewers it was still, one presumes, a fascinating performance by the two protagonists, an inspired piece of match-making. For the weary critics it was perhaps too much of an 'in-fight' and they asked wearily: 'Were these boxers really trying?'

16   Older Women

Barbara Cartland has made the *Guinness Book of Records* as the world's most prolific author with four hundred books to her credit. At eighty-four, this vivacious and fast-spoken woman, is the undisputed Queen of Romance. Her penchant for pink and purity is by now legendary, but she is not unaware of her own strong personality. As she admits: 'My children are always being asked if they are overshadowed by an overwhelming mother. It's all complete nonsense. Of course they are not overshadowed.'

Which invited the question on this cold February evening at the BBC Television Theatre in Shepherd's Bush: would amiable Terry Wogan also be overshadowed by this living literary legend? He has been described as 'the undisputed King of Blarney, ace compère of the chat show, disc jockey supremo, the man with a smile as wide as the Nile and a flow of talk like Nile water'.

In praise of older women might well be one of his theme songs, for he has always impressed by the manner in which he handles this generation of women, particularly if they happen to be rich, famous and glamorous. Maybe it's his cuddly disposition that relaxes them or his charm and bewitching smile. They don't feel threatened.

As he relaxed in his soft chair one sensed he was happy with the world; there was no Sir Robin Day leering across at him, making his life miserable. Instead, there was the impressive figure of Miss Cartland, looking radiant and scarcely her eighty-four years. One suspected Terry liked to see her there; she was a woman of achievement, she would adorn *Wogan* with her talk and her talents; she was different from many of those jumped-up film and television personalities who often had so little to talk about.

Any woman who can write twenty-two books a year commands the greatest of respect. How did she look so well? Maybe it was the effect of her black false eyelashes? Whatever it was, she sat almost upright and looked across at Terry as though he was her own son. In fact, this was the woman who was once quoted as saying: 'My dear, I didn't want daughters at all. I wanted a wonderful son, and I'd have liked dozens of them. So when I married for the second time and when Ian was born it was the most exciting moment of my entire life.'

After Terry's opening remarks, she told him with typical conviction: 'I don't like modern novels very much, they are so dirty. But they'll change, they'll change. It's only a passing phase. It's going now; things are moving in America, trends are changing, all the girls are told to write like Barbara Cartland. They're all so sweet, never kissed.'

WOGAN: What qualities do you think a romantic hero should have – should the classic romantic hero still be tall, dark and handsome?

CARTLAND: He should be cynical and caddish until he meets the girl; he changes completely when he becomes her husband.

WOGAN: Do you still think they are looking for the type of man who treats them roughly in the beginning?

CARTLAND: What they are looking for is a *man*. Men have always wanted tender women. What we have got in America is the worst of the lot: these hard women, very raucous women, pushing men out of a job until they take his place. The minute you produce anyone sweet, soft and gentle-voiced the men fall over themselves; they think it is absolutely wonderful, because women should be women. It is a very ugly period, but it will pass. We shall get back to the phase which men have always wanted.

WOGAN: What rules would you lay down for a courtship

in 1986? I mean, it does tend to be a bit rough and ready
these days.

CARTLAND: Again, that is the women's fault. A man gives
you what you expect. If you ask him to be strong and
masculine and very loving, he is. Englishmen are wonderful
husbands, but not so much good lovers. There have always
been the French. I'm told the North American can make
love for three hours without repeating himself.

(*Laughter from audience, who have taken to Miss Cartland*)

WOGAN: Are we talking about sex, or are we talking about
all this arm-kissing stuff?

CARTLAND: We are talking about love. I hate the word sex
and I hate the word romance. Everybody wants love, real
love. But of course, you want the frills with it, the flowers.
You want the people to say: 'Darling, I love you.'

WOGAN: But for how long? Is it during the first flush of
marriage or the first date? I mean, after twenty-five years of
marriage . . .

CARTLAND: A man needs a woman who is in love with
him. If she loses him it's her own fault. In America women
are so busy – I see it all the time. A reporter was interviewing
me the other day and told me privately: 'I got engaged to
be married and she said she must have a career where she
needn't have children and where she can keep to her career.'
I said to him: 'Don't marry her, drop her, she is bad news.'
I'd say that to all men who go out with women like that:
they're no use, they are not going to make a wife and a
home and they're not going to be warm. If they want a
career, what do they want the men for?

WOGAN: You are saying that all men are romantic at heart?

CARTLAND: They can be if you make them.

WOGAN: Force them into it?

CARTLAND: Not force them into it. Coax them.

WOGAN: It seems to have worked very successfully for
you, particularly commercially. But money doesn't mean
anything to you?

CARTLAND: It isn't a question of money. I've always
wanted to help people. I've tried many different ways of

doing it. I know I am helping people. I give them beauty and I give them love.

WOGAN: Barbara Cartland, it has been lovely to talk to you.

Talking to Barbara Cartland was obviously a joy for Terry, akin to talking to his own mother. His next guest also promised to be fun for the audience and *Wogan* viewers; unlike Miss Cartland, she was better known as a sex symbol. She was Eva Gabor, one of the famous Gabor sisters. Everyone knows that Zsa Zsa Gabor has gone through seven husbands and a score of lovers, mainly millionaires. Their mother's promise that 'You will all be rich, famous and marry kings' has been only two-thirds fulfilled but that steely Hungarian lady taught them to survive. If Zsa Zsa has filled more gossip columns, both her sisters Magda and Eva have had their moments.

Terry introduced Eva as 'an infusion of real Hollywood glamour, sister of Zsa Zsa and Magda'. Eva was greeted by prolonged applause. She has a sunny disposition, shapely legs and glittering eyes.

WOGAN: It's a pity you didn't bring your sisters with you.

GABOR: It is a pity, I agree. I think, though, the three of us would be a bit too much for you.

Terry pulled a wistful face and gave the impression that Miss Gabor might even be right.

WOGAN: You all talk the same – in broken English. (*He tries to imitate her accent, which has a hint of European in it.*)

GABOR: No, no we don't have broken English accents. No, we just have American accents.

WOGAN: You have a British accent?

GABOR: I haven't got an accent. (*Short pause*) Irish, aren't you?

WOGAN: Yes.

GABOR: There you go. You have a strong Irish accent.

WOGAN: I don't talk in broken Engish.

GABOR: Nor do I.

The accent on accents had grown tiresome. Terry changed the topic of conversation not a minute too soon.

WOOGAN: You lookk absolutely wonderful, just as you did in *Green Acres*.

GABOR: God knows, I try.

WOGAN: It's not that hard.

GABOR: I would like just to be a plain actress, I really would; to do a play in England is my lifelong ambition. But I've become established in America as a glamorous actress. We have to do a lot in the morning to make ourselves glamorous. I mean, our hair, our –

WOGAN: I never take off my make-up! It's not hard for you to cope with the passage of years.

GABOR: (*Aggrieved*) I don't find them passing. I find them more interesting. You see, darling, there are two possibilities in this world – you either die or you grow old; and the question is which one you will choose.

WOGAN: But you're never allowed to grow old in America, are you?

GABOR: Not really. You see, in show business you have always to be beautiful.

WOGAN: It doesn't get harder as you get older, does it?

GABOR: Beauty really comes from within anyway. Where did you get that Irish charm?

WOGAN: (*Avoiding a straight answer*) But you said you wanted to bee a plain actress. You mean you would have been happier that way?

GABOR: That's very easy. I just take my make-up off.

Miss Gabor looked disappointed that Terry had not been taking her artistic achievements more seriously. She reminded him that she had studied Shakespearean drama and once got an offer to play in *A Midsummer-Night's Dream*, but lost the audition because of her Hungarian accent, which interfered with her reading for the part.)

WOGAN: The end of Shakespeare for you?

GABOR: Unfortunately.

WOGAN: You did work with Noël Coward?

GABOR: The master! I did one of his plays, *Present Laughter*, with him on Broadway. It was an incredible joy.

Proudly she reminisced about her meetings with Laurence Olivier and Laurence Harvey.

GABOR: I was overwhelmed by Olivier.

WOGAN: (*Suddenly changing the subject*) How many times have you been married?

GABOR: How many times have *you* being married?

WOGAN: Only once.

GABOR: Look up my biography. That is all you are going to get from me.

Time was up. Eva is an amusing woman, but not as witty as her more famous sister Zsa Zsa, who remains the true legend of the family Gabor.

Later in the year, when Terry invited Zsa Zsa on the show it proved fun, with the screen goddess living up to her reputation. Introducing her as 'somebody who believes in marriage and to prove it has celebrated her nuptials with eight, or possibly, nine men', Terry told his audience that Zsa Zsa had interrupted her honeymoon to be on *Wogan*. There was loud applause as she took her seat and Terry called her the 'great romantic'.

WOGAN: You are very welcome.

ZSA ZSA: Thank you, darling. I am very happy to be here.

WOGAN: Your eighth marriage?

ZSA ZSA: Don't talk about husbands, it is so boring.

WOGAN: You can't find it all that boring, you –

ZSA ZSA: I am married because I am a very moral person and if you are moral you can't sleep with a man unless you're married to him, so I married and I sleep with them and when I've enough of them I leave.

The audience showed their appreciation of the vivacious Miss Gabor.

WOGAN: You got a lot of female support for that.

ZSA ZSA: After two years marriage gets very wobbly because sexual attraction only lasts two years.

WOGAN: Only two years! Will this marriage last?

ZSA ZSA: How can you tell? Has yours lasted?

WOGAN: Twenty-one years.

ZSA ZSA: Oh my God, how can you stand it!

WOGAN: That's a question you should really ask my wife.

ZSA ZSA: To be serious, the biggest luck in the world is to have a marriage that will last.

WOGAN: It's not your fault then? You are not difficult to live with?

ZSA ZSA: I really am a very good housewife. I cook, I love my animals. If a man is unfaithful, I don't want him, let him go to the other woman. Who needs him?

WOGAN: You have never been unfaithful, yourself?

ZSA ZSA: (*Laughing*) I have been, just once. I couldn't resist him!

WOGAN: But you are a woman of strong will, you can fight these things if you want to?

ZSA ZSA: I don't fight things. I am a very hard-working woman. I make much money and men like women who make much money. I've a couple of houses, dogs, horses, a husband; in two or three years I'm alone for a couple of years and then married again.

WOGAN: It must make your present husband very nervous?

ZSA ZSA: Yes, it does. (*Laughing gaily*) He is German, he is a prince and five years ago he decided he would marry me without knowing me.

WOGAN: It's true you wanted your horse to be the best man?

ZSA ZSA: Yes, I wanted him because he is the best man.

WOGAN: This does make it very tough on your present husband?

ZSA ZSA: Why, he likes the horse, too!

The theatre again rocked with laughter.

WOGAN: If the horse is the best man where does that leave your husband?

ZSA ZSA: You can't compare a man with a horse, can you?

At this point she talked about her movie-making in Berlin.

Afterwards, Terry remarked rather quietly: 'You remain a child bride, don't you?'

ZSA ZSA: I'm very naive because I believe that everybody tells the truth; actually nobody tells the truth. Do *you* tell the truth?

WOGAN: I tell the truth.

ZSA ZSA: You have such gorgeous green eyes.

WOGAN: Thank you.

ZSA ZSA: How many children have you?

WOGAN: Three.

ZSA ZSA: Wonderful.

WOGAN: It wasn't easy!

She continued to talk about her exploits in Germany and said she had slept in Hitler's bed. The audience were not quite sure whether to believe her. She went on to refer to one of her late husbands, George Sanders.

WOGAN: George Sanders! He was the great love of your life?

ZSA ZSA: Yeah, I loved him. George was wonderful.

WOGAN: Where is he on the list with the horse?

ZSA ZSA: (*Surprised by the question*) You cannot compare George Saunders with a horse. He was an intellectual, a wonderful, wonderful person.

WOGAN: Perhaps you should be careful of speaking about your past husbands with your present husband watching this programme?

ZSA ZSA: I suppose you're right. My present husband is very, very nice, but George killed himself, which I can never forgive him for doing. No intelligent man should ever kill himself.

WOGAN: You're an incurable romantic?

ZSA ZSA: Yes, thank God. You have to be a romantic to survive the world.

17   *Out of Tune*

The studio orchestra in the Television Theatre played *Happy Birthday to You*, and the audience applauded. It was a Monday in February 1986, a special occasion in the life of Britain's most successful chat show. *Wogan* was celebrating its first birthday. Nothing must spoil the fun.

A large birthday cake was wheeled in on a trolley by two pretty stars of *Eastenders*, and the show was soon off to a rousing start. Terry, looking in the pink, had survived the year's ordeal and was now eager to get on with the show. To the girls from *Eastenders* he talked about the sensational success of the series.

After the preliminaries, Terry introduced Elton John, who was got up in a colourful cowboy outfit and looked right out of a Clint Eastwood movie. It was a nice touch by the *Wogan* production team, for exactly a year before Elton was a guest on *Wogan* and Terry slipped and nearly fell on his face. He survived that with a shrug and a smile, like he had done when the press accused the BBC of over-exposing him.

Elton told all and sundry that 'he had just arrived from Phoenix, Arizona'. He enthused about his new single 'Cry to Heaven' and proceeded to sit at the grand piano and sing the song to his own accompaniment. The evening was living up to expectations.

ELTON: I dressed up for you tonight. I've even got frilly underwear.

WOGAN: (Handing him a slice of birthday cake on a plate) When you made that appearance on *Wogan* it was a help to your career?

ELTON: Oh, it was.

WOGAN: (*Pulling a face*) My own career took a major step backwards. (*A film clip of Terry's undignified stumble a year ago is screened*)

Afterwards, Elton handed Terry a memento in the form of a large banana to celebrate the show's birthday).

WOGAN: I shall wear it always. The old banana-skin, nobody deserves it more.

Elton had endeared himself to the audience. He is the type of person Terry likes as guest on *Wogan* – he is forthcoming and good-humoured. When James Galway eased himself into a chair opposite Terry he was made thoroughly welcome by the audience. Armed with his 18–carat gold flute, the popular Irish-born virtuoso seemed the ideal personality for the birthday celebrations. Backed by the orchestra, the flautist proceeded to play a lively polka on his instrument.

WOGAN: You must be feeling exhausted. You have just flown in from Zurich?

GALWAY: Yes.

WOGAN: A jet-setter?

GALWAY: (*Sarcastically*) It's difficult to travel any other way these days. Walking and all that takes a lot of time.

WOGAN: Particularly carrying the heavy old flute around.

GALWAY: That's the least of my problems carrying the flute around.

WOGAN: It's a good job you don't play the harp, isn't it?

There was no response from the audience. The questions seemed as forced as the answers.

WOGAN: With all this jet-setting, do you go back to Northern Ireland a lot?

GALWAY: (*Curtly*) No . . . next question.

Curious applause. It lacked spontaneity. Was something wrong?

GALWAY: I go back occasionally.

WOGAN: They don't want me back in Dublin either.

At that moment, Terry looked uncomfortable, which

seemed extraordinary: Both are extrovert Irishmen with the gift of the gab.

WOGAN: What about the old home roots? Do you keep the old roots of your working-class background?

GALWAY: (*Looking as though he had wandered into the wrong chat show*) Sure, sure. Every time I have a free day in Switzerland I leave the place and rush back to the working class; then when I have had enough of that I fly back to Switzerland again.

WOGAN: (*Ignoring Galway's rudeness*) You prefer the old champagne life – who wouldn't?

GALWAY: (*Forcibly*) No, I do not. I prefer to be myself, to do the things I like doing, the things I grew up doing, like playing the flute and sitting around and talking. Being myself. I don't prefer the champagne set, as you call it.

WOGAN: You don't like being called a flautist anyway?

GALWAY: (*Sighs*) Call me whatever you like but not too early in the morning.

As though to break the ice, Terry offered Galway a slice of the birthday cake.

GALWAY: No, thank you. I had dinner before I came out.

WOGAN: (*Taken aback*) Did you? It's a very delicious dessert. It's not a bad piece of cake.

GALWAY: (*Relenting*) OK, slice a bit for me.

WOGAN: (*Slicing the cake*) You never actually studied music or the flute in the musical way, as it were? You weren't a theorist about it?

GALWAY: You don't have to be a theorist. You just have to be a practical musician. Teachers need to know everything about theory, but musicians like us – we need to know how to do it.

WOGAN: I mean, when you auditioned for the Berlin Philharmonic –

GALWAY: They don't ask you to harmonise 'God Save the King' –

WOGAN: It was tough auditioning for Herbert von Karajan?

GALWAY: It was. (*Impatiently*) Don't ask me to tell that

story. Everybody has been sleeping on it for the past twenty years.

WOGAN: I haven't. I mustn't have seen all your interviews then.

GALWAY: Have some cake?

WOGAN: Well, you do play all kinds of music, don't you?

GALWAY: Yes.

The audience seemed bewildered. The interview wasn't going anywhere.

WOGAN: (*Pointedly*) You're a bit of a rebel, aren't you?

GALWAY: Don't let me interrupt your supper.

WOGAN: It's all right for you, you had your dinner.

GALWAY: No, you're wrong. I had a vitamin pill and a banana.

WOGAN: (Persuasively) Eat a bit of cake.

GALWAY: It's not good for playing the flute. I have to play the flute at the Festival Hall in half an hour.

WOGAN: You managed to cross the boundary that exists between the classical and the popular, haven't you?

GALWAY: Yes, it does exist unfortunately. But we have managed to cross it.

WOGAN: How have you managed?

GALWAY: I grew up in a society where people played all sorts of music. Growing up in my time, Bing Crosby was still a hit and we learned all these songs by Crosby and Sinatra, and I also played in a flute band and we learned all these marches. I played in the local philharmonic, so I learned 'The Dream of Gerontius', so by the time I was in the Royal College of Music I knew all these different kinds of music. Some people in the college thought there was only one kind of music – classical.

WOGAN: Where you come from there were a lot of musicians, a lot of flute players?

GALWAY: (*More responsive now*) Yes, you can say that again.

WOGAN: How did you manage to rise above them?

GALWAY: I suppose I practised more than they did.

WOGAN: How much practice did you put in as a boy?

GALWAY: I used to play the flute all the time. I thought there was nothing else in life to do.

WOGAN: (*More comfortable now, over the worst*) Have you a favourite piece of music?

GALWAY: It's very hard to say.

WOGAN: You did 'Annie's Song'. Was that a weight around your neck?

GALWAY: No, not at all. I think it was a very nice tune. The reason I made that record was for my former wife. I think it's a nice thing to dedicate something like that.

WOGAN: Now, you're going to make a record with the Chieftains?

GALWAY: Yes.

WOGAN: That's going to be completely different?

GALWAY: (*Sardonic laughter*) As they say in the BBC, it is going to be completely different.

WOGAN: Will you use the old tin whistle?

GALWAY: No, I'll use the old gold whistle.

At this point Terry picked up the gold flute and remarked: 'Made in Japan.'

WOGAN: Are you anywhere near hanging up the old flute?

GALWAY: (*Seriously*) I'm very near taking more time off to do projects that require more time.

WOGAN: Like composing?

GALWAY: (*Grinning to himself*) No, no.

WOGAN: You have done nearly everything that has been written for the flute, haven't you?

GALWAY: I have done a lot, but not nearly everything yet. I mean, projects like making videos, putting together certain types of shows for television.

WOGAN: I wish you luck.

It was painfully evident that Terry had caught James Galway in one of his more touchy moods; otherwise there was no easy explanation for the flautist's rudeness to his host. It is one of the hazards encountered by chat-show hosts: they can never be sure of their guests' response, no matter how superbly briefed they are by their producer or researcher.

Terry is quite aware of these hazards, the unexpected problems posed by difficult guests, the uneasiness, even embarrassment caused to a host by a supercilious or deliberately rude guest.

Most of the time Terry's professionalism and experience surmounts these difficulties; yet in the case of James Galway, he was made to look decidedly uncomfortable. But Terry quickly puts such moments out of his mind. A strained chat with James Galway did not upset him unduly. Ironically, three days after the Galway affair, the papers announced a new crown for Terry: he carried off a top television award for the eighth time, voted Favourite Male Personality in the annual *TV Times* awards. Terry said: I've found this award particularly gratifying because recently I have been the target of a fair amount of abuse.'

February turned out to be a month of awards for Terry, which was a welcome boost for his morale – and every television performer will tell you morale needs stimulating now and then. Terry again topped another opinion poll – as the man most women in Britain would like to spend St Valentine's Day with. (However, he was placed third in another list of people women would *least* like to spend the fourteenth of February with.) Men over forty figured prominently in the popularity stakes, with Cliff Richard and Clint Eastwood trailing just behind Terry.

Reports continued to circulate that soon *Wogan* would go five nights a week. Terry made it known that he had refused to consider such a likelihood because he feared being 'burned out'. He admitted that 'enough is enough', a direct reference to the thrice-weekly show, which he believed was what viewers wanted. And he warned that both his show and the hit soap opera *Eastenders* could be destroyed by the constant glare of publicity. BBC 1 boss Michael Grade hoped to see Terry (his 'favourite Irishman') on screen five nights a week as *Wogan* host, but Terry confessed: 'It would mean having to rethink the whole show, my number of appearances, my holidays, everything. If they use you as a battering ram, then even a battering ram gets blunted.'

18 *Ideal Blend*

The *Wogan* team recognise that to achieve the ideal blend of guests it is essential to have a mixture of national and international celebrities. This is difficult to achieve. A contrast is also sought between guests, for a preponderance of film starlets or egotistical authors plugging their works can lead to monotony. Terry admits that much depends on the calibre of his guests. During 1986 he was able to call on some entertaining celebrities.

There was Miss Jane Russell on Monday evening, March 3. Younger viewers may not have identified with the screen goddess, but an older generation must have welcomed the opportunity to hear her reminiscences. She was in London to launch her autobiography. In her time she was a famous Hollywood pin-up and when she made her first film, *The Outlaw*, she supposedly needed a cantilever bra.

At the luncheon at the Savoy it was hardly surprising that conversation turned to questions of cleavage. Asked about her so-called cantilever bra, Jane countered: 'The answer is simple. I didn't wear one. It wasn't right for the costume. It does get pretty boring talking about the bra forty years later.'

She was introduced on *Wogan* as a 'legend of the silver screen, a woman who became the American Forces pin-up in World War Two and in her time was considered one of the famous beauties in the world'. Terry raised his voice as he reminded his audience at Shepherd's Bush that Jane had been called the queen of the motionless pictures – all because of a movie nobody had seen. At this point a clip of *The*

Outlaw was shown. Afterwards, Terry enthused: 'Miss Russell went on to become one of Hollywood's biggest and most glamorous stars.'

The audience applauded. Obviously they love screen goddesses, anyone with genuine glamour. Jane took her seat. At sixty-four years of age, she looked a decade younger and was easily recognisable from her early films. The long, shapely legs were as beautiful-looking as ever, the chin still protruded and her keen eyes rested on a spot between Terry's nose and forehead. For the chat-show host it was part two of his theme song in praise of older women.

WOGAN: You are raring to go, aren't you?

JANE: Yes.

WOGAN: And you are looking marvellous.

JANE: Thank you.

She went on to say that she began her life story in 1976 with a ghost writer but it hadn't worked out, so she decided to finish the book herself.

WOGAN: I saw somewhere in the paper over the weekend that you are sick to death talking about *The Outlaw*.

JANE: I certainly am. Wouldn't you too be sick of it after forty years?

WOGAN: Would you like to forget all about it?

JANE: Yeah, I guess so.

WOGAN: Howard Hughes and all that? He was the director of the film.

JANE: Oh, no, I don't want to forget Howard Hughes.

WOGAN: But you are asked about him quite a lot, aren't you? What kind of furore did *The Outlaw* create?

JANE: I was pretty much divorced from it. Rumours were circulating about the film, but some of them were filtering back to me. It was said we were being preached about from the pulpit, condemned.

WOGAN: People were being told they would be excommunicated for watching the film?

JANE: Compared with today's movies, I think it is very tame.

WOGAN: Yes, I suppose by today's standards. (*Slight pause*) Did it bring you instant fame and riches?

JANE: (*Shrugs her shoulders*) Yeah, fifty dollars a week. I was under contract. I was making that kind of money.

WOGAN: I understand it was over two or three years before they released *The Outlaw*. Did you feel you had been used?

JANE: I was occupied doing publicity. I worked five days a week from nine to five.

WOGAN: Like you are doing publicising your book at the moment?

JANE: Well, I had been a model before that, Terry.

WOGAN: And, what about the great day when *The Outlaw* was premièred. Was that a relief to you? Had you forgotten you had made the movie by then?

JANE: Well, for a matter of fact we had never seen it. I remember I sneaked up the stairs to see the movie for the first time. I thought it was very slow and boring.

WOGAN: It was a very theatrical première, I mean, they hyped it up and made use of all the publicity?

JANE: We had to make an appearance on stage.

WOGAN: Had it helped you in Hollywood that the emphasis was put on your figure and your face rather than on your acting talent? Did you make any move to get over that, or could you?

JANE: No, you couldn't unless you went on suspension. You couldn't work elsewhere until the end of your contract.

WOGAN: Would it be better now if you were a major star? Do you, for instance, envy stars their freedom now to do what they want to do? Or do you think this freedom of contact has made movies any better?

JANE: It's better now, but it is very iffey, if you know what I mean. It depends on finding the right director and the right film and after that hope everything goes right for you. It is much more of a gamble today, I believe.

WOGAN: Has anybody offered you any good parts lately?

JANE: No, I did a little piece in a film, that's all.

WOGAN: Do you prefer working for television rather than working for the movies?

JANE: I prefer the cinema. At least you meet the director of the picture you're making.

WOGAN: *The Outlaw* was Howard Hughes' first movie. Was he difficult to take direction from?

JANE: It was nothing for him to film twenty-five or thirty takes, not because he had made a mistake, he just wanted another take; he ran them all later and then picked the one he liked. I suppose he really didn't know what he wanted.

WOGAN: Of course in later years he became extremely eccentric. Did you see any indication of that in those early days?

JANE: No, except that he was always very cautious – and I must say, very considerate.

WOGAN: Well, what do you think happened to him?

JANE: I don't know.

WOGAN: You worked with Marilyn Monroe, She was said to be very difficult to work with. Is that true?

JANE: She may have been later but not then. I do remember she worked very hard. I found her very co-operative, but she was a little nervous going onto the set. She was such a sweet girl. Myself, I think I was much more terrified going on the stage for the first time.

WOGAN: You worked with various heart-throbs. Mitchum was one. Did you ever feel nervous working with people like him?

JANE: I fell in love with all of them.

WOGAN: Did they know you had fallen in love with them?

JANE: They knew . . . (*Loud laughter. – The audience adored this woman of charm and grace*)

WOGAN: In those days in Hollywood I believe it was free and easy?

JANE: There was a family atmosphere, if that is what you mean? But there were bad boys, too, who got out of line.

Facing husky-voiced Miss Eartha Kitt on Friday evening, March 28, Terry must have wondered if he was in danger of being seduced. For Miss Kitt is no ordinary star. Her reputation has always been that of a strong, aggressive, dominant woman. As she says: 'I think most men who have come into my life are really looking for me to take care of them. Not emotionally but financially. I rebel against that.'

At fifty-six, Miss Kitt lives in New York – alone. She has always been outspoken and once paid the price. After she had criticised America's involvement in the Vietnam War, at a genteel ladies-only luncheon with First Lady, Lady Bird Johnson, in 1968, she found herself blacklisted, her career practically in ruins for the next ten years. She says she has no regrets, no bitterness or hatred for those wasted years. 'I really am by nature reckless: I live dangerously because I speak my mind.' In 1978, however, she returned to Broadway in triumph with the musical play *Timbuktu*, an all-black cast version of *Kismet*.

On *Wogan* she purred all over her host like a large black cat, wriggled her supple body provocatively in Terry's direction, extended all her charms, which are many and varied, and managed throughout the conversation to make everyone uncomfortable. For escape, Terry relied on the best weapon in his repertoire – the gift of the gab.

WOGAN: It is lovely to see you back.

KITT: Thank you.

WOGAN: Why don't we see more of you?

KITT: I've been everywhere. (*Audience laughter*)

WOGAN: You have to be careful of this audience.

The audience laughed again as Miss Kitt emitted some snarling sounds and then proceeded to place her feet on Terry's lap and wriggle her toes. Terry was obviously taken by surprise.

'My wife also likes her feet to be rubbed,' he essayed unsettled. In her low-necked tight-fitting dark dress Miss Kitt looked seductive and beautiful. Could Terry really withstand this powerful assault on his virtue?

TERRY: (*Rubbing her toes*) You are back making hit records again, aren't you?

KITT: What do you mean: '*I'm back making hit records?*'

WOGAN: For years we didn't hear anything of you.

KITT: What are you talking about?

WOGAN: (*Still rubbing her toes to keep her at bay*) You had a couple of big hits. Now you've got another one.

KITT: What are you talking about . . . the fifties . . . sixties . . . seventies . . . ?

WOGAN: Now you have hits in the eighties.

KITT: Isn't it wonderful?

The audience had by now taken to this unusual star. She looked capable of seducing a Roman Catholic bishop.

WOGAN: It's certainly wonderful, as you say. The stuff you're doing now is disco music. It's a different style from your usual records?

KITT: It's not different from anything I've ever done. I'm the same, it's the mechanics are different.

Miss Kitt tried unsuccessfully to recall the names of some of her songs, then when she failed she made some sexy sounds with her voice and the audience laughed hysterically.

KITT: You've not understood a thing I've said so far. What is your name?

WOGAN: I knew my name before you came on.

More laughter. The conversation was in danger of getting out of hand. Terry strove hard to reassert control. It wasn't easy.

WOGAN: Orson Welles said you were the world's most exciting woman. If he was alive today he would say you *are* the world's most exciting woman.

KITT: What do you think?

WOGAN: Who's conducting the interview? (*After a slight pause*) You only married once, though?

KITT: Once was enough.

WOGAN: You are picky about men?

KITT: I'm very choosy about friends. I'm choosy about people. I love people. I would prefer to be alone rather than around people who are trashy.

WOGAN: Do you frighten men?

KITT: You have to ask them. I'm asking you . . .

WOGAN: I think you frighten men.

Miss Kitt continued to wriggle her toes on Terry's lap. He had on option but to sit there and bear it.

WOGAN: My wife does that only because she wants her feet massaged, so if you don't mind, I'm quite practised at it. Do you think –

At that moment she leaned across and tried to plant a kiss on his cheek. To the audience and viewers it must have seemed like the moment of seduction had dramatically arrived. She was prepared to pounce, but at the last moment, as though instinctively, she held back with what appeared great difficulty. ·

WOGAN: (*Relieved that his virtue was still intact*) Do you feel there are any *real* men in Hollywood?

As she wriggled her toes on his lap, he tried to push her feet away. 'Down, down, down . . .' he exclaimed. But her feet remained there immovable.

KITT: (*Mischievously*) Do I think there are any real men left in Hollywood? It's very rare to find a man any more, that is why I'm looking at you.

WOGAN: Why did you leave Hollywood?

KITT: Nobody for me to play with.

WOGAN: What about the movies? Couldn't we have seen you in more movies?

KITT: Movies? I'm not black enough to be considered black and not white enough to be considered white and therefore I don't fit in anywhere. I want them to fit into me.

WOGAN: But you're not an easy woman to suit?

KITT: Is any woman easy to suit? Obviously this is why you men are having a lot of trouble.

WOGAN: You think aggressive women like you cause men like me to shrivel up?

KITT: At dawn?

WOGAN: Long before dawn. (*Sighs audibly*) Do you know, this has been one of the most unusual interviews I've ever – but I do thank you, Eartha Kitt.

19   *Terry's View*

Terry had by now convinced himself that television critics really served no useful function. 'I believe that the TV critic is really redundant,' he declared in one of his less whimsical moments. 'A theatre critic can help to boost or kill a show, but a TV critic passes judgment on a show that every viewer has already passed judgment on. An editor admitted to me recently that a TV critic's function is merely to confirm the viewers in their prejudices.'

But he did concede: 'You have to accept some criticism. With the popular papers here, you have no choice really. I don't want to give the impression that they are all wrong. In fact, until now I've had an easy ride because I was on the way up. Now that I've achieved this popularity, they want to knock me down.'

Terry aired his surprising viewpoint at an opportune time. There was much speculation about the forthcoming *Joan Rivers Show* due to be screened on BBC 2. The brash American chat-show hostess was coming with a formidable reputation from America to stir the calm waters on this side of the Atlantic.

There was the customary publicity hype. There was a danger that her no-holds-barred approach would put the Wogans, Hartys, O'Connors and Monkhouses in the shade. In other words, the chat show, as the British viewer knew it, might never be the same again. It seemed a good moment for the TV critics to sharpen their pens, despite Terry Wogan's declaration.

The opportunity to use them quickly arrived. The first

Joan Rivers show was generally regarded as a flop. On the morning after, Miss Rivers must have been dismayed by the critics' reaction. She cut no ice with the majority of them. It was also an opportunity for Herbert Kretzmer in the *Daily Mail* to reassure his readers that the TV critic was not redundant and that his views could still be a useful and an intelligent guide for the more thoughtful viewer.

Kretzmer expressed dismay at the Rivers show while at the same time taking a swipe at current chat shows in Britain: 'The television chat show as we used to know it is dead as vaudeville. Mike Parkinson was its last practitioner. Chat shows today have become little more than self-promotion exercises in publishing and marketing new films, plays and books. Nobody talks half-way seriously on these shows any more. When a wondrous speaker like Gore Vidal appeared on a British chat show not long ago, nobody knew what to do with him and Vidal was humiliatingly wasted.'

He argued that the Rivers show had been billed as potentially hard-hitting with the hostess intent on asking all the revealing, gutzy questions. 'What we got,' commented Kretzmer, 'was a fast, fizzy, glitzy US-style orgy of self-congratulation, with everybody kissing everybody else in a mass demo of feigned affection, and words like "fabulous" and "incredible" flying around like confetti in June. For much of the time, Rivers wasn't even talking to people in their own right, but to myths they invented. The show looked like the *Johnny Carson Show*, with a painted townscape in the background, and Rivers running things from a small desk off to one side. Occasionally, Rivers remembered she was famous for her cruel tongue. She threw in a couple of jibes at Joan Collins and Christine Onassis. Spontaneous wit was left to others.'

Undeniably, Kretzmer had made a valid point, yet it seemed illogical on his part to lump together all chat shows with the exception of Parkinson's (not showing at the time) and suggest they served as much purpose as bringing sand to the Sahara desert. True, some tended occasionally to be as shallow as their superficial guests, but more often than not they provided moments of enjoyment and entertainment. Not everyone found Michael Caine or John Huston boring, or for that matter, Wilbur Smith or Placido Domingo. To imply, as Kretzmer did, that Michael Parkinson was 'the last true chat-show practitioner' was to underrate the television art of Terry Wogan, Michael Aspel, Des O'Connor and Clive James.

Parkinson has always preferred what he calls 'the one-man show'. As he explains: 'In all the years I was doing my BBC show, the ones I enjoyed the most were those that had just one star guest. British TV has more chat shows than London has Chinese restaurants. But most have the traditional boring mix of several guests plugging their books or films.'

So the argument continued. Terry Wogan is the only host doing a thrice-weekly live chat show and he would have it no other way. As he confirms: 'I like doing a live, spontaneous and risky chat show. I prefer television with the crusts on.' The Parkinson type show does not greatly appeal to him, lacking as it does the spontaneity of a *Wogan* – and the topicality.

Russell Harty has expressed surprise that the chat show invites such 'vigorous response'. Harty seemed to be echoing Terry Wogan's view that people read too much into chat shows. He puts them in the light entertainment bracket and therefore expects the critics to judge them solely from that vantage point. However, he is careful to add: 'There's space for in-depth conversations, which we can do when we get someone big enough – like Princess Anne, Michael Crawford or Larry Hagman – but the chat show is basically trivial and light-hearted. That's what it's all about. It should be like a daily radio programme, where people get the habit of watching and one day blends into the next.'

If one accepts that chat shows are 'disposable', even trivial, then it is wise to consider the opinions of Frances Whitaker, the woman who first steered *Wogan* into the top ratings. She has no illusions about such shows. 'Accusations of triviality don't worry me,' she says. 'because there's an answer: it *is* trivial. That's the whole essence of a chat show. We're making disposable television.'

Making comparisons, for instance, between chat shows does not seem a logical exercise. *Wogan*, the only live show of its kind on British television and the only thrice-weekly show hardly invites comparisons with any other chat show. When Terry first began *Wogan*, he made it clear that it would be different from the Parkinson show. 'I am different,' he asserted. 'Parkinson interviews. What I want is conversation. He is a journalist by training. I've no journalistic training. I shall act more as a catalyst and not give my guests a hard ride. I'd like to get them away from their routine, which they've done for everyone else.'

It hasn't been easy. While there is a queue of stars and celebrities who want to be guests on *Wogan* – most of them wanting to plug something or other – Terry has been firm. Authors seldom, if ever, are permitted to display their latest books on *Wogan*, There have been behind-the-scenes rows with film producers because Terry did not permit certain film clips to be shown to publicise new films.

But he continues to attract the TV critics and he is seldom out of their columns. 'Wogan teeters on a tightrope between good-natured mockery and arrogant self-indulgence,' commented a Sunday newspaper, and added: 'Terry takes more limelight than the guests.' Probably this is what the Wogan show is all about. Often he is more interesting than his guests.

Clive James, a witty and popular television presenter, and a one-time TV critic has argued that 'one of the effects of television is to make front-men over-mighty. It follows that one of the tasks of television criticism should be to remind them they are mortal.'

Terry has repeatedly reminded the world that he is 'mortal' and does not crave 'immortality'. He swears he has never had any serious pretensions to be Director-General of the BBC, or Prime Minister. He is happy in his chat-show hot seat, satisfied that he cannot be loved by all the people in all the world. 'Popularity on television is a paradox,' he claims. 'The more some people like you, the more others hate you.' He has been accused of underselling *Wogan*, even his own role as host of the show. At times Terry feels trapped in a net of his own making. While it is important that *Wogan* is never ignored by the media, it can be detrimental perhaps when the show attracts coverage for the wrong reasons. Clive James doubts, for example, the power of the TV critic, but he sees the critic as 'influential'. It is hard to say, however, with any accuracy how influential for television itself is more influenced by programme ratings.

When Michael Parkinson was once asked why he hadn't settled in America and made a career there in television, he replied frankly: 'I found it too competitive and ratings-conscious. It was not fun. They used to sit there having suicide pacts over the ratings. It was not for me.'

One also imagines that when the fun goes out of television in Britain for Terry Wogan he may choose a different road. He is undoubtedly a performer who must enjoy what he is doing (his breakfast radio show is an example), otherwise he may find the whole thing monotonous. Like everyone else, he keeps an eye on the programme ratings, but he is not obsessed by them like some other performers. In others, for instance, a drop in ratings tends to cause a sense of panic. Terry has not experienced such an extreme emotion as yet with *Wogan*.

Anyway, he doesn't like to dwell for long on ratings. He prefers to get on with his show. An optimist, he argues that it is futile to worry about ratings, although he is realist enough to know that they cannot be ignored. Criticism, yes, ratings, no. He knows the viewing figures for *Wogan* like a banker knows how much cash he has received at the counter.

So the chat show 'creates a chummy conspiracy between host, guest and studio audience which helps disguise the emptiness of the programme's content . . .' Terry sighs when he tries to read on. 'Is there no end to the philosophising about the poor old chat show?' he asks himself wistfully in moments of quiet desperation in his dressing-room at the TV Theatre Shepherd's Bush Green. He could be forgiven for thinking that there is from time to time a conspiracy to unseat him and dump him in the River Thames.

'You'd think I was trying to be a Sir Robin Day,' he yawns aloud, as he lights another impressive cigar. On reflection, he says: 'I'm out there trying to bring a bit of brightness into people's ordinary lives. Do they want me instead to talk about Proust and Plato?' A look of impatience shrouds his smooth face but quickly the smile appears, his own panacea for the tribulations that occasionally assail him. The gift of the gab, smiles – these help to keep Michael Terence Wogan sane, insulating his glitzy world, becoming an inseparable part of his armour.

He looked relaxed on the evening of April 28 as he prepared to talk to best-selling author Maeve Binchy, his guest on *Wogan*. It was a relief for him to distance himself from critics and philosophers, to be back in his beloved theatre in Shepherd's Bush Green, surrounded by a friendly audience who knew him as 'Terry'. He told them he had just returned from a holiday in Spain. Looking suntanned, he bounced onto the set wearing a large sombrero and singing a parody of the song *Viva España*. He was in a lively mood and did not seem to mind that Miss Binchy was on the show to promote her book *Echoes*. One suspected she was there primarily because she's a friend of Terry's, also because she happens to be a good storyteller and genuine person.

WOGAN: You have become accomplished at this kind of thing, the old chat show?

MAEVE: No, I'm as nervous as a cat, as you well know. You and I haven't talked before we came on the show so I don't know what you're going to ask me. I can't bear a silence in a conversation; that's what thunder is about because nature abhors a vacuum.

WOGAN: I couldn't imagine you being lost for words.

MAEVE: Like yourself, Terry, I've never really found it

hard to find a word, it's finding the right word is the problem.

WOGAN: As you were saying about the Irish – I found this difference between the two races when I came to work in Britain; I mean, you'd go to a dinner party here and find the English were quite content to say nothing. I gabble. I am embarrassed by silence.

MAEVE: That is what has you where you are –

WOGAN: Because I'm permanently embarrassed!

MAEVE: Because you're able to keep talking.

WOGAN: Your tour took you around Britain – and Scotland?

MAEVE: You remember when you did the radio show for the BBC and you had these fantasies – cattle grazing on the roof . . . I think there is something mysterious happening on Radio Scotland because when I went there a nice lady came in and said: 'You mustn't mind us, we're all wearing helmets.' I asked her why and she answered: 'The ceiling isn't too secure'. There they were, wearing yellow, green and purple helmets. So I asked if I could have a helmet and they refused because they said when the ceiling fell it was going to fall slowly. Think about that! What kind of docile people would they have working for the BBC that would sit there with helmets on? (*Laughter from audience*)

Maeve talked at such a fast pace that she was in danger of a verbal collision with Terry. For some inexplicable reason, the chat between the pair fell slightly flat. Perhaps Terry was too intent on keeping to *Echoes* instead of inviting Maeve to tell some of her Irish stories. Furthermore, Miss Binchy, seemed uncharacteristically nervous in the hot seat opposite her host, something her friends would find hard to understand.

Soap opera stars continued to drift in and out of Terry's show. The star who followed Maeve Binchy that evening was the actor Ken Kercheval, who plays Cliff Barnes, arch rival of the scheming JR, in *Dallas*. Cliff was in England to have his marriage blessed in the Norman Church of Orston, Notts. Two weeks before he had been married in California.

WOGAN: What is it like playing the perpetual loser?

KERCHEVAL: Ha, ha, ha.

WOGAN: It's no reflection on yourself. You're an actor.

KERCHEVAL: (*Smiling*) I take exception to that. From my point of view Cliff Barnes loses but is not a loser. He always comes back.

WOGAN: He gets the seven bells knocked out of him by JR.

KERCHEVAL: But he forever stands up and starts all over again.

WOGAN: How do you feel about the character? Do you like him?

KERCHEVAL: I have to like him.

WOGAN: He's hard to like. You get fed up with him?

KERCHEVAL: I am really obligated to liking him because if I didn't like him or find a way for him to have continued enthusiasm about his attempts to get JR, the audience wouldn't believe him.

WOGAN: Cliff seems to me the most highly strung of the whole crowd; he is always bursting into tears. Is that you or is that the part?

KERCHEVAL: I am very cool. (*Laughter from audience*)

WOGAN: Have you based the character on anyone in real life?

KERCHEVAL: No, no.

One felt that Terry wasn't taking the character of Cliff Barnes seriously; if anything, he was sending up Cliff and the soap opera itself. As they went on to chat about more characters in *Dallas* and the killing-off of certain characters, the conversation was curiously dull and lacked credibility. Perhaps it was because they weren't actually dealing with real people, but soap opera characters. The irony of the thing was that actor Kercheval projected a pleasant personality and obviously believed that as Cliff Barnes he was fulfilling a useful function.

20   Vadim's Women

Roger Vadim, the film director, has been described as the world's greatest lover. His conquests include Brigitte Bardot, Catherine Deneuve, Jane Fonda, Annette Stroyberg and Catherine Schneider, but there were numerous other beauties, among them Leslie Caron. In early May 1986, Vadim was back in England doing the radio and television chat-show rounds, promoting his new book *Bardot, Deneuve and Fonda*. It was already revealed that the three stars (his ex-wives) were preparing to sue him for invasion of privacy.

At fifty-eight, Vadim is shrewd and urbane, and from a cold exterior projects charm and confidence. He is more famous today for the women he loved (and lost) than for his film achievements. His most notable love affair involved Brigitte Bardot who was only fifteen years of age when they first met, but was reputed to 'be very sexually aware'.

Vadim seemed the near-perfect guest for *Wogan* on the evening of Monday, May 5. It mattered little, it seemed, to the film director that he was being labelled 'vain and heartless' for writing about the intimate details of his marriages. Terry was prepared for the world's great lover. Fresh from his brief visit to Norway for the Eurovision Song Contest, which he presented for the BBC, he looked eager for the task.

After some initial small-talk about wines, Terry asked his guest calmly: 'Why did you write this kiss-and-tell book? There are people who'll say it's not a gallant thing to have done?

VADIM: Do you know there are a lot of books written by

women about their ex-lovers and husbands, and everybody finds that charming and a perfect thing to do. Therefore, why shouldn't men be allowed to do the same thing? Why is it considered ungallant when a man writes about his women?

WOGAN: (*To the audience*) I think he got out of that rather well. We are talking about Vadim as a husband rather than as an individual. Haven't you been swamped by the reputation of your wives?

VADIM: Actually, I do not like to live with stars. It's something I would not wish on my best friends. It's more important for me to live with a very interesting woman before she becomes a star. That's a fascinating and interesting experience and in my case I don't regret it. And I wanted people to share that experience with me, so that is why I write my book. I'm not selfish.

WOGAN: What about the accusation that you exploited these women on film and now you are going to exploit them in your book?

VADIM: I think they exploited me.

The audience laughed derisively. Terry pulled a face and appeared amazed by Vadim's remark.

VADIM: They were pleased and delighted with their successes. Nobody exploited them. They were free agents. I just helped them in their film careers. If I had a contract with them it might have been different. I would have taken a percentage. The only thing I did was to help them to become famous.

WOGAN: At least two of your ex-wives, Brigitte Bardot and Catherine Deneuve, say they are going to sue you in the courts.

Vadim seemed to turn the tables on Terry by telling him that he sent presents to his ex-wives and they still loved him.

VADIM: I do not know if they are looking for publicity or not. It's a nice pleasant book for them. I talk with respect and tenderness about them. Everyone who has read my book thinks it's charming and fair.

WOGAN: There's no hint of pique there because they all left you in the end?

VADIM: If you read the book – and one of the reasons I wrote my book is that people will read it – you will see that each case is different, each marriage is different.

Terry must have been strongly tempted to quote from the book, particularly Vadim's passages involving Brigitte Bardot and the alarming attitude of her parents to their relationship. But one presumes that a fear of possible libel and a determination to preserve good taste kept him out of the Joan Rivers television territory. From the audience point of view, and presumably that of the viewers as well, it was an entertaining *Wogan*.

Some newspaper and magazine reviewers of Vadim's book showed less restraint. When Vadim appeared on Gay Byrne's *Late, Late Show* on Irish television he was verbally mauled; he looked exceedingly vulnerable, displaying little of the composure he brought to *Wogan*. One irate woman, who took exception to his conquests, called him an unmentionable name. The whole thing made for rather hysterical television.

The *Wogan* team's reluctance to use Vadim's book on the show was well justified on libel grounds. Some months later, Roger Vadim was ordered to pay damages to Brigitte Bardot and Catherine Deneuve for revealing details about his love life with the two stars. The actresses each received £6,500, paid jointly by Vadim and the publisher. But the Paris court refused to order him to cut the offending passages from his memoirs.

Two nights later, Wednesday, May 7, Terry welcomed Bob Geldof, whose autobiography had just reached the bookshops. Looking less scruffy than usual, Bob received a particularly warm welcome from the audience, not so much for his book but rather for his achievements in the humanitarian sphere. Terry left no doubt in anyone's mind that he, too, admired his fellow Irishman for the same reason.

Curiously, Bob's book hardly received a mention. Most of

the time was devoted to talking about Sport Aid, yet another
charitable exercise to get aid for the hungry in the Third
World. It was a world-wide venture and Bob pointed on a
large map to the different world centres involved. Since he
had introduced Live Aid to a weary world, Bob Geldof had
grown in stature; he was now more sophisticated, more
confident, and aware of his own influence, which had grown
immensely. It didn't matter to Terry that Bob had been
labelled 'enigmatic' and even now 'contemptuous' in some
respects of Ireland itself.

This evening Terry was helping Bob to promote Sport
Aid and he knew that such a gesture was good for *Wogan;*
promoting the right product could do nothing but enhance
the show and make it meaningful.

WOGAN: Is it deliberate affectation with you to
underdress?

GELDOF: It is totally deliberate.

WOGAN: Millions of people saw that famine aid
programme on television, but why you? Did you ever ask
yourself why it was you who were selected to help famine
relief?

GELDOF: There were lots of things. I think time and events
conspired to make it more easy for me.

WOGAN: Did you ask yourself – why me?

GELDOF: Yes, at times in the middle of Live Aid I'd be
awake at night and wondering. But I can distance myself
from myself quite easily. It seemed at the time that events
were happening within my control but outside of myself.
At points like that you are thinking, 'What is going on here?'
I remember there was a piece in *Life* Magazine at Christmas
about Live Aid and they asked, like you: 'Why Bob Geldof?'

Geldof laughed as he recalled the magazine's attitude: 'I
think they presumed that some fallible god had come down
from heaven to find somebody who would help and
knocked on the wrong door and this guy in his shoes answered the door and they asked who is he, what will he do?
That was their attitude.'

WOGAN: Do you think it was an intervention, a deity or anything like that?

GELDOF: No. It was not glamorous. It is not that glorious a thing. It is something I wanted to do and I thought I would raise £72,000, but as you know the whole thing grew and grew. I just stayed with it, mainly because I wanted every penny to get there to help these starving people. So it grew to millions of dollars and I'm still there with it.

WOGAN: So it's now Sport Aid. People are prepared to give, but how much money? Is it really a bottomless pit?

GELDOF: Yes and no. The interesting thing is that Food Aid and things like that are still going strong long after the television pictures have been forgotten. It means that people care and not only care, they care for long periods of time. It means that they are not merely crisis-orientated or only give when they see these terrible pictures on the screen.

WOGAN: I thought you could go to the well once too often, but as you say that doesn't appear to be so.

GELDOF: This must frighten a lot of politicians. The main reason for Sport Aid is not so much the money, though that's crucial, but to focus attention on the General Assembly of the UN who, on the day after the big race, debate the crisis on the continent of Africa. On this occasion they must listen to the voice of the people who are demanding that something coherent must be done to aid these people.

Bob Geldof's eloquent appeal was well received by the theatre audience who seemed to identify with his sincere efforts to get things moving. 'A genuine guy' one could almost hear them whisper.

WOGAN: You want everyone to run in the race, right across the world?

GELDOF: We want to get everyone going. We want to get people to show they do care that these poor people are not going to be allowed to die miserably.

Pushing Sport Aid did not seem so much a plug as a worthy exercise in charity.

21 'Emotional'

Terry felt emotional. He made no secret of the fact to his audience in the TV Theatre at Shepherd's Bush Green on the evening of Friday, May 31. 'Yes,' he said softly, 'I must confess that I am feeling a little emotional on this unique occasion for the show. For tonight we are celebrating 201 *Wogan*s. He was generously applauded.

'It has been a long haul for me,' he continued, 'the boy from the Shannon. I knew that holding the door for Pete Murray would further my career. I've sat here conversing with them all – heads of state, royalty, ambassadors – Jimmy Young! I've known them all and that is why I'm feeling a little emotional. Bob Monkhouse taught me how to fake sincerity. And throughout it all there has been you . . . the audience . . . and you . . . the viewers . . . and after 201 shows you are all still here, my loyal viewers, sweet-smelling, devoted followers.'

Terry said he was pleased to introduce a star who rarely gave interviews 'and I don't know why he bothered giving one here. He has conquered America, has done some great movies like *Murder on the Orient Express*, all brought to light by his brilliant acting. Ladies and gentlemen, Albert Finney.'

Finney had just celebrated his fiftieth birthday. He was reputed to be worth ten million dollars. When queried about the figure, he joked: 'Make that twenty million if you like, although I would say ten million was rather high myself.' The fact of course is that he owns race-horse winners bred in Kentucky. Not surprisingly, 'he is in the amiable habit of forgetting fame and enjoying himself for a while.'

He once recalled: 'Growing up in Salford you didn't see too many horses, and when you did, they were pulling carts.' Since the summer of 1954, when he did his first professional job on stage, he has emerged as one of Britain's most celebrated actors both in film and on stage. At this time he was appearing in *Orphans* in the West End. Although he can be prickly at times (he didn't get on in rehearsals once with Samuel Beckett) he is, however, unpretentious and good-humoured. He has the strong presence that is synonymous with stardom. He smiled as he took his seat opposite Terry. The day before he had been playing charity golf with the host, as was another guest to come that evening, Terry Savalas.

FINNEY: 201 . . . and you look great!

WOGAN: There's scarcely a wrinkle there (*He pulls a grateful face that reveals no trace of a wrinkle*) Did you enjoy the golf outing the other day?

FINNEY: I didn't play well. I announced before the first tee that my game would be indifferent.

WOGAN: We have played golf together, haven't we?

FINNEY: You only mention it because you defeated me.

WOGAN: You're back at work in the West End?

FINNEY: Yes, I am.

WOGAN: You're not a man who works very hard, are you?

FINNEY: (*Surprised by the question*) I beg your pardon!

WOGAN: You're given to the sabbatical, aren't you?

FINNEY: I love the sabbatical. It's very important for me to get away from it all; afterwards I have a burst of work for two or three months. After that again I like to go off.

WOGAN: It has happened during your career that every-body is clamouring for you and off you go to the Amazon.

FINNEY: I like that. I think they are actually quite relieved when I do go off!

WOGAN: But what about the insecurity of the actor? You must be very self-confident to be able to turn your back on work.

FINNEY: If I was in a secure job I wouldn't be doing this,

would I? I'd be doing your job. (*Burst of laughter from audience*)

WOGAN: Do you ever feel that when you come back there'll be no work for you?

FINNEY: Sometimes there isn't any work.

WOGAN: What about this play you're involved in at the moment?

FINNEY: It's terrific. It was a play I first saw in New York last September and I was bowled over by it. I knew straight away I wanted to do it. The Americans were flattered. I remember them saying: 'Albert wants to do the play in London. How marvellous for us.' The play has done a lot for me. Now and then in one's career you do things which really give you a fillip, I mean personally, and this play has done it for me.

WOGAN: You've got to do a Chicago accent?

FINNEY: Yeah . . .

WOGAN: We had people on here telling how difficult the Chicago accent is.

FINNEY: The place where the play started was in Chicago. I got a cassette and I listened to it. I listened to it a lot during rehearsals. Also, when I was a kid I used to go to the movies a lot, to those gangster movies, so it's part of the conditioning really.

For a while the conversation stayed with accents, when perhaps Terry might have questioned Finney about the films he made and his co-stars.

WOGAN: Your father was called 'Honest Albert, the punters' friend'? Did you ever think of taking up book-making like your father?

FINNEY: If I had, I'd be a rich man today.

WOGAN: You have an interest in horses?

FINNEY: I love horses. I own race horses.

WOGAN: Any tips for the Derby?

FINNEY: Well . . . (*He ran through the names of a few likely winners provided the going was hard.*)

WOGAN: After the play, and the Derby, will you take another sabbatical?

FINNEY: Oh, no. I may go over to the States, where some of the horses will be racing. I might get involved in a film project or a play.

WOGAN: What time are you on stage to-night?

FINNEY: Whenever you like . . . (Laugh from audience)

Time was up. Finney had a date on the West End stage. It was regrettable in a way, for there were many things left unsaid, but waiting in the wings was another actor, the quintessential American, Terry Savalas, easily recognisable by his magnificent bald head. To viewers he is better known as the television tough guy with the heart of gold – Theo Kojak. He was greeted with the kind of applause reserved for household names in movies and soap operas. He came on wearing a great broad smile, projecting affability by the ton.

WOGAN: They love you. You're looking very bronzed. Where have you been?

SAVALAS: It's high blood-pressure being on your programme.

WOGAN: How did you play today?

SAVALAS: You heard what Albert said – well . . .

WOGAN: You're just back from Las Vegas. You've been doing a little gambling?

SAVALAS: They have this world championship in poker going out there.

WOGAN: Do you come from a well-off family?

SAVALAS: I come from a destitute family. No, I'm kidding. I come from a kinda class family. My father . . . there was a consistency to his personality that made him exciting.

WOGAN: Your mother was connected with the arts?

SAVALAS: My mum, apart from being one of the most outstanding and beautiful women in this world, she . . . do you know it's a strange thing when you have got a mum like I have, she still advises you. If it's snowing outside she'll say: 'Hey, Terry put on your boots, take care of yourself, you're not eating right.'

WOGAN: You have an uncle who is a shrink?

SAVALAS: (*Laughs*) My uncle is a shrink, a total nut. He might bring patients into the family house for the night.

WOGAN: You have a reputation for embroidery?

SAVALAS: I am of Greek stock.

WOGAN: Are you a Greek?

SAVALAS: I grew up in the streets of New York. I am not responsible for what the press writes about my ambiguities, but most of what I say is true, except don't believe it for I might change it again.

It was difficult for the viewers to know what to believe. It is one of the hazards of having a funny man like Terry Savalas on your show. He's an old campaigner at chat shows and knows when to send the host the wrong way. You can't signpost a man like Terry Savalas. He was having fun at Terry's expense.

WOGAN: You owe your first break in your career to Burt Lancaster?

SAVALAS: Burt saw me do a television show and said: That guy might be good for my picture'.

WOGAN: Were you bald then?

SAVALAS: I came into life bald and I hope to go out the same way.

WOGAN: You're not really bald, are you?

SAVALAS: No, no. But if I let my hair grow I'll never work again.

Terry was enjoying a successful run with a mixture of national and international celebrities, thus ensuring that there was abundant contrast from Monday to Friday night. On the evening of June 4, he seemed to take particular pleasure introducing an actress who was a Hollywood star at the age of nineteen. At sixty-one, Lauren Bacall has the air of a woman considerably younger, with green eyes and incredible legs. When she laughs, it is a laugh that comes from deep inside her slim, shapely body.

Terry said he had 'waited months' to get her on *Wogan*, telling his audience that he had always had a soft spot for screen goddesses. Miss Bacall was in London starring in the

Tennesse Williams' play *Sweet Bird of Youth*. Married years before to Humphrey Bogart, she has a clear view of life: 'You have only one time round – so don't waste it.' No one could accuse her of wasting it, ever since she made her debut in *To Have and to Have Not*, based on Hemingway's novel, winning instant fame with the film. More fame followed when she co-starred with Charles Boyer in *Confidential Agent*.

When she married Bogart he was twenty-five years her senior, older than her uncles.

WOGAN: You brought the good weather with you?

BACALL: Yes.

WOGAN: I am somewhat disappointed. We sent a bouquet of flowers to your dressing-room and you didn't seem to like them?

BACALL: I didn't mean to give you that impression. I actually love flowers. The problem was that it's such an enormous presentation that I didn't really think it was for me. I am not used to receiving so many flowers.

WOGAN: I shall take umbrage if that is the way you feel. (*Audience breaks into laughter*) The role created for you in your first film was to be tougher than Bogart, but you weren't exactly like that were you?

BACALL: The idea was to have a woman who could give as good as she got and was able to stand up against somebody who had an all-encompassing personality. Bogie had, but I've had to live up to this image ever since.

WOGAN: You're not like that in reality, are you?

BACALL: Oh, no. Tough wasn't the word, insolent perhaps, someone who wouldn't take it, a woman who could stand up for herself.

WOGAN: A kind of liberated woman?

BACALL: I've always been liberated.

WOGAN: Did you resent having that kind of image foisted on you?

BACALL: No, I don't think in terms of images. I really don't understand what it means, any more than I understand what legends mean. I always thought legends were dead so I don't identify at all with legends.

WOGAN: I was thinking of doing the introduction again and leaving out the legend bit. You were married to Humphrey Bogart. Was his off-screen – I won't use the word 'image' – was his off-screen persona similar to his screen's? –

BACALL: Not at all.

WOGAN: He wasn't a tough guy?

BACALL: Not at all. He was a very emotional, sensitive man, actually brought up on the right side of the tracks. He was always considered a gent (with a doctor as a father and an artist as a mother), he was always a well-read and intelligent man. What was wrong with him? Just a minute. (*Audience laughs*) He was marvellous in that first film with me because I was so terrified. I was terribly nervous doing it. I am nervous now. I am always nervous.

WOGAN: You mask it well. You were both independent spirits? You both had trouble with the studios?

BACALL: Independent spirits usually have that kind of trouble, don't you find?

WOGAN: Yes.

BACALL: Jack Warner's attitude was that actors were employees and he thought we should do as we were told. Unfortunately he hadn't a lot of taste as regards films, so if you wanted to do something and showed taste in choosing particular film parts you were in trouble. You ended up under suspension and didn't work for months, but in spite of that films then were wonderful, terrific in fact. Warner Brothers produced some of the best films ever made.

WOGAN: You are not suggesting, are you, that there's something to be said for Warner Brothers' treatment of actors as employees?

BACALL: No, no. I don't think there is ever anything to be said for that. I think, though, there were a tremendous number of talented people making films then.

WOGAN: Do you detect a great difference between then and now in the making of films?

BACALL: There is a tremendous difference – in costs, in

the number of films, and in the concentration of talent in one place. That doesn't exist anymore. You go where the work is. You seldom work where you live. There are still many talented young people in films, but I don't think as many as in my day. They don't build stars to last.

WOGAN: It's very difficult to become a film star. I mean, we go out to a movie and see players and established actors, but they don't become stars like they used to.

BACALL: They don't last. Stars to me are people. Having your name over the title for five minutes isn't being a star in my book.

WOGAN: You were nineteen when you were a star?

BACALL: I was a wee kid. It would have been harder to handle if I had not met Bogie, I'm sure. I had a very solid upbringing; my feet were quite firmly planted on the ground.

WOGAN: Are you glad it happened to you then?

BACALL: I am glad it happened at all. I think I am lucky it happened at all. I was told once by Moss Hart: 'You understand of course that you have no way to go but down?' And he was absolutely right.

WOGAN: I don't think that's true.

BACALL: But it is true. If you are praised beyond your capabilities, as young people very often are, you can't live up to that praise.

WOGAN: Your original ambition was to work on the stage. Do you prefer it to working on movies?

BACALL: No, I just prefer working to not working.

WOGAN: If you had a choice?

BACALL: I would do both. One has to. I think one should. Each medium has something different to offer. I would do everything. But the best thing about the theatre is that it is happening then, it's live, and the best thing about a film is that you have a better life, not that relentless eight shows a week, fifty-two weeks a year.

WOGAN: You need stamina at this stage?

BACALL: Yes, you do.

WOGAN: There's not a frail cowering woman behind that facade?

BACALL: No, but there's a very vulnerable centrepoint. One can feel intimidated.

WOGAN: Do you get offered many roles?

BACALL: I am not crazy about that question. What kind of roles have you in mind?

WOGAN: They don't allow me to offer anybody any roles here in the BBC, but you do get offered many interesting parts?

BACALL: There are not many wonderful parts written for women; in fact, there are some terrible parts written for women. It is very difficult to find anything that is interesting. Maybe it will change. I find there is better stuff to do on stage than in movies.

WOGAN: What about television?

BACALL: I don't think the level of work is good enough. I don't want to be trapped in a soap opera for four of five years. I think it would drive me mad. Some people can handle it better than others. I don't think I have five years to spare. If I went into soap opera I wouldn't be able to come to London to talk to you. (*Audience applauds*)

The interview was too short. One would have welcomed more insight into Miss Bacall's views of Humphrey Bogart and the stars in her later films. But lack of time, as usual, was the enemy.

22 Royal Wogan

No one would have been surprised if Terry had received an invitation to the July wedding of Prince Andrew and Sarah Ferguson. For weeks on *Wogan* he had joked about a grand possibility and as usual nobody quite knew whether to take him seriously. After his lively interview with Princess Anne, people talked about the success of the show and how freely she had chatted to him. Later his conversation with Prince Philip would be less happy, prompting him to admit to me: 'When you interview royalty, you interview them with both arms and your tongue tied behind your back'.

Terry realises he is not expected to be a Dimbleby or a Burnett, but plain, enduring Terry Wogan with the dazzling smile and witty asides; in brief, the viewers' Everyman. As an Irishman he can scarcely rank as an Establishment figure in the same mould as Sir Robin Day, nor does he want to. Like Clive James or Frank Delaney, Terry is doing a job and happens to be loved by the great majority of viewers. Eamonn Andrews was once honoured by the Palace for doing much the same thing.

Inevitably, the Wogan show zoomed in on the royal wedding on that July day in 1986. Everybody was talking about it. Romance was in the air. More importantly, it was a royal romance and the English love nothing better than a Royal occasion. It was all that mattered to millions of women, and the media, realising it had gripped the imagination of the nation, gave saturation coverage to the hectic lead-up to the great event. With the shortage of American tourists in London, it was clear that the stage would be left to the two stars of the show or, as the tabloids called them, Fergie and Andy.

Would people tire of the whole razzmatazz before the wedding even took place? Of course not. A royal romance lifts a nation, puts smiles back on tired faces, turns drabness into colour, and reminds every loyal English man and woman of the value of the monarchy as an institution. Forgotten is the thriving divorce industry, what matters is two young people in love, hopefully for ever. The television channels recruited all the best talent available to ensure that their millions of viewers got the most memorable words and pictures. So did Fleet Street and Wapping – indeed, in the romantic surge towards the big day even the bitterness generated by Wapping seemed for a while forgotten.

On the evening of Monday, July 21, Terry announced briskly to his audience in the BBC Television Theatre in Shepherd's Bush: 'This week could be a lifetime for my next guest. The royal wedding has been claiming everybody's attention for some-time, but for Fleet Street and Wapping it has become a circus, a relentless chase for pictures, articles, fact and fiction as everything and anything you ever wanted to know about Fergie and Andy is regurgitated for your delight. Whatever they are going to fill the papers with next week, doubtless pictures of the wedding and the secret honeymoon hideaway, taken more likely than not by my next guest . . . *The Sun's* ace lensman . . . Arthur Edwards.

Edwards was greeted by prolonged applause.

WOGAN: Arthur, it's a big day for Fergie and Andy next Wednesday and almost as big a day for you. It's make or break day for you really. If you don't get the pictures, you're dead?

EDWARDS: Yes, if I don't get the picture of the kiss I'm dead . . . and that's the picture I'm going for.

WOGAN: The kiss on the balcony?

EDWARDS: That's right.

WOGAN: So where are you going to be for that?

EDWARDS: I'm going to be on the Queen Victoria Memorial with the other photographers.

WOGAN: How does one recognise a royal photographer?

EDWARDS: You'll recognise me because I'll be traipsing down the Mall at about six-thirty in the morning with huge lenses, huge tripod and my aluminium ladder.

WOGAN: How many photographers will be there?

EDWARDS: There'll be about thirty facing the balcony.

WOGAN: They'll all get the same shot then?

EDWARDS: Well, if you blink you could miss out. A lot missed last time. I wasn't there, but several did miss it, I'm told.

WOGAN: So are you going to go on honeymoon with Fergie and Andy?

EDWARDS: Oh, yes. Windsor Travel. (*Laughter from audience*)

Terry examined some of the royal photographs Arthur Edwards had taken for *The Sun*, then exclaimed: 'That's not the most flattering picture I've ever seen of Fergie! It's a bit cruel, that?'

EDWARDS: (*Unmoved*) Not really, because she does make full expressions and does try to give you a different picture; in fact that was at a flax works in Northern Ireland and the smell of the place – you'd pull a face like that too . . .

WOGAN: How do you think she's shaping up in the short time that she's been under the enormous pressure you chaps put on her?

EDWARDS: She's certainly shaping up . . . and shaping down. She's desperately trying to lose weight for the wedding.

WOGAN: How do you know that?

EDWARDS: Because I photographed her in the beginning when she was fat and I photographed her this morning and she was thin.

Edwards' touch of humour brought laughs from the audience.

WOGAN: I suppose that is a compliment in a way?

EDWARDS: It's a compliment to her. She's really looking super.

WOGAN: Had you being following her for a long time

before – had you with your newshound's nose worked out that she was going to be Andrew's bride?

EDWARDS: When I first saw her at Ascot last year I didn't think in a million years he would marry her.

WOGAN: (*To his audience*) I thought Arthur was a bit dismissive there, didn't you?

EDWARDS: His track record before was always models and actresses. I didn't think this girl was his scene but I was told before Christmas: 'Have a look at this girl, she is definitely going to be the one.' So after that I took a huge interest in her.

WOGAN: Are you implying that the marriage was somehow arranged, that Sarah wasn't necessarily his choice?

EDWARDS: No, no. Fergie is definitely his choice, but she was so different from the other girls with which he associated.

WOGAN: You think he had decided to settle down?

EDWARDS: I do – and he's picked a super lady; he's the lucky one.

WOGAN: Is there any jealousy between Princess Diana and Sarah Ferguson? Or is Di still the star of the show?

EDWARDS: Oh, Di is still the number one. Di is one of the most beautiful ladies in the world and coupled with the fact that she is going to be the next queen of England, she's going to be the superstar for a very long while to come.

Terry looked over more royal photographs in Arthur's picture album and remarked: 'Now that – did you do this deliberately?

EDWARDS: No, she does –

WOGAN: Oh, come on –

EDWARDS: No, no –

WOGAN: That is an unglamorous shot of Di.

EDWARDS: That I think is a pretty nice picture. She turned up at a polo match wearing a head-scarf and she teased us all afternoon. She went around with her head down and turned away and was giggling. But just before she departed she gave us that picture and that is the way with the royals –

you get one chance and if you miss it, it's too bad. I think it's a cracking snap. I think I'll enter it in a competition.

WOGAN: Diana might not agree with you, but obviously she has a sense of humour. What was your first big scoop?

EDWARDS: Believe it or not it was Prince Charles' bald patch.

WOGAN: (*Examining the picture*) That's a bit cruel, Arthur. You wouldn't do him any favours by showing that to him.

EDWARDS: I couldn't believe it when I saw it either, in fact, I realised next morning that this was the sort of picture that was wanted, not the stuffy, boring pictures we had been doing of the monarchy up to then.

WOGAN: Do you think that is what the public want?

EDWARDS: I think so, yes.

WOGAN: Do you think they would want them if you didn't give it to them?

EDWARDS: That is a funny question, Terry.

WOGAN: It's a chicken-and-egg situation. Are you creating the demand or are the public demanding that you show them these pictures?

EDWARDS: I think it's a little of both. We've got to get better and better pictures, that's the standard, otherwise they won't get into the paper.

WOGAN: Seems there is much more coverage of the Royal Family over the last ten years and certainly since the last royal wedding. Is it a public demand that is creating that, or is it Fleet Street seeking more and more sensational photographs and articles?

EDWARDS: I think it changed when Princess Diana came along. I mean she was such a super, beautiful girl and she was going to be the next queen and that created an enormous amount of interest. Since then it has got bigger and bigger and the Royal Family is getting bigger and the younger ones make great pictures too. So it is going on and on.

WOGAN: You don't think that these kind of pictures, or indeed this kind of press attention, trivialises the Royal

Family, turning them into a kind of Carrington family of Denver and Ewing family of Dallas?

EDWARDS: No, I don't think so at all. The proof is when they go on public engagements huge crowds turn up in Britain and overseas.

WOGAN: Do you think the Royal Family welcome huge crowds or would they be happier with the little crowds they used to get before you gave them publicity?

EDWARDS: I think they love it. They love the crowds. They're in show biz. I've always said you don't get any picture they don't want you to get. They know you're there and they know what they're giving you.

WOGAN: Well, Arthur, I hope you get the kiss.

EDWARDS: So do I. If I don't I won't know what to do.

WOGAN: Have a good wedding.

Arthur Edwards had proved a genial and intelligent guest. The *Wogan* production team had found an unusual angle for highlighting the royal wedding and Terry's effortless chatty style took care of the rest. The show further illustrated the marked change in the BBC's attitude towards the Royal Family. That Terry and his guest could talk about them freely, though always in good taste, showed that in certain respects the royals were no longer sacrosanct. As Arthur Edwards might say, that's the way the Royal Family wants it to be in the 'eighties, not projecting the pompous image of yesterday.

Terry's cheery style tends to put the rich as well as the royals in relaxed mood. As their host he is respectful without being reverential. 'I would love to chat to Princess Diana,' he has said more than once. 'I think she would be a marvellous guest.' Terry is aware how far he can go with the British royals, although he has experienced one or two awkward moments.

Chatting to European royalty should give him more scope to be probing, yet when he faced young Princess Stefanie of Monaco in the TV Theatre in Shepherd's Bush Green he showed unusual restraint. One presumed he would have asked about the odd wayward royal who seems no longer interested in observing traditional protocol; or her own views of the changing attitudes towards royalty today. As we shall see, Terry took a soft approach and, although pleasant for the viewer it tended to provide dull television.

WOGAN: (softly) You've said you are a princess of thhe twentieth century. Is that because you dress the way you want and because you can pursue your own career?

PRINCESS: I think it is the way I was brought up. I have a lot of things to do and I dress the way I like. Nobody says anything about it.

WOGAN: You weren't brought up in a strict, formal manner – I mean, to wear proper royal clothes?

PRINCESS: Of course on certain formal occasions I do wear the appropriate dress, that is, for instance, when I'm representing my family.

WOGAN: Do you find that a strain?

PRINCESS: No.

WOGAN: You are designing swimwear. Isn't that mainly what you do? Is designing going to be your career?

PRINCESS: It is one of my careers. But I love my artistic career as well, my singing. It is my life.

WOGAN: Would you like to be a pop star?

PRINCESS: No, a singer.

WOGAN: A lot of pop stars are singers.

PRINCESS: Depends on what you are singing.

WOGAN: The first time we saw you as a career girl you were a model.

PRINCESS: I was a model and enjoyed being a model, but I don't want to do it any more.

WOGAN: It wasn't due to any family objections, was it, that you stopped being a model?

PRINCESS: No.

WOGAN: Did your mother, Princess Grace, encourage you to go into show business?

PRINCESS: Yes. My mother had me tap dancing and singing when I was a child.

WOGAN: But nobody said to you first and foremost that you are a princess and you must behave with more dignity?

PRINCESS: My parents brought us up in the knowledge that there were different avenues open to us and that each of us was a personality. Our personalities are different. My parents did not force us to do certain things. They let us do the things we enjoyed. I think this was important.

PART FOUR

WOGAN '87

In two years, *Wogan* has become so much part
of the television furniture that it is
difficult to remember what it replaced or
to envisage what could be done instead

—DAVID BERRY in *The Listener*

23   'Under Siege'

Shepherd's Bush Green wore a shabby look. Shops and houses appeared in urgent need of a splash of fresh paint. On this wet March afternoon in 1987 the modern blocks of high-rise flats at one corner of the Green seemed curiously out of place. Below, the pigeons flew low across the green grass and deserted tennis court – an ominous sign perhaps? All the time, vehicles roared by, passing on their way the BBC TV theatre on which the name 'Wogan', in red lettering, was clearly visible on the canopy over the front door. That was important. As Terry Wogan had said in another context: 'If you are not on the screen you're dead. I happen to be in the game, so the point is to be there.'

He was still King of Shepherd's Bush Green, with, one presumes, more friends than enemies. For three days each week, Mondays, Wednesdays and Fridays, the theatre was virtually his home; here he met with the *Wogan* production team, ran through rehearsals, greeted his guests and audience, and usually ended his evening in the Hospitality Room sipping a glass of wine and puffing on a large cigar.

At five minutes to three I was admitted by the stage door to the theatre. My meeting with Terry promised to be unusual, for I had come to find out if the great man was actually under siege, embattled. Rumour and counter-rumour filled the air and appeared to be encapsulated in at least one Fleet Street tabloid heading: 'MY SHOW WILL NOT BE AXED, SAYS WOGAN'.

The rumours looked paradoxical after Terry had been voted television's favourite male personality of the year –

for the ninth time. When he first won it in 1978 it had come as 'a complete surprise'. Receiving the '87 award from Shirley Bassey, he took a swipe at the critics: 'For people like me, they're the most important awards as they are the public's.'

Earlier in the year he had incurred the wrath of some Fleet Street critics by stating that he was worth more than the £350,000 a year the BBC paid him. As he explained: 'They say I earn this kind of money. I don't think that's much. Per programme it makes me the lowest-paid worker in television. There are people earning £10,000 a time, so I'm doing for peanuts a live show where I could "die" at any minute.'

For weeks afterwards the sniping continued, with suggestions that the Wogan show might be axed because of falling audiences. Newspaper reports highlighted a 'major slump' in the ratings for *Wogan*, saying that he was being beaten by his ITV rivals at 7.00 pm – *Wish You Were Here*, *This Is Your Life* and *The Newlywed Game*. It did not seem nearly enough that *Wogan* was attracting 7.6 million viewers a programme.

Suddenly Terry Wogan seemed vulnerable. Newspaper readers could be forgiven for assuming that he was embattled in the TV Theatre in Shepherd's Bush Green. Their fears seemed to be confirmed when it became known that the BBC's top brass had asked for a revamp of *Wogan*. Scrapped was the long-running signature tune by trendy pop star B. A. Robertson, to be replaced by something new from seasoned songwriter Harry Stoneham. Also changed was the *Wogan* studio set, but perhaps the most significant change was the appointment of experienced producer John Fisher as series producer.

Terry was aware of the storm clouds over Shepherd's Bush Green. He defended the changes: 'They're just subtle changes. A slap of paint here and there, new graphics over the opening titles, a new coffee table to replace the old battered one and things like that.' On a more personal note, he told a reporter: 'I'm going to be around for at least the next couple of years.'

In television circles it was hinted that the BBC was worried by the return to the screen of chat-show host Michael Parkinson, who over the years had chalked up an incredible 1,500 TV interviews. His new talk show would go out on ITV once a week. But Parkinson, a friend of Terry's, said there was 'no conflict' between them. And he added: 'Wogan is the hottest property in British TV. The only thing wrong with his show is that it should go out five nights a week, so that it can be a rolling show. I am a late entry into the 'eighties chat-show stakes, and I don't want to be in direct competition with Terry. I don't want to be tied down on a weekly basis. This show burst of eight shows is just what I want.'

Evidently, Michael Grade, BBC TV boss, had had a hand in the Wogan show changes. It was generally known that he wanted John Fisher as the new series producer. While confirming that Wogan was an absolute fixture, Grade sounded a warning when he stated: 'There are too many plugs in a lot of the shows. I hope it will provide more human interest stories in the future, rather than the round of celebrities. I'd like to see more members of the public involved.'

Terry would say that Michael Grade had discussed the show with him and they agreed on certain proposals aimed at improving Wogan. The BBC boss had always been a champion of Terry's style, but it was obvious that he wanted the show to make the top fifty, which it sometimes failed to do. Gloria Hunniford, on the other hand, was jubilant over the success of The Newlywed Game, and commented: 'This is terrific news. It's great to see off the old rogue. Terry and I will stay the best of mates, but there's no love lost when it comes to winning the viewers.' Her ratings success was the latest round in a long-standing rivalry between the two. Terry used to call her 'Grevious Bodily Hunniford'.

Shortly after three o'clock Terry breezed through the stage door and, without stopping, beckoned me to follow him to his dressing-room, which is off a narrow corridor on the ground floor. Once inside, he lit a cigar, poured himself a Perrier water, and sat himself comfortably on the long couch. At that moment he didn't appear like a man embattled or under siege. He exuded confidence, managed a smile or two, and revealed not a trace of uneasiness.

The rumours and counter-rumours had no place in the confines of this dressing-room. If there was a conspiracy afoot to purge him, either Terry hadn't heard about it or he was disguising the fact superbly. The whole thing seemed preposterous, the figment of Fleet Street's vivid imagination, the concoction of little minds. It was obvious that the Bard of Shepherd's Bush Green was alive and well, and eager to address himself to the world.

Before he began I reminded him that a year ago the critics had accused him of over-exposure on TV; now it was a question of disappointing ratings.

'Over-exposure?' Terry uttered the word calmly but firmly after a quick sip from his glass. 'That's all in the past – and they were proven wrong, you know! As regards this talk about ratings, we attract nearly eight million viewers per programme and on Fridays often nine to ten million. How can they call that a slump?'

He paused to draw on his cigar. 'Nonsense,' he continued. 'There is no way we are failing. The number of viewers is terrific. I always think it is a compliment to the show that ITV fling against us as many strong programmes as they can. Obviously, this is a deliberate policy. No, there is no question of being embattled or under siege. By now we have a hard corps of viewers who watch *Wogan* three nights a week. If we could do what *Eastenders* does, and compile together all the weekly viewing figures then the overall figures would look an impressive twenty million plus.'

'So there's no feeling of panic?' I said.

'Panic?' The word seemed utterly alien to him, as though I had touched on a sensitive nerve. Terry broke into a short laugh. 'Why should there be panic? We are talking about a successful show. I admit that all the shows cannot be as good as we want them to be, but I think that *Wogan* has its moments.'

How significant was the appointment of John Fisher as series producer to Wogan?

'A new producer will always bring his or her own ideas to a show,' mused Terry. 'Frances Whitaker, who was here before John, implemented her own ideas; now we are seeing more emphasis on newsworthy subjects, or more matters relevant to the day. Change is good. It achieves what I like it to achieve – it keeps the show fresh.

'The show in terms of viewers is no more successful than it was a year ago. It keeps its audience. After all, that is all you can hope to achieve. After doing it for over two years you can't expect suddenly to jump to twelve million viewers. A talk show at seven o'clock in the evening is never going to get the kind of viewing figures, say, of *Coronation Street*.'

Terry was in full spate. His voice sounded easy on the ear. One felt he could go on talking about the show for ever. He emphasised: 'Doing a show like mine, one has got to avoid certain pitfalls. It mustn't become monotonous. It must try to be different. What you are hoping for is that it will become regular viewing. The great hole you fall into is making it predictable.'

It had been suggested that since the new *Wogan* production team took over, interviews had tended to become 'harder' and 'more meaningful.' There were fewer giggling starlets. One of the interviews that aroused a lot of public interest involved Miss Sara Keays, which in a subtle way underlined the important new emphasis. It will be recalled that the Westminster secretary whose love affair with Mr Cecil Parkinson caused him to resign from the Tory Cabinet made 'an electrifying outburst' on the Wogan show and attacked Prime Minister Mrs Thatcher for her morals and her attitude to the private lives of her ministers. Had Terry anticipated such an outburst? 'I suppose I did expect Miss Keays to be explosive; she is a forthright woman and pulls no punches. She feels she has been wronged.'

'Is that why you invited her on the show?'

'The reason was she had been misquoted and, in her own words, "misrepresented" in a woman's magazine and we decided to give her an opportunity to answer back, which she gratefully accepted.'

'Are you normally taken aback when a woman like Miss Keays explodes in rage on *Wogan*?'

Terry shrugged and finished his drink. 'It's up to me to handle it. That's the whole point of a live show like mine – you'll get these spontaneous outbursts and it can be exciting television. Such an interview stretches me and affords me an opportunity to get behind the person I'm interviewing. I think the occasional in-depth interview is welcomed by the viewer. But long chats aren't the essence of *Wogan*. You must remember it's screened early in the evening, after the news, so viewers want to be entertained. In the main, people in this country may not sit down to watch the show, but if someone on the box catches their eye they will watch and stay with it. If it happens to be a good interview they will sit down and watch it. *Wogan* must always have elements of light entertainment.'

I was by now inclined to the view that the great man wasn't under siege, or at least he hadn't shown any outward symptoms of stress. Surely, though, in view of recent newspaper reports and rumours, he must be experiencing certain personal pressure on him and the show. Unlike some actors who proudly boast they never read critics' notices, Terry has always kept an eye on what the papers say.

He looked composed as he reflected: 'I do not feel pressure on me or the show. I think this is because one knows when something is succeeding and when it is not. I would be the first to know it the show was failing. I would not be here. The BBC would have taken *Wogan* off the screen. But of course nothing succeeds for ever. For instance, I can't think where I'll go from here, for there is not much more I can do on television. I'll probably slip slowly into senility. I've been lucky. Some day a new face will come along and do the show better than me.'

The art of interviewing has long fascinated him. Ever since

Bill Cotton asked Terry to do the thrice-weekly *Wogan* his
chat-show style has been under scrutiny. At times he has
been described as 'self-indulgent' and 'sometimes missing
interesting follow-up questions, thus allowing experienced
interviewees to get on their hobby-horses without being
seriously challenged'.

Yet everyone agrees that he has accomplished the tricky
art of putting guests at their ease. Some of his critics feel
his softly-softly approach sometimes lets him down. Had he
ever considered adopting a more aggressive style? He was
emphatic: 'No. I can only be what I am. It's too late for me
to try to be something else. I am exactly what I am and
that's how viewers have come to accept me. I can't change
at this stage of my life. More important, perhaps, is whether
viewers would expect me to change. I continue to win
awards as I am, but for how long more I cannot say. Of
course the day will come when I won't win them and for
some people that will indicate I'm sliding quickly down-
wards. They'll jump on poor old Wogan. Other television
stars who don't win awards will not experience the same
thing.'

Inevitably, the conversation reverted to the Wogan show.
He did not deny that he had certain preferences regarding
potential guests on the show. He gave top priority to Princess Diana. 'I think she would be marvellous and with lots
to say, but the royal household keeps itself to itself and the
royals naturally curtail the amount of television exposure
they are prepared to permit. I haven't done so badly,
though. I would also like Margaret Thatcher, if only to probe
the woman behind the politician; that would be fascinating,
don't you think?'

At 3.30 there was a tap on the dressing-room door. It was
time for Terry to run through the scripts with the producers
and programme consultant. He would have read the
researchers' notes and studied the questions. The
researchers play a very important role in the Wogan show.
For instance, one of the guests that evening would be John

Stalker, the ex-Deputy Chief Constable of Greater Manchester. For more than a week a young researcher had been to Manchester to compile detailed biographical notes.

When Stalker arrived at the TV Theatre that afternoon he was accompanied by the researcher, who would stay with him right up to the start of the show. As one researcher put it: 'We are expected to look after the guests we have researched. We have two research teams, one working on show day, the other preparing material for the following week. It works very smoothly, though there is a lot of work involved. We also supply a list of questions to Terry, which he may find useful when he is framing his own. He grasps script details very quickly and misses nothing.'

On the set, meanwhile, the technical team were doubling as the host and his guests to check lighting and camera angles. At five o'clock Terry himself took the chair for a rehearsal, illuminating the bank of screens in the director's production gallery. At six it was time for guest John Stalker and then Terry to receive the finishing touches to their make-up.

That morning before he left Wogan Towers, Terry had worked for some while on the introductory words to the show. He always regards them as important to the success of *Wogan*, for they set the right mood and, if witty and topical, manage to put the theatre audience into good humour, and hopefully the millions of viewers. Occasionally, as when he returned from holidays, Terry is inclined to let the introduction run and indulge himself. But in recent weeks it had tended to be more brief.

In the Hospitality Room I was introduced to some of the guests and their relatives. John Stalker, in his immaculate suit, cut an impressive figure and for a man who had gone through his own personal trauma he looked unruffled. His brother, looking much younger, and his wife informed me they were both members of the police force. As people sipped glasses of wine in the rather confined room, there was a buzz of conversation. At that moment John Fisher made his first appearance in the room and had a few words with the researchers. He seemed satisfied there were no last-minute hitches.

John Fisher is tall and rather intense. A polished speaker, he has brought to the Wogan show a wealth of experience. On the invitation of Bill Cotton, he arrived at the BBC in 1968 after an Oxford education, working for five years as a researcher, then as a producer of the Parkinson show. Nowadays he is author of two much-praised show-business books, and a magician to boot. James Gilbert, Head of Light Entertainment at Thames TV, and a former BBC colleague, described Fisher to me as 'a tremendous worker and fine producer'. He felt he would be good for *Wogan*.

John Fisher found that when the Parkinson show was established there was no problem getting guests. 'But the important thing was to choose the right guests. The chat show itself is in my opinion the most flexible and versatile format on television, for you can devote a whole show to one person, or you can have individual interviews, or else people sitting round in conversation. I think that Parkinson was the first person to make the single interview important in the chat-show context. David Frost, for instance, had been very good conducting a forum, but Michael Parkinson set his stamp on the personalities.'

With his analytical mind, Fisher has given a lot of thought to what makes the chat show work. When he left *Parkinson* he found himself producing the *Paul Daniels Show* and later *Joan Rivers*. When Frances Whitaker left *Wogan*, he was not surprised when he was asked to take charge of *Wogan*. He recalls: 'I think the powers-that-be thought my experience in the chat-show sphere would be useful for the Wogan show. The prospect appealed to me. I had met Terry only once and that was across a crowded hospitality room when he was a guest on *Parkinson*. I came to the show with no preconceived ideas, for doing a live show three days a week was something new to me. I also arrived uncertain about the Wogan mythology. I think one had been led to believe that Terry wanted to interview one person at a time, but after a few weeks on the show I found that this mythology had been thrust on him. For here was a man just waiting for the additional challenge. I think he has welcomed that challenge – the tougher interview, tackling issues as well as personalities.

Fisher quickly concluded that the show must always reflect Terry's personality. 'The wonderful thing about Terry is his total versatility. He can come on and talk to a soap opera star and sound just as convincing as though he was tackling a serious issue. There are few people in television capable of doing that. He is always himself. He doesn't become a Parkinson to interview a film star or a Robin Day to talk to a politician. He brings to the chat show a charisma that is unique. He exerts this fascination within the public for wondering how that person is going to react in the presence of Terry Wogan. He does bring a special quality to the show that is difficult to define; others bring it to their own shows but not to the same degree as Terry.'

John Fisher agreed that the ideal blend of guests was a mixture of the national and international, although on occasions the unknown guest could create a surprise. 'I think the show is big enough now not to worry about the race to get the big name.'

He was aware of the importance of ratings, although not obsessive about them. If the figures for *Wogan* were to drop below the present level, however, he admitted he would be worried. At the same time he would be delighted to see them rise significantly. The *Wogan* team, he said, was devising a different kind of show and he thought it might take the public a little time to respond to what he hoped would be a better quality show. In time he believed the experiment would pay off with increased viewing figures. 'We are certainly now obtaining a higher appreciation index than the show was getting earlier in the year.'

Fears had been expressed in some television circles that there was a danger of the Wogan show losing its light entertainment appeal by 'hardening interviews' and touching on current affairs and politics. It was noticeable that more politicians had joined the guest list. John Fisher saw no such danger. He preferred to apply his own golden rule for success: 'Never book anyone who doesn't have something to say.'

The danger of keeping the show in the orbit of show business was, in his opinion, merely living within a diet of marshmallow, although he would concede there were show-business people with something interesting to say. Sometimes in the past, where starlets were concerned, there seemed to be confusion as to whom Terry was interviewing, whether he was talking to the actor or the part the actor was playing. 'What we needed was a degree of roughage being infused into the show providing the human interest.'

The policy pursued by the *Wogan* team prior to the appointment of John Fisher was to entertain, not educate. The team saw a distinct danger in a 'mix' of current affairs, politics and show business. The team believed that Terry's style was best suited to lighter subjects and that it wasn't wise to ask him to excel in 'specialist' fields like politics, economics and current affairs. But it was now obvious that Michael Grade had given his blessing to the change of emphasis on *Wogan* and had invited John Fisher to implement these changes.

There were obvious risks in the new policy. Fisher, for instance, agreed that the Sara Keays interview was important to the Wogan show. As he explained: 'I think there is no harm in inviting a guest along who is going to be talked about. You must remember that Terry is not being the political interviewer.'

Meanwhile, back in the Hospitality Room Terry had briefly joined the guests to say hello, nothing more. He makes it his business not to talk to them before the show. At about five minutes to seven he slipped out of the room and along the back seats of the balcony, which by now was full. With glass of wine in hand, he walked down the balcony steps until he faced the audience. Heads turned to catch a closer look at the great man. Some people had come a long distance for the privilege. Terry flashed a smile, then said: 'Greetings! Hope you are all happy tonight. Enjoy yourselves. We need your applause. Cheer up, let you, and look happy. Pretend you're enjoying it. That's the main thing in this programme – pretence.'

Word had gone out that one of the guests that evening would be John Stalker, whose name was much in the news. As far as *Wogan* was concerned he was 'a catch', for he had not talked on television about his experiences. He was part of the new policy being pursued by John Fisher. Stalker was bound to have something to say, but since another police officer was conducting the inquiry into allegations of misconduct against Stalker, he would be limited in what he could reveal.

WOGAN: Back in civvy street after thirty years?

STALKER: Yes, indeed.

WOGAN: How does it feel to be outside the comforting womb of the police force?

STALKER: Strange, I suppose, because I've been in the force since a teenager and you do become accustomed to a wall around you, but I've to get on living the same kind of life everybody else has to live.

WOGAN: It all started in 1984 when you were asked to investigate the Royal Ulster Constabulary.

STALKER: Well, in May 1984 I was asked to undertake a very difficult and complex job – certainly the most difficult and complex I ever had to do. Two years later I had almost completed my work when I was removed from duty for ten weeks.

WOGAN: Were you aware that you were treading on dangerous ground? Was it made clear to you that you wouldn't get all the co-operation you wanted?

STALKER: Not in so many words. It wasn't spelt out, but anyone who reads the newspapers knows there are no winners in Northern Ireland.

WOGAN: Did you feel you were getting close to the truth?

STALKER: Whatever the truth is, I was certainly peeling away at the onion. How near I was, I'll never know.

WOGAN: Your suspension from the force – it came out to the blue?

STALKER: I was literally told that 'you are removed from the Northern Ireland inquiry while we investigate innuendo, rumour and gossip.'

WOGAN: All sorts of theories grew up in the newspapers, even mention of an MI5 conspiracy and internal police jealousy. What do you think?

STALKER: I have obviously drawn some conclusions. All I know is when I started out that investigation I was a successful and ambitious and presumably a promising youngish senior police officer; now I am out of the force. People have to draw their own conclusions. I have drawn mine.

WOGAN: Why not tell us what they are?

STALKER: First of all, there are still pieces of the jigsaw to go in.

WOGAN: You were cleared by the Greater Manchester Police Authority. Were you welcomed back to work?

STALKER: Well, the welcome was a bit frosty from some people.

WOGAN: Is it true that your chief's door wasn't exactly open to you?

STALKER: Not as open as it had been before. But there again, people do change. Life changes.

John Stalker so far had been calm under questioning, displaying no outward emotion, no rancour and no bitter disillusionment. He was determined to let the viewers judge for themselves. As expected, he could reveal little or nothing of importance. But Terry's forceful – yet friendly – interviewing ensured that it was good television, though never sensational. Here at least the new *Wogan* policy was working. The mark of John Fisher was apparent in the interview.

There was an amusing touch towards the close when Terry asked: 'It looks like somebody was out to get you?'

STALKER: Well, you can be forgiven for thinking that.

WOGAN: You think that as well?

STALKER: If you ask me as a policeman, I'm not sure. If you ask me as a man, yes, I am sure.

WOGAN: John Stalker, thank you.

24   Wogan's 'Crime'

It was 7.45 when Terry – his face still a rouge colour from the make-up – sauntered into the Hospitality Room smoking a cigar. It's a little ritual he never cares to miss, mostly out of respect for his guests. Once or twice he has been known to skip it after a particular guest had been deliberately rude to him on the show. But this evening he was in a genial mood as he moved between the small gathering with a few words for everybody. Missing, though, was John Stalker who had had to dash back to Manchester.

For a man who in his time had been accused of egomania and arrogance, Terry's attitude now made a mockery of these accusations. Could it be that his critics had confused arrogance with professionalism, egomania with showmanship? At that moment, as he chatted with a young researcher, he did not look like a star about to throw a tantrum. When someone asked if he had ever thought of giving up cigars, Terry joked: 'They are among my few pleasures in life.'

Later, in his dressing-room, where we resumed our conversation of that afternoon, he expressed quiet satisfaction with the evening's show. He was enjoying the new challenge posed by John Fisher. To get his mind off the show I asked why he had decided to buy a patch of bogland up in Scotland. 'Your Irish friends,' I told him, 'thought you would buy an Irish bog.' He laughed and shook his head. 'Buying bogland in Ireland would not qualify me for tax relief,' he said, 'but it does in Scotland. It has been going on for ages – Steve Davis and Alex Higgins did the same thing as me – but it didn't make news until someone wrote that I had purchased six hundred acres. Tree plantation, they hope, will create new jobs. It will happen in Ireland also. Now I can also do some shooting if I wish.'

Buying bogland wasn't the Wogan 'crime' however, although a few Fleet Street papers claimed Terry would be gaining annual tax relief of over £150,000 by his investment. His 'crime' was something far more esoteric than bogland. It arose out of a thoughtful piece in *The Listener* in which David Berry took the opportunity on the second anniversary of *Wogan* to examine the show. It had quickly proved to be the BBC's most popular chat show ever, he reflected. *Wogan* had become so much a part of the television furniture that it was difficult to remember what it replaced or to envisage what could be done instead. That was Terry Wogan's success.

Berry argued that in *Wogan* Britain emerged as still essentially one nation. Despite the country's decline, there was still much in the British character they could celebrate. Wogan was a champion of the acceptable feelings viewers had towards people in the public eye. Voyeurism was replaced by curiosity, hatred by admiration, envy and resentment at success by a good-natured respect for the successful. It was no coincidence that *Wogan*, in contrast to other chat shows, was extraordinarily personalised: how Terry Wogan felt about what his guests said mattered a great deal. That was because unlike, say, Michael Aspel on ITV or Gay Byrne on Irish Television, Wogan did not simply facilitate the talk but acted as a filter and a packager, taking out everything that might disrupt easy viewing. 'We are not watching his guests but watching how his guests react to a short chat with a likeable bloke,' Berry said.

Terry admitted he had read the piece in *The Listener* and considered the argument unjustified. It is a reflection on his personality, though, that he continues to be the subject for discussion in serious as well as lightweight newspapers and magazines. David Berry's summing-up raised a few more pungent points: 'It is little wonder, then that British viewers find relief in *Wogan* after the early-evening news, for he is really saying that things are not so bad, that nothing is too serious to get in the way of trivia and laughter and entertainment. In an important sense, *Wogan* could only be done by an immigrant, by someone who has not been brought up with the contradictions of recent British history, someone who can see from the outside the desire of the British public to escape from present uncertainties back to what made Britain great: the fortitude and modesty of her people. Only an Irishman could see this and at the same time, gently mock it in a way which comes across to the British viewer not as an attack but as a celebration

'This, then, is Terry Wogan's achievement. In two years, he has built a rapport with viewers by confirming our need, amid the challenge of other cultures, to be proud to be British. It is, if nothing else, a distinct achievement.'

At that moment in his dressing-room Terry sighed, as though David Berry might possibly have read too much into *Wogan*. Intellectual argument tends to make him wary. In a year's time, on the third anniversary of the show, *The Listener* might well argue that viewers preferred the old-style *Wogan* instead of the 'newsy' *Wogan*.

Terry remarked with a short laugh, 'You saw what Bernard Levin said about me? String the bastard up, that's what he said – meaning me. I don't know whether to take that as a compliment or an insult.'

Levin, in his *Times* reply to David Berry, prefaced his piece by telling readers that once on the Wogan show he had been invited to display his knees to the nation in close-up, so at least the columnist knew what it was like to be sitting opposite Terry on the stage of the BBC TV Theatre in Shepherd's Bush Green.

Levin claimed that 'Mr Berry took a long time to pinpoint Wogan's crime, in fact too long.' Levin himself was more succinct: 'String the bastard up, that's what I say; Wogan's popularity and success have clearly been earned by painting a wholly spurious picture of Britain. Nobody but a lunatic would deny that there are many things wrong with this country: sloth, obstinacy and cowardice on both sides of industry, a rising tide of political as well as physical violence and intolerance, a level of public lying for which we would have to go back many decades . . .'

Wogan's crime, Levin argued, was to disguise the fact that the country was done for, yet he conceded: 'Wogan does indeed represent true values, those attitudes, those aspirations which were so politely put down by Mr Berry and which elsewhere, amid foaming hatred, are proclaimed evil. But, in doing so, he is a prophet, and more truly embodies the future of a Britain proud of herself than those who declare, with relish, that there is nothing to be proud of in Britain, and that those who feel such pride are enemies of the people.'

Most nights Terry leaves the BBC TV Theatre before 8.30 but this evening he was in the mood for discussion. Obviously the Berry-Levin arguments intrigued him; it could be said they constituted one of the few occasions when his show was properly analysed. He himself argued that he wasn't showing a Britain without warts. Nor that all was fine in the country. As he stressed: 'I don't think we do that in *Wogan*. We have interviewed all kinds of people and touched on serious issues of the day. To say that we paint too nice a picture, as *The Listener* claimed, is unjustified. When Bernard Levin says I should be strung up he fails to appreciate that the show is screened early in the evening, after the news, and must have elements of light entertainment. I think the British public is intelligent enough to realise what we are doing. They now see that there is a new emphasis.'

Terry lit another cigar and looked relaxed. I reminded him of the charge made against him not so long ago by Frank Delaney, who accused him of selling out to commercialism. Terry had read it and the memory made him chuckle. Commented Delaney: 'Wogan's a very bright guy but he was always interested in broadcasting for money. I wasn't. I could have gone that route – the money route – I was asked to do the Parkinson show but I was too interested in writing.'

Delaney had added: 'I don't know why Terry is doing *that* TV show. I love him, but he's gone down the money road and I don't think that's right. I really don't. I mean, what is he doing there? How many more times can he have the girl from *Eastenders* on? I believe he feels embarrassed at having let down his own sense of intelligence. Wogan's a millionaire several times over, and sometimes I have to scrimp and scrape – oh, God, yes. But I would not do something that is really down-market just to get the money.'

Frank is a friend of Terry's. Now Terry reflected: 'What Frank is saying is that I am more commercial than he is. He is right of course. I don't deny that. I think he is essentially a writer. I'm lucky that I have been able to present popular programmes. I would like to be an artist as well, but I can't afford it. Frank can obviously afford to be an artist.'

Delaney is inclined to snub the world of light entertainment because it is a *popular* art form. Terry Wogan took a long time to convince some of his own people that he wasn't a Day or a Dimbleby, but the presenter of such shows as *Come Dancing*, *Song for Europe* and *Blankety Blank*, all of which helped to shape his successful television career.

But Terry too is in demand as a writer. His witty and often original turn of phrase makes his pieces in glossy magazines most readable. As a satirist he can be amusing. When, for example, he was asked to look at the Irish, he observed: 'The Irish are the only people I know who can combine sentimentality with cynicism. Maybe that's where "the tear and the smile" come in.' Or: 'Nobody spots a fake quicker than the Irish, maybe because most of the time they're putting on a bit of an act themselves.'

Once when he was asked why he hadn't tackled a humorous novel or an epic on the life of Wogan, he said candidly: 'I prefer the short pieces. I haven't the patience or the stamina yet to tackle the epic.'

It was nearly time to leave the dressing-room. Terry harked back for a moment to the time when he was accused of being over exposed on television. 'All of that was nonsense,' he now said. 'By the 'nineties when satellites begin to circle all over the place, telly will be crawling with chat shows from America, Japan, Australia – you name it. The chat show in Britain will be on five nights a week. Don't you know that at the moment America is full of chat shows, morning, noon and night? Maybe viewers will get too much of them and be bored to tears. It's cheap television to produce, like quiz or panel games, so they are popular with television chiefs.'

Outside on the footpath some people had waited for Terry to sign their autograph books; he obliged with a smile and a quiet word of encouragement. Then he hastily took his seat beside his chauffeur and the car sped away from the theatre. For Terry, it had been a long day but he was happy with the way the *new* Wogan show was progressing. Michael Grade had expressed satisfaction with the guests and fewer plugs. Soon, however, Terry would be back in Wogan Towers and in the privacy of his house. It was the world he cherished.

Spring by now had come to Wogan Towers. The daffodils were in bloom, the greens looked verdant. In more recent years Helen Wogan has derived great pleasure attending to the flowers and plants, although she left the main work to their gardener. Today the talk was about the oak tree that a storm had levelled to the ground and which the gardener was making arrangements to have cleared from the area around the house.

Helen has managed to carve out her own lifestyle. She always reckoned that was important. When Terry is busy in Shepherd's Bush Green she might join some lady friends for a round of golf. She finds satisfaction in the garden or going into London to shop. At weekends she entertains Terry's friends or they attend dinner-parties together. 'I always find something to do,' Helen would say. She usually watches *Wogan* and the new format pleases her. She feels that Terry welcomes the challenge of more stimulating inter-

views with politicians, writers and people generally with
something worthwhile to say.

As much as Helen and Terry Wogan would like to claim
that they have succeeded in shielding their children from
publicity – there are fewer recent pictures of the three children – they confess it is virtually impossible, now that their
sons are growing up. Helen conceded there was growing
pressure on them. 'There is no point in saying this is not
true. Sons and daughters of celebrities experience this
pressure and in turn it can affect parents, although I try not
to take it seriously. I don't. Yet it is hard not to take notice
when gossip columnists write about your children. A boy
or girl need be only involved in a minor incident to have
the story blown out of proportion.'

In recent times both the Wogan boys, Alan and Mark have
been in the news. It was reported that Alan, a first-year
philosophy and psychology student at Warwick University,
had joined other students in a rent protest. It was claimed
that the rebels were refusing to pay £15 a week rent in 'a
bitter row over their bedsits'. Young Wogan was quoted as
saying: 'There is nothing I want to say about this.' A friend
revealed: 'Alan does not want to comment and cash in on
his dad's name. He is making his own way in life.'

Helen had read the report and was astonished. 'As far as
we know, Alan paid his rent,' she said. 'This is the kind of
thing that can annoy one if you let it.'

There was a story that Mark Wogan was said to be finding
the pressure of living in his father's shadow so great that
he was considering leaving Britain to complete his studies in
the United States. And according to another curious version,
Mark was thinking of joining the Army to escape the
pressure.

Mark was attending Freefolk House, an exclusive
boarding school in Basingstoke, Hampshire. The head-
master, Mr Conrad Rainbow stated that it was inevitable
that pressures on a man like Terry Wogan were going to
rub off on his children and Mark's ambition to go to America
could be a a reaction to that. He described young Wogan as

'a sensible sort of lad' and said that Mark hoped to sit for American university exams after finishing his O Levels in the summer.

The Wogans took the news philosophically, although Terry was surprised at Mark's premature decision. 'I don't think we can say it's final,' he said. The Wogan family is a close-knit unit and Mark's announcement was bound to be a talking point. Helen saw the newspaper story as yet another example of the pressure that can be put on the children of celebrities. Ever since they went to school the Wogan children have had to live with this kind of pressure. Occasionally in the early days they became the victims of taunts by some children.

Terry has given much thought to the possible stresses facing his children. Friends say he has always been protective where his children are concerned; a few claim he has been over-protective. Today, he admits he is worried for their sakes. As he says: 'This pressure on them is getting worse, almost running out of control. As any parent would be, I am worried about it. In the case of Mark, or any sixteen-year-old, he does not know what he wants to do. I was exactly the same at that age.'

Terry has always been interested in young people. Every week in his mail he receives letters from boys and girls eager to get into broadcasting. 'I don't think there is any answer,' he says. 'I got into broadcasting by answering a newspaper advertisement. We have researchers on *Wogan* who are over-qualified, I mean Firsts at Oxford and Cambridge, so the competition for places is extremely tough. I find it hard to give exact advice to these young people, except to tell them to keep trying.'

I once asked Terry if he would object to his own children going into showbiz. 'Not at all' he replied. 'If that was what they wanted, I'd do my best to help.' Helen Wogan feels the same way. Katherine, their only daughter, has shown interest in a modelling career and her mother has no objection, but it's a case of school exams getting priority.

As the spring sun filtered through the clouds and lit up

Wogan Towers, it was hard to believe that its occupants could be affected by external happenings. There was a serenity about the place, even if one missed the Wogan children playing tennis or splashing in the pool.

However, the sniping continues in the popular press and the criticism penetrates through the rafters of Wogan Towers. When Terry was accused of being big-headed, Helen was obliged to say: 'He gets plenty of stick from me and the kids at home so he wouldn't stand a chance to get big-headed anyway. To us he's just the same as he's always been – the success has never gone to his head.'

Terry can become impatient with his critics, often believing they are unfair to him. 'The criticism would get to anyone – and after all, I am human. You'd have to be made of wood not to let snide comments hurt your feelings. It seems there are weeks when the whole world is queueing up to have a dig at you. What I loathe most of all is the extra pressure it puts on my wife and children.'

If Helen is sometimes inclined to dismiss as 'rubbish' some of the things written about their children, she can become furious occasionally when verbal swipes are taken at Terry. She sometimes wonders how he has been able to take it without exploding. As she says: 'There seem to be so many people out there who want to get at Terry, but when they're getting at him they're also getting at us. I don't think they realise this. It's something we've had to live with for so long – but sometimes it gets to you and invades your life and home.'

Helen and Terry have always tried to exclude these things from life at Wogan Towers. Their dinner-parties are usually delightful affairs, a mixture of Helen's exquisite cooking and Terry's lively wit, ensuring the guests go home contented. Of course Terry has other consolations. He derives a lot of fun from charity golf games, or reading through his mail and finding words of encouragement and praise from fans. 'My fan mail shows that people like what I do on TV. Their letters are terrific.'

A realist, Terry knows he's got to pay the price for success.

'There are days when you look around and feel the price is very high. I know most people would love to have what we have and the kind of acclaim that goes with it, but could they stand the constant barrage of abuse and criticism?'

25   *New Challenges*

Terry Wogan is happiest as the flamboyant chat-show host in the familiar surroundings of the BBC TV Theatre in Shepherd's Bush Green. To millions of viewers of *Wogan*, he brings a touch of unique glamour to a show that in other hands can seem complacent, even dull. The fact is that Terry enjoys himself – and it shows. He doesn't dwell on problems; he leaves them to John Fisher and the show's crew. While other chat-show producers complain that there aren't enough guests to go round, particularly as most shows insist on exclusives, the *Wogan* team claim they don't experience any such difficulty.

There is unanimous agreement that Terry is perfect casting for *Wogan*, so much so in the view of the vast majority that it would be hard to imagine him as interviewee rather than interviewer. Would it not curb his irrepressible personality, affect his charm, stifle his flow of blarney? The risks he would face are enormous. Yet this miscasting occurred on a March evening when he appeared on the first series of BBC's *Network*.

The new series was designed to invite criticism of BBC programmes; not only that, it helped the aggrieved viewer-critic make his own video to drive home his points. When Terry took his seat opposite presenter Anna Ford he was introduced as being not too keen on television criticism programmes but 'tonight he has agreed to come on *Network* and to hear what viewers say about Terry.'

FORD: What's this about you not enjoying programmes about TV?

WOGAN: I think TV has a tendency anyway to inspect its own navel with the result that programmes like this may be counter-productive. They may make programme-makers and people like me more introspective.

Terry looked rather ill at ease as he essayed a half smile. He listened as Anna Ford announced that the first of the video-makers was Jane James. Her video was entirely devoted to the Wogan show.

Jane prefaced her remarks with: 'Apart from sport and politics there is one other thing that everyone in Britain has an opinion on – and that is Terry Wogan. Like many others, I watch our national institution three times a week. In one particular show his three guests included Lord Soper and Jeffrey Archer and afterwards I telephoned the BBC – something I never did before – to tell them how much I enjoyed that *Wogan*. At other times, though, the show can be mediocre. Having worked in a number of shops in my home town, I got to hear what local people thought and I was surprised to find so many saying how much they enjoyed the show with Lord Soper. The guests on that occasion were able to develop their conversations, for all too often they are not allowed to do so. Don't get me wrong, I do like Terry. Recently, however, when he was talking to singer Burl Ives he could not resist the temptation to interrupt.'

Miss James wondered why Terry and the *Wogan* team could not come up with different angles about guests instead of well-known facets. She had heard Kenneth Williams tell the same joke on the Wogan show as he had told on Michael Aspel's show. She wondered how deeply they researched their subjects.

JOHN FISHER: (*On Film*) I think the programme can go as deep as possible. Part of the fascination of the Wogan show, given the charisma that surrounds Terry, is the public's fascination of seeing people from all walks of life in his company.

JANE: This would suggest that sitting any guest opposite Terry Wogan would produce a good show. Let me say that you can't but be impressed by the production of the show in the TV theatre, but this adulation and excitement shouldn't hide the fact that it is the viewers at home who are important.

FISHER: It is said that Terry tries to upstage his guests, something I've found a complete fallacy. There have been occasions when he has been trying to save the situation.

JANE: Do you think it has become more of a habit with him to jump in and cut across what the guest is saying?

FISHER: Since I took over the show it has hardly happened at all.

JANE: I don't think this is true. I've seen Terry interrupt very interesting guests with unnecessary comments which may please studio audiences but just leave viewers annoyed.

In his role as listener Terry appeared uncomfortable, as though someone had cut off his gift of the gab. Since he confesses not to look at himself on television, looking now at Jane James' video must have made him wince inwardly. Anna Ford did nothing for his ego when she looked across and said: 'Well, Terry, there's a viewer that sees more in you than meets the eye.' Turning to Miss James, he said he was flattered by her video and her interest in the show. In the same soft voice he continued: 'It is difficult for someone to sit in this chair and say: "No, I'm a wonderful interviewer," for at worst it can sound like egomania and at best bombastic. All I can say is that in the course of two years and well over three hundred programmes I can name interviews of which I have been very proud. I have managed perhaps to get more out of the guest than someone who asked questions in an abrasive tone. *Wogan* is an extremely easy programme to criticise because it is on thrice weekly – and it's live. It's not edited and polished once a week for an hour and then cut down to forty-five minutes. What you see is what you get.

ANNA FORD: Is the show too often for you to be able to be interested in nine interviewees a week?

WOGAN: No. I think the essence of all talk shows is repetition. I always felt when I did the *Saturday Night Show* that it had to be a feature. *Wogan* is light-hearted, hopefully informative, occasionally intelligent. But it's on three nights a week; the best you can hope for is one out of three good shows.

GIRL in audience: *Wogan* to me is the equivalent of a cheap tabloid newspaper.

WOGAN: Oh, thank you.

GIRL: It doesn't go into serious topics and I think that is why it does work. Another reason why it works is yourself, Terry. The PR people have done a wonderful job, built up a wonderful person. It's got to the point where it doesn't really matter who goes on – it's the Terry Wogan show. I think it's a nice show for the personalities who go on. They know it is going to be safe, they're not going to be pressed to reveal anything –

WOGAN: (*Slightly agitated*) What should they be pressed to reveal? Press them on that, and they'll just throw down their microphones and walk off. I resent your suggestion that I am the creation of some PR firm. I am me. I am what I am. I am not putting on an act. I am not being artificial.

Shortly afterwards Terry rose, thanked Anna Ford and walked off. He looked unhappy, sensing perhaps that he was miscast. The fears he had earlier expressed about such shows had been well founded in his own case. He is happier as a performer. Under scrutiny he can look uncomfortable and annoyed. It is true of many performers. The fact is of course that Terry doesn't enjoy criticism and probably finds it tedious and rather a futile exercise anyway. His motto is to get on with the show and if it falls short, hopefully the next one will exceed popular expectations.

For viewers – and especially the studio audience – *Network* provided a useful platform to examine shows in some depth. Never before, for instance, had the chat show come under such close appraisal. *The Observer* gave Sunday readers an insight into the chat-show kings – Wogan, Aspel, Harty, O'Connor, Parkinson, Monkhouse, Young, Kilroy-Silk and Nicholson. Commented the writer of the piece, Andrew Duncan: 'A lot of stars no longer want to appear on *Wogan* because all they do is feed his self-image.' The *Wogan* team would deny this allegation. 'We can get most people we want,' said a spokesman. 'There is no shortage of guests.'

James Gilbert, who gave Terry his first big break in television in Britain when he chose him to present *Blankety Blank*, has continued to watch Terry Wogan's progress and is in no way surprised by the Wogan Phenomenon. He cannot think of any other person who could front the seven o'clock show as successfully as Terry. Gilbert reflects: 'What he has brought to television is a mixture of the common touch and a superior intelligence. When I first met him at the BBC, I thought he was a little wasted in the *Breakfast Show*. As Head of Light Entertainment, it was one of my duties to make a presentation to the winner of a *Song for Europe*. Terry handled the whole thing so well that I remember saying to myself: "I must get a television show for him as quickly as possible." He had done shows that hadn't exploited his talent, but when we found *Blankety Blank* I knew we had something worthwhile for him.

'I think Terry learned a great deal doing *Blankety*, and he was to carry this experience into his weekly chat show and later *Wogan*. He has this marvellous gift of communication and he is able to adapt to people, and of course he is very versatile. You can do a chat show or you can't. It's as simple as that. I have profound admiration for Terry.'

But Gilbert remembered also the criticism levelled at Terry in 1986. 'The reason for this was because he was focusing on the cameras too much, and he also began to exploit certain mannerisms. Doing a thrice-weekly show these become noticeable, but he has corrected them and is sailing along to more success.'

James Gilbert is impressed by the team Terry has around him in *Wogan*. 'John Fisher is one of the best in the business and there is nothing he doesn't know about chat shows and he is a strong personality who can debate points with Terry. Since the show is almost totally dependent on the host, it is important he gets the right projection – and the best guests available. From time to time there will be criticism and this can be hurtful to star presenters, but often it isn't justified. In Terry Wogan's case I feel some of it is certainly not justified.'

He recalled that *Blankety Blank* was severely criticised even within the BBC, but no one worried because it had a huge audience and high appreciation. As far as the *Blankety* team was concerned it was being watched and Terry Wogan, as presenter, was doing a super job. While some stars can be affected by criticism and some are very sensitive to it, they should not allow it to affect their performance. 'I don't think Terry Wogan let it get to him in any serious way – at least it didn't show on the screen.'

Gilbert is convinced that Terry can go on successfully for the next ten years. 'He has learned to withstand criticism. There is a freshness about his style that never permits complacency. He is shrewd and intelligent, and will eventually know when to call it a day.'

Like James Gilbert, Marcus Plantin moved on from the BBC and is now Light Entertainment Head of London Weekend TV. As director of *Blankety Blank,* he came to admire Terry Wogan's spontaneity and his gift at ad libbing. 'We had fun doing the show. Watching Terry match his skills against his panellists could be exhilarating. *Wogan* wasn't quite the same; he has had to depend on the calibre of his guests and sometimes these didn't always measure up. But he has done some great shows. He is splendid with people. I am not surprised that he has become a superstar of television.'

Nor is Alan Boyd, who was the producer of *Blankety Blank*, surprised at the Wogan Phenomenon. 'I think any of us who worked with Terry in *Blankety* knew the sky was the limit where he was concerned. His kind of talent is scarce in television.'

At the BBC TV Theatre there was a new buoyancy, a fresh enthusiasm generated by the hardworking John Fisher and his production team. However, the Fleet Street tabloids continued to give Terry dubious space in their news columns. One boldly asked its readers to telephone with their views of Wogan and when the majority suggested he should quit, Terry's comment was: 'Well, most normal people are hardly going to telephone the *Sun* to say what they think of me. That's the reaction of show-offs and obsessives, or people who have a lot of time on their hands. But as far as the public is concerned, I'm still number one, and human nature being what it is, they like to see number one being kicked around. That's par for the course, but I'd be mad if I thought I deserved success or had the right to be enormously well known and terrifically well paid.'

It was evident at this point that Terry was becoming somewhat annoyed by the reaction of the BBC itself to criticism. He was to say: 'The BBC is of course a target and has become an embattled organisation continually looking over its shoulder – but so is all television; it's pathetic. At the moment there are about eight programmes that invite viewers to say what they think about television, but I preferred it in the good old days when it had enough confidence to do things without constantly asking the public: "Did you like that?" It's running scared and not at all the self-confident organisation it was even ten years ago.'

His words mirrored the more thoughtful side of Terry Wogan, who has for nearly twenty years been a star act at the Beeb. It is true that he rejected lucrative offers from rival TV channels, but he was determined to stay at Broadcasting House. Yet his words on this occasion, which surprised not a few colleagues, obviously found a response among many BBC employees. Not that Terry has lost confidence in the BBC. 'I have always liked the organisation,' he told me once. 'As far as I am concerned there is no distancing; I mean, as you work through the system you meet the people that matter. I can see no divide between me and the various heads of departments. Bill Cotton and Michael Grade regularly discuss *Wogan* with me. It makes one feel part of the organisation to have someone take an interest in what one is doing. I think that is the essence of running a TV station.

It is not full of mandarins who don't communicate with one another.

'When I referred to the BBC's attitude to criticism I was voicing a personal view. A lack of confidence in individuals and shows can undermine any organisation and often results in a drop in programme quality. I do hope the Beeb soon gets back its old confidence. Up to now it has always believed in its own judgement. It doesn't need to have to look over its shoulder.'

The pressure on him of presenting three live shows a week has given Terry scant time to ponder what his critics have had to say. But the newspapers have noticed the subtle changes taking place in *Wogan*. The show is concerning itself more with day-to-day happenings, like the teachers' dispute. Terry interviewed two young teachers and managed by a sensible approach to put the problem into perspective. As if to balance the act, he had as his guest a few weeks later Kenneth Baker, the Education Secretary. Baker is a smooth individual and reckoned 'a highly political Education Secretary', so clearly he would have the advantage over Terry, who is no specialist in the education field. As the interview began, it soon became evident that this was not light entertainment but rather current affairs. The questions could have been compiled by a researcher for Jonathen Dimbleby.

WOGAN: The main argument for the strike is that you have taken away the rights of negotiation?

BAKER: The teachers have been badly let down over the past two years by their negotiators and I want to say again that I want to move to a better system of negotiation.

The interview continued in this vein, with Terry finally asking the Minister what his own early education was like. Was this the kind of chat show, though, the average viewer wanted at seven o'clock in the evening? Michael Grade has welcomed the 'journalistic input' into the Wogan show, yet cannot be satisfied with the result so far. The show has not increased its audience. It would be wrong perhaps to judge Grade at this stage, for some of his programme concepts

have been enormous successes like *Eastenders* and, until its
demise, *The Late, Late Breakfast Show*, and of course *Wogan*.

It has been argued that such interviews 'stretch Terry
Wogan', but there is a body of opinion that he is more at
home with an Albert Finney in the opposite chair than a
Kenneth Baker. The shrewd Frances Whitaker, who master-
minded the success of the early *Michael Parkinson Show*, felt
strongly about the ingredients essential to the success of the
Wogan show. Entertainment figured top of the list.

As if to prove the point, Terry some time later was infi-
nitely more himself with Alex Higgins as his guest. Getting
him was a scoop for the show. A tribunal had just heard
charges against him and now the findings were to be
revealed to *Wogan* viewers by Higgins's manager. As it transpired, the 'Hurricane' was suspended and fined.

Higgins looked calm and in the pink of health. Terry
welcomed the chance to talk to the controversial snooker
ace.

WOGAN: Are you sorry about what happened?

HIGGINS: Of course I'm sorry. I think the incident could
have been defused.

WOGAN: When I met you for the first time in Scotland you
were the epitome of gentleness and kindness to my children.
How do you reconcile the reports we sometimes see in the
papers about your behaviour. Do you have a dual
personality?

HIGGINS: I have a very short fuse. There's a lot going on
beneath the game than meets the eye.

WOGAN: Will you be able in the future to control your
temper?

HIGGINS: It's up to me to do that.

As an interview it made for entertaining television, the
kind of thing viewers enjoy – and Terry himself enjoys. At
home in Wogan Towers, Helen Wogan had watched the
show and enjoyed it. A shrewd judge of what makes a
successful show, she likes guests who are forthcoming and
have something interesting to say. Occasionally she has
expressed disappointment when guests were unresponsive.

*

Late in March, '87 the new Parkinson show was screened on ITV and obviously caused a stir even in the somewhat complacent world of the chat show. 'We are not in opposition,' remarked Terry when I talked with him about the show. 'Michael's is a short series, mine goes on and on. And mine is live, his is not quite that.'

Jack Lemmon made an entertaining guest. Commented critic Mary Kenny in the *Daily Mail:* 'It is wonderful to have Parky back in the chair that has never been adequately filled by a successor in the chat-show stakes, though Wogan sometimes comes very clos- '

Parkinson had expressed some trepidation about returning to his old job: 'I'm not sure it's sensible to play an innings after the "final" one. I'm nervous of what people might think seeing this guy coming back five years more haggard. But it's the best job there is. The programmes are called things like *Parkinson* or *Wogan*, which improves your commercial value, and if you're a journalist it's the only job you can do without learning how to be a magician.'

To Parkinson, the single interview is everything. As he explained: 'We offer a proper chance for an interview, and as it's not live there isn't a dreadful scramble like there is at the end of *Wogan* to talk about a guest's film or book. We make absolutely sure that it is built into the interview, but the trick is to do it so that it doesn't look like a huge plug.'

Unlike Parky, Terry loves the excitement of the live show. 'A live show should be live with all its spots, boils and pimples left in it.' So there is really no competition between the two shows.

Terry was back once more on his favourite ground – Wogan Towers – and at peace with himself. Helen was in the garden attending to the flowers. Terry was in casuals, his usual attire around house, an indication that he was relaxing. He reflected on the luck that he had enjoyed in broadcasting in Britain since he left Ireland. He achieved most things he set out to achieve – success in radio and television, a stable marriage, and children.

'My life is geared to my home and family, and that is where I want to be all the time,' he would say between drawing on his cigar, his famous legs stretched comfortably across a chair. 'There's nothing else I really desire. My ambitions are mainly for my children – that they should be happy and succeed. My ambition for myself is that my wife and I should continue to be happy and healthy.'

As he approached the age of fifty, Terry no longer had any illusions about television: 'People are not glued to the set as they were in the fifties, sixties and seventies. Now they are not impressed by television, technology or anything else and will hop in and out of a programme. Ratings and all that are meaningless because of videos.'

He rose and stared across the broad fields of Buckinghamshire with Windsor Castle in the distance. It was a misty day, so on his own admission he would be unable to wave at the Queen. On the lawn outside the house could be seen the symbols of his success – a gleaming Rolls Royce and Helen's Mercedes sports car. Yet Terry will say that he is not happy with the trappings of fame. 'The advantages of being able to get the table you want in a restaurant are outweighed by the number of people who are boring holes in the back of your neck. It would be nice if at times you could cut yourself off from all the attention and relax.'

Not that Terry does not enjoy life – he does. His love of rugby football, which he first cultivated in Ireland, has stayed with him and he still pops over to Dublin when Ireland is playing a match. He enjoys the sunshine of Spain and the comfort of his villa there; above all, he enjoys people – and good food and good wine.

A millionaire, he doesn't *have* to present *Wogan* with all the attendant hassle, but one presumes he will not be entirely happy until the show is screened five nights a week, thus making it another first for Terry. As he says: 'I'm not saying that I could physically stand up to that, but I'd like to try it.'

Anything is possible where Michael Terence Wogan is

concerned. As his mother, Mrs Rose Wogan likes to say:
'Terry never stopped surprising me.'